To: Mum . Mothers Day '99 .
Love Janice
G000113702

Over the Mountain

Over the Mountain

MARYANNE KERR

Illustrations by Stephanie Daniels

MICHAEL JOSEPH
LONDON

MICHAEL JOSEPH LTD
Published by the Penguin Group
27 Wrights Lane, London w8 5tz
Viking Penguin Inc., 375 Hudson Street, New York, New York 10014, USA
Penguin Books Australia Ltd, Ringwood, Victoria, Australia
Penguin Books Canada Ltd, 10 Alcorn Avenue, Toronto, Ontario, Canada m4v 3b2
Penguin Books (NZ) Ltd, 182–190 Wairau Road, Auckland 10, New Zealand

Penguin Books Ltd, Registered Offices: Harmondsworth, Middlesex, England

First published 1996
1 3 5 7 9 10 8 6 4 2

Copyright © Maryanne Kerr 1996

Set in 10.5/13 pt. Monophoto Sabon
Typeset by Datix International Limited, Bungay, Suffolk
Printed in England by Clays Ltd, St Ives plc

A CIP catalogue record for this book is available from the British Library

ISBN 0 7181 4087 7

The moral right of the author has been asserted

For my children, both here and there
(with a salute to Mullaghash)

Some names of places and people
have been changed in this account.

I went back. Back to the bogland that had spawned me. To the slow cold stream at the foot of the mountain where I'd paddled my scraggy feet and where, egged on by my whooping brothers, I'd gleefully landed my first trout.

It had lain there in the sodden grass, its one topaz eye transfixing me for ever as I stood over it in the watery summer sun, wrecking – in its last paralytic moments – the whole of the rest of my life, for all things mute and sacrificed. Years later, in my singing lessons, one of the pieces was Schubert's 'The Trout', a tinkly, sad little ditty which instantly brought to mind the images of that dismal day. I sang it with such fervour in my final exam that the poor examiner was moved to shed a tear. It was, without a doubt, my soulful rendition of Schubert's 'Trout' which alone won for me his commendation for a scholarship to study opera in Milan – the first of many squandered opportunities that would befall me.

Afterwards I never sang the song again. Nor indeed heard it. Until quite recently, nearly half a century later, as I stood at an early-morning bus stop in a far Australian town, the lovely melody floated out and over me from a nearby chemist's shop. It caught in my throat. And as clear as the miraculous day before me, I saw again the eye. It was softer now. Filled with light. I knew then the forgiveness to be complete.

PART ONE

Mullaghash was the mountain out our back. These days it looks rather more of a hill, but in our day it was a fine laid-back lump of a mountain, the nearest one in the Sperrins – a range of hills that straggles across the county of Derry in northern Ireland and then away, wavering uncertainly into the dim, dazy distance of County Tyrone.

We lived in the Schoolhouse, that extra chunk of building tagged on to the side of country schools for the convenient living of the headmaster and his family. Altogether the whole structure presented a fearsomely solid edifice of whitewashed brick, its tight little windows painted bottle-green, the doors and window-sills dung-brown. Across the blue slate roofs, from out the chimney tops, summer and winter, floated a constant drift of pungent smoke from the turf fires below.

It was all set in a great hotch-potch of wilderness, with a Tarmacadamed road forming a rough boundary one side and an endlessly wandering lane separating us out front from the farmers' fields beyond. The lane was special. Edged in by trees and an entanglement of bushes and nettles, it provided us with limitless possibilities for the playing of houses, the hiding and seeking, and the gathering in the faint autumn evenings of hazel nuts and berries. Its way was rough and pockmarked, full of stones and clumpy tufts and unexpected small gushes of spring water, squirting up out of the gravel and spraying into a myriad of tiny rivulets across our path. Sometimes, when it rained, these trickles would gather a wonderful momentum, gurgling up and cascading over themselves in a splendid torrent of river, filling the lane with tempestuous flood before finally propelling themselves helter-skelter into the dank belly of the ditches – there to bubble and brood and worry for days.

Around the back of the school was a commendable stretch of vegetable garden. Rows and rows of potatoes, beans and peas

I

were laid out in military precision alongside the lettuce and shallots. There was never a weed in sight, the tending of the whole affair being considered part of the school curriculum, a pretty crafty ploy of my father's. As it happens, most of us revelled in our hours of horticultural dalliance, a merciful escape from the unrelenting drone of sums and grammar. Two ones are two, two twos are four. I am, you are, he she or it . . .

Then there was the bewildering scramble of scrubby fruit bushes, totally untended, but always managing to produce, year after year, a bumper abundance of white, red and black currants and, well-hidden in the undergrowth, a resplendent assemblage of ploppy yellow gooseberries. What the birds and us lot didn't get, my mother picked. And the jam for the year was secured.

Roaming all over the place, pecking and poking and stabbing at everything, were the hens. Not too many, just enough to keep us in a goodly supply of eggs. Meat was a luxury, reserved mainly for the Sabbath and Christmas, so eggs in one form or another provided the main dish of the day. Everything else was complementary and arranged under or around them – the toast, the potatoes, the lettuce, the baked beans, the gobbet of melting butter. Fortunately our hens were copious layers, amply sustained as they were by the discarded remains of some seventy or more lunchboxes. They scraped and scratched in the flute of trickled water from the pump, and then over and across the midden by the big back gate, into the field of corn behind the lavatories. It was a great life. Happy for them, though, that they had a limited supply of memory cells.

A couple of times a year, my mother would get the notion into her head that we'd have roast chicken for dinner. There followed the most awful commotion out the back, the hens scattering in all directions as she raced around the yard, hatchet in hand, hell-bent on decapitation. No one ever dared ask why she couldn't simply wring their necks. Certainly not me. When I'd see her coming out of the coalshed, wielding the axe, and that predatory look on her face, I'd run as fast as I could up the lane and hide in the treehouse.

Nevertheless those chicken dinners, with the mashed potatoes piled high and cabbage and peas and thick brown gravy all around, remain to this day some of the most succulent meals I have ever tasted.

Climb the gate, cross the road, over the meadow with no cows, tumble and spill my way through the stream and already I am in the heather. As children, one of our summer excitements was to be taken picnicking up the mountain, squelching through the bog in our wellington boots, stumbling in and out of potholes, our fingers trailing through the bobbing feather heads of the white bog cotton. It was a lot of hard work getting to the top – a good two thousand feet's worth of circumnavigation, but making it to the massive boulder cradled in the very tip was our goal. This was the rock thrown in a fit of temper by my friend Finn MacCool, a giant of great renown. It seems he was passing the time of day with another lesser giant, probably a Protestant, in the county Fermanagh, when a profound philosophical argument started. One thing led to another and Finn, being of a hot-blooded disposition, scooped up a stone (thereby incidentally creating Lough Erne, nobody ever told me which of the Lough Ernes – there are two) and let fly at the lesser individual who was, of course, by now halfway across Scotland. The stone either fell short of its mark or was arrested in its course by the peak of Mullaghash.

The imprint of Finn's big gentle hand spread across the rock's surface and we would sink our small weary bums into the palm of it, squeeze our eyelids tight shut and wish away to our hearts' content. What I wished for then must have been fairly obscure. We had no idea what went on in the rest of the world, except for what we learnt from our geography lessons, and that was pretty unimaginative ... longitude and latitude, height above sea-level, mountains, rivers, towns and what was manufactured therein.

But I do know that from a very early age I had a terrible restlessness in me. And Mullaghash, in its rugged sweep, with the joyous wind zinging through its crags, epitomized for me the sweet ecstasy of freedom. I wanted not only to climb up to Finn's lofty pinnacle, but to soar with the eagle right over the top and discover for myself the boundless infinite beyond. Most evenings, when we had finished singing – my father always ordered a singsong round the fire after tea – I would slip out the back and carry on the performance for my mountain. Standing in the same little spot between the pump and the coalshed, the night black and full of stars, I'd send my voice skimming over the lavatory roofs, away beyond the road and meadow, straight into the sleeping heart of the heather. It was, for me, the supreme comfort of my childhood.

We would have been six children in all, but one died so we were five. I was the only girl. The three eldest, Patrick, myself and Joseph, had barely a year between us. My mother used to sigh happily, 'Like steps of stairs they are' – as if it was something to be proud of. I suppose, in our upright Catholic environment, it was. If a woman failed to produce every year, she was regarded with suspicion by both neighbours and relatives, never mind the parish priest and curate. It was a sin worse than mortal, and her salvation was heavily dependent upon the regularly recurrent swing of the rocking cradle. When we were early teenagers it seems she went through a series of miscarriages, but we were never aware of anything untoward. Except for one middle of the night when I woke up, desperately wanting to pee but too terrified to use the po in case I'd be heard downstairs. There was obviously something awful going on, that I had no business to be hearing. The sounds came from the sitting room, painful whimpers from my mother and my father's voice placating, muffled, desperate. I knew something was up. Bad, bad. And I was suffocated by an overwhelming sense of shame and guilt.

Like most country women, my mother had her children at home, the local midwife and doctor in attendance. For the births of the last two, the deliverers arrived during the day and Patrick, Joseph and I were hurriedly whooshed away up the lane to play and then off to the farm to fetch butter and milk – anything to get rid of us. How they managed to cover up the whole proceedings I cannot imagine, but during those early years of birthing I know that I accepted without question the same old yarn that the doctor had very kindly brought us a new baby.

My mother was tough. She scrubbed and polished and dusted, knitted, sewed, cooked, made bread, jam, cakes. Washed, ironed

– and scolded. She was perpetually going on about something. Or some one. Her tongue could be vitriolic in her castigations, but I don't think there was any real harm in her. It was just that she liked to hear herself talking.

She was a most beautiful woman, lovely eyes, fine cheekbones, small neat nose and a wide pleasant mouth. Her clothes were few, but they were expensive and made to last for years. They were ultra-conservative, well-pressed dark greens and browns. Except when it came to hats. These appeared on her head in an astonishing array of shapes and colours, big, with feathers, flowers, veils. Everyone turned when she appeared. Her jewellery, too, was an amazement – a gaggle of earrings glittering in kaleidoscope under the curled brown hair, chains and charms and ornaments clustered at the wrists. My father bought her these things and the extravagant perfume which she wore on Sundays and Holy Days and upon all grand occasions. He was monument-ally proud of her and adored her with a passion that was dimmed not one whit by the hardship and adversity that periodi-cally afflicted them during their long lives together.

He was the quiet one. At least in the home. The total sum of his energies went into teaching, so in the warm smoky kitchen he would let her clatter on with it, and nurse himself and his book and his pipe in the corner, humming to himself, every so often spouting forth at us, in his finest oratorial voice, some lofty snippet of verse.

Sometimes she'd leave what she was doing for a while and sit down on the sofa beside him, head back, eyes closed, in a long sigh of weariness. He would take her hand. She would comb his hair. Finely thinning hair. Patting it carefully into place.

Often they'd get up suddenly and announce, 'We're going for a walk now. You stay here and behave yourselves and you, Mary, you look after the house – there's a good girl.' And out they'd go, up the lane, arm in arm, like the two sweetie-pie lovebirds they were.

I have one stinging memory of those walks. It was high summer and I was dangling on the swing when a couple of brothers and a friend came catapulting down the lane, giggling, bent over double, wild with mirth. They refused to tell me what was up and went on and on. Then suddenly I heard a whisper:

'Did you see his hand on her . . .?'

They didn't say what, but I guessed it was one of the more sinful parts of the body, the ones we weren't allowed even to contemplate. Immediately I was filled with a hot, seething jealousy, furious that they should do such a dirty thing, and furious with my brothers for having caught them.

Knowing little or nothing of sex, how could I guess that my parents had to take advantage of every opportunity they had to be alone? Their bedroom had a cot in it. Permanently. Next door was ours, also with a cot plus a small put-U-up and, taking over most of the floor space, the most colossal bed I have ever seen. We children piled into it at night, heads to feet, squabbling and whingeing, pinching and punching, and calling names and heaving and yanking the unwieldy thick grey blankets over us.

There was also the 'spare room'. It was off my parents' room, a tiny damp squib of a room that nobody could live in without catching pneumonia. Or even *double* pneumonia. Nevertheless my parents, every once in a while, would have a diligent go at fixing it up. For me, the only girl. Alas, it was never to any avail. During the nights the paper, with its pretty flowery border still attached, would quietly undulate back down the walls again and come to an exhausted flop at the bottom, the paint would crumble and flake and flutter to the floor. In any event, it was so dark and miserable I felt it was haunted and, even though I dearly wanted privacy, I was too afraid to sleep in it.

It never occurred to anyone that the downstairs sitting room, hardly ever used, could be utilized as an extension of the sleeping quarters. It was a plumpy, cushiony room, the only carpeted space in the house, and could easily have accommodated the odd small body or two. But the sitting room was 'the parlour', the showing-off room, the taking thereinto of visiting important persons – like priests, the doctor and curates, the Schools' Inspector, and the more toffee-nosed aunts and uncles.

Us lot were allowed to play in there on Christmas Day, the whole day – untrammelled – starting at dawn when we crept down in the shivering cold to find, arranged around the fireplace, the surprising and not-so-surprising goodies of Santa. We could sit on the separate detachments of the three-piece, trying them out for size, push them together to make trains, bounce up and down on them, pick at them. Spill lemonade on the carpet, finger the trinklets on the mantelpiece and in the glass china-cabinet, fold and unfold the three-legged dining table in the corner. The window was expansive and generously curtained. You could stand within its orb of pale light and, skimming the pump and the midden and the henhouse, keep a benevolent eye on Mullaghash. Or in the evening you could gather the drapery around behind you, shutting out the lights and sounds of the room, transport yourself up up into the hollow of the great rock and just wish and wish and wish. An altogether enchanting room, and one that entirely captivated me.

That is, until the age of six. Then something happened that was to put me off it for ever, plunging me always into a sombre disquiet each time I had to pass its dim-lit doorway by the foot of the stairs.

It became the room in which my mother chose to administer to me the worst beating any of us children had ever had to endure. I screamed and screamed. The others too were crying, huddled together outside the door, begging her to stop. But she had gone completely crazy, hitting at me with a savage fanaticism that was totally out of control, so that even when the blood came she couldn't stop.

In the aftermath when all was still I lay curled on the floor, utterly destroyed. There was an awesome silence. The house listened. Darkness came down, slowly, into the room. Through the window the hulk of Mullaghash sat serene in its constancy. And a fierce hatred began to well up in me, taking hold like a canker. I vowed that one day, one day dear God, I would kill that woman.

As it happens, an unremitting forty-five years later, as she lay on her deathbed, I almost did. But at that moment it was to ease the pain of my father. He who could no longer bear to watch the suffering of the woman he loved so much.

Even on her deathbed, though, as I stood looking down on the woman who had so surely marked me for life, I still couldn't find it in my heart to forgive her. Nor she me.

It was all to do with sex.

Although we lived and slept in such close proximity, seeing each other naked was a definite no-no. And perhaps *because* there was so little privacy, we went to great lengths to keep ourselves covered up. In the bedroom we undressed with the light out, or we put on our pyjamas in the half-light of the landing. My mother gave herself a full wash-down in the scullery every single afternoon of her life. She was very clean. The heavy pot of boiling water was carried out from the kitchen stove, the door was closed and that was that.

I was twelve before I was allowed to be present at her ablutions, and that only briefly. She was washing the top half of herself and had called out for me to bring her something, but the sight of her small sorrowful breasts, slippery with soap, sent an acute spasm of humiliation through me. I knew she was trying to tell me something, realizing that my own young buds were beginning to stir, but the words wouldn't come out. I stood on the mat and stared straight through the window, as if we were having a pleasant cup of tea.

Us lot had the full hose-down every Saturday night in front of the stove, its window thrown open to blast our finicky shivery bodies with a solid swathe of heat. We took it in turns, in the heavy aluminium bath, starting with the eldest, the rest of us playing outside or biding our time in the scullery. The same water did everybody with a top up from the pot in between. There was no such thing as shampoo, of course. A wholesome slab of Lifebuoy soap covered all eventualities, from the top of the head down to the toe tips, then a brusque rough-over with the towel and finally the haphazard pat here and there with the sweet powder puff of apple blossom.

It was inevitable, then, that I didn't have much of an idea as to how the male of the species should look. I'd had the odd sighting, accidentally, and was truly mortified. And full of sin. But it didn't stop me wanting more. The problem was solved for me by the arrival of one Danny McGuigan upon the scene, and the setting was some whin bushes up the lane on the occasion of our mutual sixth birthday.

Danny was one of a sprawling family of brats belonging to the woman with the consumptive husband who owned the only grocery shop between us and the village. The children ran wild, were unkempt and sickly and were always getting into trouble of one kind or another – their unfortunate mother having little or no time to care for them. The shop sold everything: paraffin, sacks of flour, turnips, cigarettes, sweets, bags of coal, and, even though it didn't have the slightest pretensions to cleanliness, with sticky buns and candle grease and loose tealeaves all over the counter, it did a roaring trade. The trade was especially blooming on a Sunday morning, with the chapel round the corner and full houses for the nine and eleven Masses – never mind Benediction in the evening, and a fair sprinkling of funerals, confirmations and weddings. We were one of their best customers, both my parents being desperate smokers, apart from the numerous other things we were forever running out of. Between our house and theirs there was an incessant toing and froing, the short-cut over the braes a muddy path with the constant trips we made.

Danny, like the others, was not the most appealing of children. There was something wrong with his nose. A globule of glistening snot kept dropping down from one of his nostrils, and he'd quickly sniff it back up again instead of giving his nose a positively thorough and final blow, like the rest of us. It meant that he was beset by a persistent case of the snuffles. However, he was endowed with one powerful attribute – a headful of rampantly blazing marmalade curls.

He always smiled at me in a kind of sly, snivelling sort of way, but the fact that he actually noticed me more or less made up for his lack of social graces. He was gentle, whereas my brothers were not. Brothers were infinitely tiresome, forever teasing me, hitting my dolls. I ached for a baby sister, and although I'd been posting diplomatic reminder notes through the doctor's letter box for nearly a year, he obviously had no heart whatsover and had recently delivered to us the fourth male infant. I was still upset.

So when Danny offered one afternoon to carry some of the shopping back home with me, over the braes, I took a mite of comfort in it. We had got to the whin bushes, a whole hedge of them up the side of the lane near the house, when Danny stopped and suddenly asked me if I would like to see what boys looked like. He dropped his short raggedy pants and stood in front of me and I stared. It wasn't a pretty sight. His small peduncle was a rather daunting shade of livery prune, like a turkey's neck – and a dead turkey at that. I was disgusted. Nevertheless, for days after that I tortured myself by going back for more of the same. Danny would wait behind the bushes and as soon as I appeared down would come the pants and there it was. Specially for me. Sometimes he'd finger it around a bit, I suppose to give it a life of sorts, but it still looked miserable. And it still fascinated me.

It was, catastrophically for us, right in the middle of one such clandestine tryst that my ever-vigilant mother took it upon herself to creep up on us. Whether she herself had suspected what was going on, or whether the brothers had peeped and told was immaterial. We'd been caught. You could hear her screeching the other side of the braes. Danny ran for his life.

When I saw her charging across the yard, headlong through the line of flapping sheets straight for the tree from which she always tore the sally-rod, I knew I was in the vilest of trouble. No excuses, no long-winded explanations, no stuttering. Nothing and no one could get me out of this one. I wished I were dead.

Unhappily for all of us, the punishment didn't end there. Over the next week, in the classroom and in the playground, I slowly began to realize that I had become the laughing-stock of the entire school. Small clutches of children would collect at every break-time behind the blackboard, over by the fruit bushes, at the back of the henhouse, huddled together in secret whispering connivance. When I approached they scattered. I knew exactly what was going on, but was powerless to stop it.

In desperation I ran away. Up the main road, sticking tight to the hedges, ready to dive in should anyone appear, clutching a brown paper bag with my favourite doll, pyjamas and a wedge of fruit cake stolen from the secret tin in the scullery. A few miles along and I found what I was looking for: the gypsies. They were my friends. They weren't actually aware of the relationship yet, but I felt quite confident they wouldn't object to an extra small body about the encampment.

I stood at the edge of the field where they'd arranged themselves and their caravans and washing lines; horses and ponies and a bandy-legged goat or two grazed nearby. I tried to muster up the courage to approach them. They were a rum lot. A wood fire smoked low on the corn stubble. Raggedy children ran hither and thither, laughing, crying, cavorting. The menfolk hammered and hacked at glinting metal – gypsies were always tinsmiths by trade – their women pummelled clothes, poked up the fire for the cooking pot, shouted orders, harangued. It was a lively scene. But one which, for the time being anyway, I wasn't venturesome enough to participate in.

I turned away. And walked straight into the arms of my father. Too often in the past had I threatened to run away to the gypsies. He'd known exactly where to find me.

The following afternoon the entire school was told to collect in the junior classroom. It had never happened before, and we knew that there was something calamitous afoot. There was a sudden hush as my mother appeared in the doorway. Throughout her years as the schoolmaster's wife, she had never been known to place a foot across the threshold of the school. Always one of those flamboyantly noisy women who can put on a great show when flanked by a strong supporting cast, she unaccountably went to pieces when confronted with a situation where she had to go it alone. She was trembling as she stood up front and faced the crowd and I could have felt a terrible pity in my heart for her if I hadn't known what was coming. It was a deadly warning to one and all. Shut up. Shut up that terrible dirty talk about her daughter. Or else. She was a brave, brave woman.

As for me – the hapless instigator of the affair – had I been aware of the word 'suicide', and the blissful expeditious oblivion it incurs, I would in that instant most certainly have committed it, mortal sin or not.

My First Confession took place when I was seven. We had several practice run-throughs before the real thing, which was on the evening before our First Holy Communion, and after that one it behoved us to preserve the mind, body and spirit in a composed state of Grace for the acceptance of the Host the following morning.

I looked forward to my First Confession. For a whole year I had carried around the guilt. As I knelt my side of the confessional in the ice-cold chapel, I sent up a quick hosanna of thanks that it was the old parish priest in the centre box awaiting my outpourings, and not one of his young stroppy curates. The parishioners would get tetchy at the Sunday Masses when it was the old man who was saying them. He was unbearably slow, fumbling and mumbling his doddery way through the proceedings, forgetting the most important happenings such as mixing the water with the wine, confusing the poor long-suffering altar-boys. When it came to sermon time, several people would develop fits of faintness – quite easy, actually, when one considered they had to fast in order to partake of the Sacrament. His sermons were a penance in themselves. He rambled on and on, often right off the subject, and could suddenly lapse into a little reverie of sorts, silent, staring out of the stained glass windows near the altar, oblivious to everything. It was irritating in the extreme.

But for confessions the man was a veritable walk-over. More than a little deaf, you could whisper to him a great walloping mortal sin and all he would say was, 'All right then. Anything else?'

Whether he understood its gravity or not was immaterial. The sin was confessed, absolution imparted, the soul scoured like bleached bones in the desert.

My particular sliver of dynamite – 'I looked at a boy's thing' – I managed to slip in pretty neatly betwixt an act of disobedience and an elaborate theft from the biscuit tin. The Act of Contrition, and I was out. Out into the chapel, out into the world. Free at last.

For my First Communion my mother made me the prettiest white dress, with a fine knife-pleated accordian skirt, puffed sleeves and rose-bud trimming – the whole rage at the time. With my tiara headdress and veil, I forgot that heavenly morning that my hair was cropped and ugly and my shape squat and podgy. For those few hours, O Lord, I was beautiful. A princess. Filled to bursting point with the shining new light of God's forgiveness.

I was very much alone as a child. My brothers and I had nothing in common and the presumption that an only daughter is thoroughly spoilt by parents and siblings alike most certainly did not apply to me. Instead I was expected, as another female, to help my mother with the stacks of housework and washing. The fastidiousness of the woman was ridiculous. Every single bit of wood in the house had to be polished every single day. Some of the furniture was rather ponderous, with elaborate knobs and twirls. These had to be rubbed and buffed and polished until they gleamed like burnished satin in the firelight. Then the linoleum on the floors was washed. It, too, was given a wipe-over with wax and shined to perfection, even though one or other of us was always slipping on the rugs laid across it.

The washing water collected in a wooden barrel placed under the scullery window, where it caught the rain from the roof drain-pipe; the barrel was always full. The water was boiled up on the stove, and for years my mother and I, of a late Saturday afternoon, would be bent double in the scullery washing the jerseys and shorts and long thick socks from the savage mud-logged Gaelic football jamborees of my brothers.

I actually disliked my brothers in those days, all of them, that is, except the last one, a good deal younger than me, whom I immediately pretended was my longed-for sister and took to dressing up as a girl. Every chance I got, I would wheel him up and down the lane in his pram, up and down, him grinning away in his frilly bonnet and bows. He was an amiable child and didn't mind in the least. For some reason neither did anyone else. I suppose it kept us both amused – him quiet, and me out of harm's way. I had a special tender spot in my heart for my baby brother and I grew to love him very much. I still do.

But for the others, they teased me about my fatness, wrecked the houses I made, hid or broke my dolls and laughed at my distress. When the word 'Utility' came into use near the end of the war, they immediately nicknamed me 'Utility Liz'. It made no sense and meant nothing to anybody, but I loathed it. If I hadn't been such a softie, I could have given them a few names back. But I never did. I was forever in fear of them. My mother tried sometimes to interfere, to reason with them, but she too was a softie. Soft on her sons. It was the way with Irish mothers in those days. To have a son become a priest was the greatest gift the good Lord could bestow on any human being. It was every mother's dream to be so blessed. And so her sons were gently chided, nurtured, guided. And utterly, utterly spoilt.

When the winter came and the snow lay deep, they had one special game that they played, using my small cardboard school attaché case. They would place it out front on the snow, in view of the kitchen window, scatter breadcrumbs in the bottom of the case and prop the lid open with a ruler. Attached to the ruler, through the top of the kitchen window, would run a thread of cotton, the spool end held fast by them as they sat in control around the table. In due course, sensing food, the birds would home in. I used to watch in trepidation as they stepped gingerly around and about the case, leaving skinnily delicate prong marks in the snow, bravely staking out the possibilities, but ready to dart off at the slightest sound. My brothers would wait, breathless, spool steady in hand, poised for the master stroke. Suddenly, unexpectedly, in would hop a bird. Yank would go the thread. Soundless would drop the lid. And much celebrating, with moronic yelps of delight all round.

They would let the birds go again, so it was only a bit of harmless fun. It was just that I, far too sensitive for my own good, couldn't bear the thought of them being trapped in the dungeon of the case and terrified so unnecessarily out of their tiny wits. I felt I had a way with birds – rather I was *working* on having a way with birds – and any other animal who happened along, fancying myself often as the female version of that guy from Assisi.

I talked to myself a lot, there being no one else much to converse with. I would write plays and perform all the parts myself, in either a high or a low voice depending on the sex. Not having television and being, as it were, untravelled, I knew little of regional accents – little of any accent for that matter. My stories tended to be of the frog-turned-prince and the lovely flaxen-haired princess swooning into his waiting arms variety. I made a wonderful princess, pretty, reed-thin, long wavy tresses tumbling to my waist.

My mother kept the boys' and my hair really short, mainly I suppose because of the ease with which we picked up fleas from the other children at school, but also perhaps because she was a compulsive scissor wielder. Indeed, in later years, when they'd moved up in the world, into a terraced council house in the village, with not only an inside loo and tiled bathroom but a hedged front garden, one of my brothers, back from Canada, took a picture of her executing the final trimming to the already close-sheared lawn with her fiercely sharp dressmaking scissors. So she kept snitching at our hair and any time we happened to be sitting still, like when doing our homework around the table, and she noticed one hair longer than its kin, out would come the scissors.

My hair she kept cut to half way up my ears, with the back of it shaved. It was white-blond, almost albino, wispy and straight and fine and I suppose could have been quite nice, given a chance.

But cut like that it was ugly, and I knew it. I kept pestering her to let it grow, longing with a fervent passion, more than anything else in my small world, for long ringleted hair. So I dreamed of it instead. As I dreamed of many things.

Most of my dreaming was indulged in on the swing.

The day they put up that swing was a rapturous one for me. I watched every move with a tingle of excitement reaching down to the very tips of my fidgety, hopping toes. I guessed it would almost exclusively be for my personal use, the boys being mainly concerned with ball games of one kind or another. Ably assisted by the brothers and a couple of friends, my father did his level best to make a professional job of the operation. A poet by inclination, he was born ham-fisted and always got himself into a state when trying to put things together. The seat was a good thick slab of wood and, with a red-hot poker stabbed intermittently into the innards of the stove and much spitting, he burnt two holes each end, nearly but not quite setting fire to the whole shemozzle. Next a fine strong rope was pushed through the holes and knotted securely underneath, then the ladder and a lot of arguing and throwing and pulling and adjusting and splitting of hairs to get the thing properly balanced and hanging correctly from the magnificent corpulence of the ancient oak tree the far side of the lane. They got me to test it out – it was one of the moments I felt I loved them all – and pushed me carefully back and forth, back and forth, easy does it. Oh, the unbounded joy of it! And, oh, the halcyon times spent thereon.

I sang and wrote poems and embroidered and knitted and composed sad little songs and performed my plays, all on the swing, summer or winter, rain or shine. I also read a lot, although where the books came from I don't know. There was no library and we certainly couldn't afford to buy books, but there were always books around. Lots of fairy tales and Tennyson and Dickens. I feasted on everything I could get my hands on. My mother complained. It was her constant moan: 'Stuck with your nose in a book all day. Out you go for some fresh air.' And I'd be whooshed out of the house. My favourite reading place was behind the water barrel, tucked in by the wall. I was hidden there and sheltered against the wind.

Boxes of watercolours, brushes, drawing paper and exercise books were easy to come by as they were supplied free to the school, so I painted a fair bit too, though in fits and starts. If something wasn't showing promise, I'd abandon it and not pick up a brush again until the urge came upon me, which might be a considerable time hence. For some reason, my mother never objected to my painting. I think it was because she'd had an uncle who had become a famous painter somewhere in Donegal. *Terribly* famous, she kept telling me as she eyed what I'd done. He was a natural, it seemed, and had never been to school of any kind. He just sat and painted watercolours all day long. And sold them. And lived, or survived one way or another, on the money he made from them. God, how often did I wish I had known him – that wraithe-like obscure relation of mine, dreaming and water-colouring away there in his lonely hutch in the hills, or by a lake maybe. All forlorn, but happy, happy, I was sure. On our kitchen wall my mother framed and hung her favourite paintings of mine: some soothing landscapes I had done, and an exact copy of 'The Age of Innocence', the little girl in a blue dress and a head of soft fair curls, as I remember it, looking out into the distance. We both loved that particular picture, and she'd point it out to the visitors with a 'Our Mary did that', followed by a mention of the famous uncle.

But what I really needed more than anything else in the world and couldn't have was a special friend with whom to play and confide my secrets in. The girl to whom I took a tremendous liking was called Claire. We were in the senior classroom by then, with my father teaching us, and she liked me too. I would rush out of the house in the morning and the two of us would already be installed in the back row, giggling and gossiping, by the time my father arrived. Da was an excellent teacher, although a tough disciplinarian. He had a reputation country-wide for producing more scholarship pupils than anyone else but, to achieve those results, he utilized his own Christian Brother training and indoctrination, resorting to the harshest punishment for the slightest misdemeanour. Our classroom walls were covered with gigantic maps – he was mad on geography – made of soft greasy oilcloth fabric, yellowed with age and peat smoke and supported top and bottom by long wooden poles. It was with one of these poles that he hit us, hard, across the palm of the hand.

During the lessons he demanded full concentration, no rustling, no whispering, no conniving. Absolute silence. Inevitably, though, when he turned his back to us to work on the blackboard the odd half-suppressed snigger would escape, enveloped immediately by a cacophony of camouflaging coughs, cutting across the lone scrape of the chalk on the board. He would swing round, exploding with rage, savagely bent on annihilation.

Too often, Claire and I were the unfortunate ones who copped it.

'Kerr and McGinty, come up to the front.' Using our surnames to add further affright. It was an accepted fact of school life in those days that teachers were tougher, and moreover *seen* to be tougher, on their own children so they could never be accused of showing favouritism. My father was no exception.

Nevertheless, although I had a brother in the class either side of me, I was the one who got punished the most. Everyone was aware of it and I oft times got pitying glances, but nothing could be said or done about it. My father's stick intimidated the most intrepid. The pain of it would shoot up the centre of your arm, bringing instant tears seconds after he struck, stinging into the very core of a million nerves right the way to the shoulder. The agony of it was paralysing, leaving you benumbed, in a state of aching stupor for the rest of the day.

I could never fathom my father. About the house, with my mother around, he was a clumsy, inept, pleasant, easy-going sort of ditherer. Put him in front of a class of schoolchildren on his own, however, and a weird metamorphosis took place. He stood tall, the dictator, uncompromising, pitiless. During school hours I felt an intense enmity towards him.

At other times I found there were moments when I thought he favoured me, his only girl. He would single me out for a particularly dramatic rendition of some delectable piece of verse that would light his fancy, knowing I could respond with an equally impassioned appreciation. He would ask me – me and no one else – to go into the parlour and sing for the visiting important persons. He invariably marked my long rambling essays with an

'Excellent', and read them out to the class as an example of how it *should* be done.

Perhaps it was my being with Claire that set him off. Claire with her pearly alabaster skin, so fair and so creamy. Just like the buttermilk she always drank . . . no tea, no lemonade like the rest of us. A rare child. And gentle. Why, therefore, my parents refused to accept her as a possible friend for me was beyond our comprehension. She was quiet, well-behaved, never a sight of a flea on her, her homework produced on time and correct. A model pupil. Yet they wouldn't have her stay on to play at our house after school, or allow me go to hers. I would stand by the swing and wave at her, as the solitary dainty figure of her trotted down the lane, tossing the satchel over her shoulder, singing a silly song, happy enough. But leaving both of us, until the morning when we'd meet up again, unequivocally and woefully alone.

She lived with her mother about half a mile down the road, over a field, in a tiny, lost single-storey cottage by the river. Her mother was seldom seen, not even at Sunday Mass, and Claire did the shopping, or it was brought to the field gate once a week – as it was to most of the houses in the countryside – by the big mobile grocery shop van from the city. Sometimes on Christmas morning, she would be there at Mass, near the back, head bowed low in a dark headscarf, but she'd scuttle out with Claire at the last gospel, before the throngs began to collect themselves for the grand exodus.

I was well into my teens and the memory of Claire with her lovely buttermilk smile dimmed but not forgotten when someone told me that her mother was getting married. 'Again?' I asked. 'No. Married.' Married for the first time. Only then did the whole painful truth hit me. It seemed that when she was found to be pregnant as a young girl, the mother's family had disowned her completely, banishing her to the cottage, there to live out the rest of her days, alone with her bastard child, in enduring and isolated shame.

When I made the discovery, the hurt and frustration and anger I felt against my parents made me want to weep for a very long time. For Claire and for me.

*

Christmas was a grand occasion. We had to be careful not to snack at the remains of orange squash and biscuit crumbs left by Santa on the sitting-room table from the offering laid out for him the night before. The partaking of Communion was obligatory on Christmas morning, and not even the minutest droplet of water was allowed to relieve our fasting stomachs. After Mass, hurrying back up the road we'd come in the cold crisp dawning, still carolling 'Silent Night', to the toasty kitchen and breakfast fit for a king. My mother cooked us sausages, big fat ones, multitudes of them, spluttering and jumping out of the pan. Then the plum pudding, in the making of which we'd all had a stir, fried in butter, sweet, fruity, oozy thick slices, delicious delicious, burning the tips of our tongues.

The dinner was held sometime about mid-afternoon, the turkey desperately carved up by my father, who sawed and hacked away as best he could. We made fun of him, offering to help, but inevitably he insisted upon doing it by himself, proving that for this once in the year he was master of his own household.

We had one guest to dinner. Every single year of my childhood. She was known as Miss Mohan, Minnie Mohan, a cantankerous wizened old woman who lived down the road, tucked away in bushes up a little private lane of her own. No one knew a single thing about Minnie Mohan, except that she had always been old. Her cottage was the most diminutive tumbledown scrap of a place with one and a half rooms, the half being a shop. It was an unspeakable shambles, with a high lumpy bed, stuffed away in a shadowy alcove under and behind a musty festoon of drapes and curtains and nets and dishcloths and coats and longjoins and huge dusky-pink flanelette bloomers, the lot of them for sale. And stays and combinations and outsize corsets, with laces and stringy tape and fraying ribbons hanging down.

There was a bench which served as a counter of sorts, with cardboard boxes overflowing with zip fasteners, and pop fasteners, and safety-pins and sewing needles and knitting-needles and wool and all colours of cotton reels. Finally, there were the sweets. Heavy jumbo-size bubble-glass jars of them. Liquorice Allsorts, strings of liquorice, jelly-babies, brandy-balls, dolly-mixtures. She had cut-up squares of newspaper which she'd twirl round with her nubbly fingers into a cone shape called a poke. You could have a poke of sweets for a penny.

The whole place was filthy, smelling of mothballs, as was the living room part, one wall of which was taken up with a great open fireplace with inglenooks at the side that you could sit in. There was no grate. The fire happily blazed away there on the floor, always well-stacked as people felt sorry for her and kept her more than adequately supplied with turf and wood. On the hob hung a black cast-iron kettle so encrusted with age and years of flame-licking you didn't dare drink the tea she made from the water in it. She was always offering tea, being lonesome I suppose. She would move half a mountain of stuff off the only chair – apart from her rocker – so as to hospitably accommodate your person. But we were afraid of her, the possible witch in her, and, although out of politeness and not a little fear, we would sit ourselves down, we'd be nervous and anxious to get off.

I imagine that the Christmas dinner at our house was the highlight of her year. She was in raptures every minute of it. After the eating rituals were over, we'd be packed off to the sitting room again, which we were pleased about, and the three adults would continue to celebrate in the kitchen with full glasses of pink lemonade. After a while we could hear my father beginning to sing, and after a longer while my mother would come in and ask the boys and myself to escort Miss Mohan home. It was dark by now and we'd link her down our lane and off up her own bit of a lane, full of shadows and spooky waving branches. She'd be muttering and scolding and singing to herself the whole way.

We, who knew nothing of alcohol – the word was never mentioned in our house – had no idea, even in the early teenage years, that the pink lemonade, Christmas in and Christmas out, was, in fact, sherry.

There was one Christmas that I shall never forget. That was the one when I found in the early-morning dimness, propped up and grinning at me on the three-piece sofa, the biggest and most beautiful doll the world had ever seen. She was as tall as me, dressed in frilly skirt, knitted jumper, petticoats, pinny, shoes, socks, bonnet, bangles, necklace. Everything. But the crowning glory was her hair. Long, long yellow hair made of soft squishy wool. That hair! I brushed it, combed it, plaited it and replaited it. I put my mother's curlers in it and every conceivable kind of bow and clip and hairgrip. It was the first Christmas that we had begun to doubt the existence of Santa. That, and the fact that I recognized some of the materials, combined to prove to me that my mother had actually made the lovely creature herself: knitted the top, embroidered the pinny, gathered the petticoats, stiffened the shoes, painted the pretty face – hours and hours of painstaking work.

Young as I was, in my confused way I recognized in the gift of the doll my mother's own confused way of telling me – something that she could never have got out in a million years – that she loved me anyway. No matter what.

Making music was the one pursuit from which we all derived the most consummate joy. Both sides of the family were remarkably musical and my parents and ourselves all possessed the capacity to sing in particularly melodious, strong, clear voices.

Sunday mornings in the chapel, and again for the evening's Benediction, we would take ourselves up the rickety staircase into the choir box high up at the back from where we could spit down upon the heads of the congregation. My father would settle himself neatly on the piano stool facing us, push away the tattered scrap of moth-eaten green felt covering the harmonium, derange a scattering of music sheets here and there over the top and on to the floor, heave and ho a few stops, and proceed – with joyful relish – to pump out a selection of rousing improvisations on the creaking old contraption before him. He was in love with his music; indeed the whole family delighted in it. When we sang, the seven of us together, our voices would blend in a rich harmonious swell, entwining, locking, weaving in and out, re-sounding against the walls of the church in a splendid rhapsody of celestial grandeur.

It was through music that my parents met, and often I begged my mother to tell me the story. I never tired of it.

They were both taking part in a Feis, the music festival of the Irish language which was held every year in the city of Derry. My mother was dancing, wearing the pretty, saucy short-skirted costume of the set-dancers. He was a soloist in his school choir. The ornate brooch attaching her cape at the shoulder fell apart. He was standing near, having already noticed her – she had great legs – and immediately proffered his new tie pin.

I used to sit and nurse the image of that first encounter in my mind. It was so beautiful, a true fairy-tale romance, exactly the way I wanted it to happen to me, when my turn came.

I myself used to sing in the annual Feis, and I often won. If I didn't, though, my father – who had coached me well and was highly competitive – would go to pieces, arguing with and putting the blame on everyone, declaring in a loudly obstreperous voice how it was 'all fixed'. I would be mortally embarrassed.

But I too cared if I lost. To me it was yet another symbol of rejection.

The war didn't affect us particularly. My father had acquired a wireless from somewhere and he used to sit in the corner of the kitchen of an evening, with his better ear fully atuned, listening to the voice of Lord Haw-Haw. He had a passion for Haw-Haw, sometimes repeating what the man said, imitating his accent, badly. It was most annoying. We would go 'Haw-haw, Haw-haw' baying like donkeys. But with restraint. Normally we kept well out of the way, lest we instigate the start of homework.

One night towards the end of the war we heard the planes go over really low and rushed up the braes to watch four bombs dropping on the city of Derry, some fifteen miles away. We children were wildly excited, but the parents got themselves into a state of near dementia. The relations, dozens of them, lived in Derry. Both mothers were there – the fathers being dead – sisters, brothers, cousins, second cousins, nieces, nephews: they all lived in the city. Hitler would have been hard put not to have hit at least one of them. We had no telephone, so my father took the next day off school and both he and my mother went in on the bus to investigate the devastation, leaving us to look after ourselves. Some relations indeed had experienced a direct hit, their houses being flattened, but had been safely ensconced in the air-raid shelters at the time. There were no casualties, but it was considered imperative that both my grandmothers get away from the firing line and come to stay with us in the comparative safety of the mountains.

Everybody arrived back in the evening, ably piloted by my uncle Gerry, a car mechanic by trade and so with easy access to transport – a chirrupy, smiley man with black curls, florid of cheek, and a salubrious appetite for the drink. My father was singing to his heart's content. We unloaded the luggage, an assortment of brown paper bags, hat boxes, veteran attaché cases, and carried the lot upstairs to my parents' bedroom, where the mothers were now to play houses for a while, the sitting room at last being taken over by my parents.

There followed a trying time for everyone. The two women were irrevocably different in every imaginable way. And they had to share the double bed. Da's mother was big, a coarse woman, blowsy, held together with corsets, an ex-teacher and bossy. In contrast, my maternal grandmother was a rather sedate individual, tiny, piping thin, frosty silver hair in a strict little bun sitting on the back of her immaculate head, a bunch of violets pinned to her throat, a delicate waft of lavender all around. But she was prone to attacks of asthma, when she would cough and spit out everything into a brown paper sugar-bag she kept adjacent to the chamber-pot her side of the bed. It was revolting.

Their presence in the house rapidly began to dominate our lives. We were constantly required to fetch and carry for them and got the snappy end of both their tongues if we didn't behave ourselves. Fortunately they didn't tarry long. I was delighted when they departed, having taken to neither of them.

People lit fires in the mountains, hoping the Germans would mistake them for towns and disgorge their bombs thereon. My mother made blackout blinds using sacking bags which she dyed from blackberries we gathered up the lane. Blackberry gathering became a good sideline for us that autumn. We sold them by the tin bucket-load to McGuigan's, upending them into rough wooden barrels of already stinking, maggot-crawling fermentation lorried up for the journey to the city.

My father, who had a modicum of sympathy for the Huns – he too being not over-fond of the British Empire – at times became rather perplexed by events, not certain which side he was on. My mother obviously denounced them both, plus a few others including America and France and almost every country she'd heard of, holding them, without exception, responsible for the continuing shortage of such necessities as sugar and marmalade jam.

But I was growing up. There was a rumour going around the school that babies were *not* brought by the doctor. This was intensely more interesting than any old war or rationing or gas masks. We were in the grip of the most exciting discovery of our small lives, with much conjecture and bawdy rumour and speculation spiralling through the schoolyard in a whirlwind of salacious innuendo.

It was the collapse of the Age of Innocence.

In our house, education was the thing.

'You don't want to end up like John Quaker,' my mother would mutter darkly. Wagging the finger. The sour bone of contention between her and the in-laws was always sitting there, raw, upon the kitchen table. Da had married beneath him. 'A little Littlewood's girl' his side of the family called her upon occasion. They were a forbidding, contumelious lot, three sisters of them plus the big mother, teachers all of then, overbearing, powerful women capable of squashing everything before them. Ma despised them with a grand passion and she could outbrazen them, too, ordering them out of *her* house with commendable equanimity many's the time. Nevertheless, their contemptuous opinion of her with her lack of scholastic niceties remained a constant thorn in her side. So much so that she was education-mad. And John Quaker, unbeknownst to his simple self, was the poor unfortunate who was held up as an example to us, an example of what we *could* turn out like were we to let up for any length of time on the learning.

John Quaker was a man of the hills. He lived with a scattering of sheep, a dog to keep an eye on them, a goat for the milk, a hen or two for the eggs, and all in together now in a little thatched sprout sunk deep in the soft far backside of Mullaghash. On the last Friday of the month the muffled sounds of his coming, down along the back road, would reach into our floating cocoon through the pearly mist-washed curtain cretonne, stirring us with the scudding of jostling sheep, the meh-eh-eh of their skinny bleating puncturing the cold morning air. He was on his way to Dungiven, a small town five miles further on from us, to the Fair Day.

Late afternoon we'd hear them on their way home, a muted patter in the distance, nearer and nearer till they reached the back gate. There they'd stop. The sheep were free to wander – all over the road, squeeze through the hedge into the meadow, pick their way across the midden, nuzzling and munching and skipping and cavorting about. A few smart directions to the long silky collie, push open the big gate and up and into the house.

'Sit down there, John, and take the weight off your feet,' my mother would say, patting a chair. The feet were often bare. He could and did walk miles in them and over the years they'd become as tough as the old boots he wore during the hard winters, the same crusted brown with as many cracks and crannies. My mother would top up the teapot on the range and offer him the best cake from the biscuit tin. He'd sit there for a while, thawing out, in the peaked cap and carrying the blackthorn stick, happy just to be at ease. Then, from some innard pocket, out would come 'the Form'. John Quaker was one of several farmers who couldn't read or write. Through the years my father had become their redeemer. He'd fill in 'Forms' – for the sheep, the cows, the harvesting, the turf, the sheep-dipping, the wool-shearing. And most importantly, the *will*, the Last Will and Testament, their greatest secret. Then they'd sign themselves 'X' on the dotted line to finish off the job. In return for my father's good work and guaranteed sealed lips, there'd be sacks of potatoes and avalanches of turf delivered to the back door the year round.

So it was imperative, in my mother's mind anyway, that none of us ended up in similar illiterate straits. As soon as the tea things were cleared off the table, therefore, it was 'get stuck into the books'. No excuses. No offering to run over the braes for fags. Father would supervise everything. A self-taught man, his head was full of wondrous things. He could talk with blythe volubility on every conceivable subject – excepting of course sex, or anything pertaining thereto. Above everything else though he loved the Irish language, the Gaelic, but this particular passion

26

was shackled to his fanatic patriotism, the dedication to free Ireland at any cost and get rid of the 'Brits'. In the middle of an otherwise pleasant interlude, he'd spoil it all by shooting a question at me in Irish, '*Conas tá tú*? How are you?' The most simple thing.

'*Tà mé go maith*. I am well,' I'd respond sullenly.

I despised this most annoying habit of his, as I despised the language itself. Indeed I harboured a great disaffection for learning of *any* sort. Rather would I while away my waking hours cogitating with the trees and hedgerows, playing houses, confiding in my dolls, dreaming . . . dreaming. I would sit at our kitchen table in those interminable cooped-up evening sessions of erudition, gnawing and sucking the end of my pencil to a moist pulp, watching through the window the half-light play upon the coalshed and over the smooth grey flank of the great oak, the hens in slow motion taking a last desultory stab at the earth. I knew other children were out and about, climbing trees, running wild, heedlessly free.

But we were different. Us lot. We were going to secondary school. We were destined to *be* somebody, make our marks in the world. In order to achieve this, it was necessary for the five of us to get scholarships, there being no free further education in those days. So from about the age of eleven, through our last year at primary school, cramming was of the essence. Patrick was the first to go, winning the Education Department's grant plus a half-scholarship from St Columb's, the boys' Catholic college in Derry, entitling him to the first three years free, plus boarding.

I swiped the lot, getting not only the Education Department's grant, but a whole five years' free boarding at the Convent of the Sisters of Mercy, some miles out the far side of the city. Unwittingly, with my wandering romantic style of essay-writing and the colourful swirls and eddies on my geography maps, my work had appealed to the artistic inclinations of the good sisters. And then for good measure they topped it up with free tuition in singing and pianoforte during my stay with them.

When we got the results, my mother sang the house down for a whole day and baked a jam sponge. Minnie Mohan arrived in the afternoon, to pick up the details.

'Isn't she the clever one now, isn't she?' Ma kept repeating. And Minnie nodded, sat at the table around the second-best china, supping the tea, a goodly slice of the sponge on her plate, ruminating over the individual strawberries in the thick jam.

'Aye, aye, she is that. She is that . . .'

'*Three* scholarships. *Three*, she won,' my mother enthused. 'The best of the bunch. Brilliant, the examiners said. Completely brilliant.'

This was a fat lie. She was off on her exaggeration course, taking wing. By the end of the week she'd be way up in the clouds, the embellishment going right through the roof. I didn't mind. Nothing could trouble me now. I was leaving home. Escaping at last the loneliness. Going to live with a group of other girls, amongst whom I was bound to find at least one friend. A brand-new world of adventure lay ahead. My imagination had already taken fanciful flight. For some time now I had been devouring soft squishy little novelettes that fairly sizzled with spirited tales of secret passages and jolly midnight feasts and frolicksome escapades down the drainpipe. I would have all this and more. My joy was supreme.

Towards the end of that summer when I was twelve, my mother took me on the bus into Derry one Saturday in order to purchase the necessary attire and accoutrements for my new school. Just the two of us. There were items like knickers and a first brassière, and some roll-ons to keep the stomach in and the stockings up should the garters fail – articles of apparel quite unmentionable in our household. The males, therefore, including my father, were left behind to look after the house. My mother's bras and pants had never been seen by anyone, except sometimes me and, one presumes, her husband. The other washing flapped away merrily on the line day and night, but the secret stuff, hers and mine, she dried in the dark of night, arranging it neatly on brown paper on the open oven door.

We'd had a list of the mandatory requisites for the school uniform, a most lengthy list upon the sight of which my mother had had a fit. *Six* pairs of navy wool knickers, *six* pairs of long black stockings, *six* vests . . .

'What do they think we're made of?' she'd cried. '*Six!* Do they think we're right eejits or something?', taking a pencil and substituting in a singularly determined fashion a three for every six. 'We'll soon see about that, we will . . . *six.*'

She persisted in her invective, shaking the head disbelievingly. I was distraught. If they said six, they meant six. I'd be mortified, be seen to be the pauper I was. I'd be made an example of, sent home. I started to cry, my lovely new life suddenly in tatters around my feet.

'There, there,' she said. Soothing. 'It'll be all right, pet. We'll just get these for the moment. If you need more we'll buy them. See how it goes . . . there, there.'

I knew then she was going to miss me. Even if only a little.

We had to buy the uniform at a particular store. I tried it on. The navy gymslip was far too long but that was because she was going to take it up and let it down by bits as I grew. A royal-blue girdle. White blouse and tie. Black stockings to be held up by the roll-on or garters or both. The school blazer, also royal, with the Alma Mater crest on the pocket. The turned-up pudding of a hat. The outdoor shoes. The indoor shoes. The gym shoes. Poor woman. She it was who carried the household purse. My father never had a penny in his pocket. No need. She purchased his simple pleasures for him – the fags, the tobacco, the pipe cleaners. Today the domestic purse was a deal lighter. A *great* deal. But she didn't seem to mind. She hummed a cheerful little tune to herself and swung the bags nonchalantly, in harmony with the dancing earrings, all the way back to the bus depot.

I hugged my delight to myself. Sweet, sweet loveliness! In the long shop mirror, I had looked upon a different person. I was *somebody* now. A somebody to be reckoned with. No longer the plain little shy body from the bog.

Alleluia! Utility Liz was dead!

The day I left for the convent, the whole family came along. It was a day of extremes, a day of excitement, a day of celebration. And a day full of tears. We saw Patrick off first, at St Columb's for the start of his second year, my mother sobbing herself to distraction as she fluttered the fine lawn handkerchief in a last farewell from the big iron gates. Then we took another bus out on the road towards Donegal, through the setting sun, along the banks of the lovely River Foyle. The convent was some five miles out and stood in its own majestic grandeur amidst sweeping lawns inlaid with flower beds and darkening swathes of rhododendron and azalea. Everywhere there were trees. Big ones, pine, cypress, oak, reaching way up into the sky. I had never seen any place so beautiful.

The convent itself was very old, grey chipped stone, with tall thin windows and turrets and statues and minarets and a belfrey – straight out of my story books, indeed, but even better! I was enraptured. But also, suddenly, very afraid. I was being set down amongst strangers, far away from the comforting familiarity of the old bog road. We all started crying again. The good nun who'd received us took over.

'I think it's time you went now,' she murmured gently to the parents. 'It's best you don't loiter. I'll take her up to the dormitory and she'll meet some of the other girls. She'll be as right as rain in a minute . . .'

Along a shiny, lofty hall with holy pictures hanging, the Crucifixion, Saint Teresa of Avilà – my favourite saint. Past an open door with clattering of kitchen things, a statue of the downcast Virgin on a far shadowy corner pedestal, freshly flowered, a mellow light unfolding the slender blue fall of her mantle. Up two flights of stairs, round and round, the heavy black serge of the nun's skirt swirling over the polished smooth heels of her shoes.

The dormitory was at the very top of the house, plain white beds up both sides, a handful of girls sitting or standing around, some weepy, others laughing, talking. Clothes everywhere.

'This is yours, Mary,' the nun said, indicating a middle one. 'And this is your locker.' That was it.

At the door, she turned.

'Supper will be ready in half an hour, girls,' the voice cut through the chatter. I'll send the Prefect to fetch you. And punctual, please.'

Sister Gertrude, the head nun of the boarders.

I placed my new cardboard case on the counterpane and, looking up, caught the eye of the girl next door. Crystal shining blue eyes, wide friendly smile in a face the prettiest I had ever seen.

'I'm Patsy,' she said, coming over and sitting down on the bed. 'Do you need any help?' She didn't look as though she had the energy to lift a finger, a big girl with an easy languorous grace. I liked her immediately.

'I'm so frightened,' I whispered. 'I've never been anywhere.'

She laughed, a low, warm, cuddling chuckle. 'Neither have I,' she said. 'But my older sister's here, so it's not so bad for me.'

She was from Dungiven, so we were nearly neighbours. At least no distance from each other that a bike couldn't handle.

Together we went down to the refectory and together we joined the other first-years at one of the long wooden tables. I looked around at the faces. Round, square, pretty, not so pretty, cheerful, nervous, chatty, lost. But all of them – every single one – acceptable as potential friends by my parents.

*

Morning call was the figure of a nun with a tiny tinker bell swishing through the dormitories in a rattle of rosary beads and a bright 'Morning, girls'. Mass was at seven, breakfast – which we ate in silence – at eight, school at nine. The school buildings were quite modern, purpose-built and practical, at a little distance from the convent along a neatly sculpted path. I was allocated a place in the highest grade of three classes of first-years, most of them daygirls from the city. I suppose this group were considered exceptionally bright, the cream of their year. But scolastic prowess impressed me not one whit.

I was immediately dismayed by their uppity looks, the glossy, suave, supercilious airs of these city smoothies, the smart haircuts, the style, the money. I was small again, plain, awkward, countri-fied – and completely out of place amongst these demagogues. There seemed to be one particular batch of them, a job lot as it were, transplanted from the same primary school, an established, exclusive, whispering, giggling clique. It was an inauspicious start.

Even worse were the new subjects that had been chosen for us, for our particular class. To me they were downright academic, the last thing I wanted: physics, chemistry, history, with compul-sory damned Gaelic thrown in. I wanted to paint and make cakes and sew and embroider and play around. But this was a class of *brains*, and because of my high exam results in arithmetic, reading, writing and geography – although achieved most certainly by my father's merciless cramming – this was where I was presumed to belong.

On that first morning, too, the teachers chose the Head Prefect. And not surprisingly, the snottiest of the snots was elected. I could have cried. Then, to my astonishment, I heard my name called. They had picked me as Second Prefect. Me. A boarder. There were only about fifty boarders in the school, compared to a couple of hundred daygirls. It was an honour indeed. And when they pinned the prized blue ribbon to my gymslip, the young mountain chest underneath rose to the happy occasion in a gladsome perky uplift. After that, I feared none of them.

Our days took on a pleasant routine. In the classroom, thanks to my father's coaching, I was way ahead in the regular subjects and so had little to learn. Irish I hated as much as ever. The teacher was diminutive, like a doll, Sister Agnes, she of the nimble brain and giant volcanic temper. We clashed. A whole lifetime later, when she was in her late nineties and confined to bed, I had occasion to visit the convent. In the small peaceful room where she lay, bolstered upright in the bed, calmly awaiting the final curtain, the life in her zinged through the space between us. She remembered me, remembered my defiance, *her* defiance. And we laughed together. For the first – and last – time . . . dear lovely old crotchety Sister Agnes.

French was taught by the round rosy Dorothea, a young nun of temperamental disposition, too beautiful, we decided, to be wasting herself away in a convent. Many were the rumours of her broken heart, of the love she had left behind – her unpredictability blamed entirely on the churlish behaviour of some capricious recreant, perhaps a rogue Parisian, in her hapless past. She was an excellent teacher and we learnt well.

The science laboratory overlooked the playing fields at the back and, right from the first lesson, the very sight of the place rendered me impotent. The stench of the chemicals, the terror of potential explosions from substances the components of which I couldn't even begin to understand, the bland sonorous voice of the teacher inflicting itself upon my impervious eardrums, together provided a sure-fire guarantee that my comprehension of the sciences would remain forever bemuddled.

Next door to the science room, however, was the glorious assembly hall, my favourite place in the school. With three walls made entirely of glass, the views were stunning – the smooth lawns, disappearing pathways, trees and shrubs in a myriad hues of green – giving it the spaciousness of a very grand concert hall. This indeed was the room where the school concerts were performed, where we said our morning prayers and sang the school anthem and where we boarders, in the recreational hour of the long dreary winter evenings, would awkwardly learn to dance with each other to the lilt of an old Viennese waltz played on the piano by Sister Imelda.

Ah! Sister Imelda. Poor woman. Her face, her skin, was a wretched disaster, stained a fiery vermilion and erupting periodically in angry Vesuvius-like sores. The hair, which should have been completely hidden, kept sticking out from under the coif in straight coarse grey tufts, the eyes behind black-rimmed glasses cold, unyielding. At times one could have felt pity for her had it not been for her fierce combustibility. She could flare up into a temper without warning, irrational, and an entire roomful of girls would go down under the meteoric blast.

Unfortunately she was my music teacher, which somewhat dampened my initial enthusiam for this fanciful new preoccupation. I was having two lessons a week in both singing and piano. The singing was fine, but the boredom of scale-practising I found most vexing, especially as the blessed Imelda wasn't beyond administering a sharp reminder across young knuckles should they have the misfortune to place a tentative finger tip upon the wrong key. Nevertheless, in time, I grew to like and respect her. Her enthusiasm for her particular subject was so infectious I couldn't help but get caught up in it. Imelda was a perfectionist, a teacher of superior merit who demanded – and received – the utmost from her pupils.

We had two tennis courts, a netball court and a vast expanse of hayfield in which to wield our thumping great camogie sticks. I was hopeless at everything. The vagaries of tennis, the one sport in which I would dearly have wished to excel just for the snootiness of it, escaped me, as did most of the balls, soaring past the ungainly swipe of my racquet with a murderous certainty I couldn't hope to control. My ability to run wasn't quite up to form either. In no time, after a few erratic sprints across the court to retrieve dead balls, I'd be lamentably out of breath. It was a losing battle, but I stuck with it, determined to crack it. Inevitably, though, the half-decent players backed off me. In singles my opponent, having let fly with an almighty thwack, would be left staring at the sky, racquet tapping the ground in a temper, whilst I ran amok into the chicken wire. Doubles was worse. We always lost.

I had made the mistake of trying to keep up with the demagogues! However, when Patsy and some of her friends, also from Dungiven, took me on everything changed. Patsy's standard of performance was similar to my own, but with her lackadaisical ways and soft beatific smile, no one could get mad at her. When

Patsy missed she just stood there where she was and folded over in foolish laughter, and I was perfectly happy to be her trusty runaround.

Patsy, Patricia, Fedelma and I. We decided to call ourselves 'Our Gang' – the rather pedestrian title of a group of daredevil characters, boys all of them, in a comic which was popular at the time. What the purpose of this exclusive coterie was I'm sure none of us knew, but there was very definite and joint intent to partake of midnight feasts and run rampant through the profusion of overgrown paths down to the river in the sloe-dark night. The wide graceful curve of the River Foyle meandered along the entire far limits of the convent grounds on her enchanted journey to the north Atlantic. We loved that river and the walks we took there, two by two, in the leisure time between last lesson at school and the evening study hours. From the main walkway, tumbling down to the water's edge, through a labyrinth of tangled brushwood and boisterous tropical plants, ran a myriad of paths, some laid in a mosaic of slippery stepping-stones, others scattering free into the undergrowth. Weekends we had time to explore and from the banks watch the rusty old barges shuffle past, creaking and coughing their slow laborious way upriver. It was a place of magic.

On weekdays study time started at five, when we gathered into one classroom and proceeded in absolute silence to do our homework. Up front, at the teacher's desk, sat a nun, a different one each day. She read her breviary or glided like a spirit up and down between the rows of desks quietly telling her beads, the black wooden rosary that swung clickety-clack from the polished leather belt. Sometimes, too, a hand would caress the crucifix, the bronzed desolation of the hanging Christ tucked into the belt below the breast. There was no curve to the breast. Whatever form it may have taken in that other life was now amorphous, forever inviolate under the starched white front.

At six, through the trees, came the sonorous dong of the bell from the convent chapel.

'Angelus, girls,' she would say. Rising. Heads down, hands joined, we would pray.

Then it was supper and with happy release and a terrific

chitter-chatter we'd be off over the path to the convent. In the refectory silence had again to be observed until Grace was said. It was a cosy gossipy time of day, the best time. After supper we'd troop into the chapel for yet *more* prayers, then back over to the school to finish our homework.

My piano and singing practice were three half-hour periods in the week, taken during the study hours, usually at round five o'clock. The piano was in the convent music room, a most elegant jade-green parlour with French doors leading out on to resplendent lawns. It was the time of evening when the sisters gathered together in the chapel to pray in unison, and I could hear the muted voices rise and fall in suppliant chant.

'Mother have mercy, Christ have mercy, Mother have mercy, Christ hear us . . .' Their lives mystified me: the austerity of it, the frugality, the fastings, the interminable praying, the repetition, the excruciating boredom of their existence, the same old routine day in, day out.

I knew they could hear me singing in the music room, songs like 'Who is Sylvia?' and 'The Lass with the Delicate Air', the set examination pieces, but I never felt in the slightest bit inhibited. Often one or other of them would remark on the enhancement of their worshipping hour. What *nobody* remarked upon, except the cunning Imelda, with her foxy ear to the job, was my piano-playing. I was supposed to practise my scales. Instead I worked out a few harmonious chords and toyed around with these as an accompaniment to my voice. I never did master the pianoforte, possessing I suppose neither the talent nor the impetus, and in the end even the indefatigable Imelda gave up.

On Saturdays we could receive visitors, and my parents would come every two or three weeks, bearing gifts of fairy cakes and pancakes and sweet homemade jam. We each of us had a tuckbox which we kept in a cupboard in the refectory and from which were shared out the goodies amongst our friends. I was considered the lucky one, for some of the girls, for various reasons, had a visit perhaps only once a term.

But I didn't consider myself fortunate. I wanted to be exactly like everyone else, no better, no worse, no different. I was awkward with my parents and they with me, and promenading up and down the path, me between them, or sitting around the table in the cold beeswaxed reception parlour, I gabbled on relentlessly about Our Gang, the teachers, the food. My father in his turn would report a death here and there or somebody on his last legs, my mother the latest gossip from Minnie Mohan. Then we'd retire to the chapel for a small prayer and I'd walk them to the gate and it was cheerio again for now.

Letters in and out were unsealed and pocket money was handed over for safekeeping to Sister Gertrude. Each morning after breakfast she would take up her position at the top of the first flight of stairs, an assemblage of keys – like a jailer's – cascading from the waist. There, from a massive wooden cupboard, a kind of mini-shop, she would serve us with our needs, totting up the monies meticulously. Very soon I learnt about sanitary towels and their purpose, and my memory winged back to the torn-up sheets, the rags hung to dry on the range door in the stealthy depths of night. She'd swipe them away in the morning, in frantic haste, before anyone was up and about. I had often wondered what the fuss was about.

I wondered now, and worried about how to tell her that I knew. Knew about *that*. I was thirteen. In our dormitory one of the main topics of nightly dissertation before lights out was periods, along with period pains, pimples, blackheads, greasy hair, burgeoning breasts, boys, babies and all such fascinating matters. It was wonderful. I felt part of a family, comfortable, warm, needed and liked. I had never been so happy.

It was part of the boarders' curriculum that at some point, some morning after the shopping ritual during our first year, Sister Gertrude would take us aside, one of us at a time, into a small cubby-hole of a corner for the purpose of sorting out any problems we might have, and there in the semi-darkness she would deliver her short pep talk. When my turn came, I assured her I knew everything. We stood close together, facing each other, and I stared hard at the big crucifix reposing in the highly polished but time-worn faded leather belt. I couldn't look up. She was a tall woman, thin, and held herself upright with a fearless dignity of which we were all in awe. She commanded respect, and got it. I was beginning to fall in love with her.

Oh, dear beautiful Sister Gertrude, where are you now? You were the inspiration of our formative years, the kind, wise and fair omnipotence that sustained us when all else was disintegrating around our juvenescent feet, you with your soft brown doe eyes and perfect face and a light shining out of you which wasn't of this paltry world, the radiance of a soul dedicated to that suffering Christ for whom you had joyfully sacrificed everything. We knew nothing about you. You were a being apart, enigmatic – a distance between you and others that no one ever dared cross. But you were there. For us. And we loved you.

Christmas and Easter holidays of that first year were good. I knew now that there was more to life than the bog, some escape at the end of it. Our Gang wrote copiously to each other and talked of visiting in the long summer ahead. I waited for my mother to speak, give utterance on the subject of my impending womanhood, the momentous astronomical change which was about to take place in my pubescent body. But she didn't. I waited and waited and then finally, a few days before returning to the convent to start my second year, the moment came. She was making soda bread on the kitchen table, kneading and thumping the dough with industrious assiduity, flicking the hair back, bangles jangling, talking to herself. My father and the boys had been sent to McGuigan's to fetch some groceries. I went into the scullery to do something. And out it came . . .

'Mary, has anything happened to you yet?' she called.

I yelled back. Quickly. 'No. Not yet.' Rooted to the spot, trembling with the fear.

There was a pause. The bread banging had stopped. Then the crack of a match as she lit a cigarette, and suddenly the fear had gone.

'It's all right,' I said, coming back into the kitchen. Calm. 'I know about it. We had a lecture at school.'

'Oh, good. Great. That's great, then.'

I thought she was about to start singing. Her back was still turned to me, a straight back, tight. But in moments like these helpless in its impotence – a terrible contradiction of a woman. She lifted the rolling pin and brought it down hard across the lump of dough.

'Make us a cuppa tea then, there's a good girl,' and the humming started.

Filling the kettle, I knew with a surge of heady relief that the deed – the imparting of the knowledge of the facts of life, something we'd both been dreading for over a year – was finally accomplished. Finished. For ever. We would never speak of these things again.

My first period arrived when I was fourteen. I hated it. Periods were an embarrassment to us, and although we talked about them it was still a precarious subject, something to be hidden, something to be ashamed of. The Curse. I never told my mother, but when I returned home that year for the Christmas holiday she pointed to the dresser doors in the scullery one day. 'If you want anything,' she said, 'they're at the back of that cupboard behind the tea set.'

Later I found them, an unopened chunky packet hidden way behind the best china. I also found a book with yellowed silky pages, very old, a picture of a curled foetus on the front cover. I couldn't wait to get the house to myself and at the very first opportunity dived in. I felt certain she hadn't meant me to find it, had actually forgotten about it. The pages were falling out, becoming unthreaded from the cotton that held them together, fusty, mildewed, damp to the touch. But what a find! It had to do with babies, not with the creation of them – there wasn't a penis in sight – but the development of them within the womb, the birthing, the umbilical, the suckling. I had never seen my mother breast-feeding although I'm sure she must have done so. It hadn't even entered my head that breasts could be for that. *That!* I was dumfounded. And couldn't wait to share it with my new friend. My new *dirty* friend. Her name was Bernadette.

Bernadette had appeared from nowhere, marching up the choir stairs one Sunday morning before Mass and more or less *demanding* of my father that she be permitted to join us.

'Fine,' he said. 'Fine.' Bernadette was hard to refuse. All of sixteen, she stood tall, boyish, handsome, arrogant. And she could sing. There was something different about her, quite unlike any girl I had seen before. The girls at the convent, even the Demagogues, were somehow just girls, lumpy, spotty, much of a muchness in the same old navy serge uniforms. This one had real class.

I caught up with her after Mass outside the chapel door. It seemed the family had recently arrived from Derry to take over her mother's old homestead, a small farm in one of the townlands a couple of miles from us. Her father was a policeman in the city and Bernadette was attending a technical college there, learning shorthand and typing. We liked each other immediately, and visiting rights were established.

It was a friendship which was not to be allowed to last. Some months later my father heard that *her* father had been a Protestant and although he had converted to Catholicism in order to marry her mother, it was soon observed that he had yet to make an appearance at Sunday Mass. Besides, in our part of the world policemen were deeply suspect, not because of their occupation but because the community was almost exclusively Catholic and the half-dozen or so policemen were Protestants to a man. Nobody liked them and they were seldom seen, keeping themselves under cover in a ugly white sepulchre of a barracks away behind the village.

So it was, with double-edged condemnation, that the discontinuance of my association with the inimitable Bernadette was decreed. As it happens, in this instance my parents were right. But I took no heed. I had a mind of my own now, a *will* of my own, the rebellious adolescent, defiant, devious. These days it took but a little effort and simple planning on my part in order to deceive them. Most afternoons I walked over to the village to post letters or hang about at the coin box for telephone calls from my friends, so it was easy for me to meet Bernadette.

It was at the crossroads below our house, leaning against a telegraph pole of a late evening, that I finally learnt, in coarse and shocking detail, the facts of life in their entirety.

She took me to her house that holiday, too, and in her bedroom we played dressing-up games – a lifetime removed from the dressing-up games of my precious lost childhood. She had an old trunk overflowing with ancient theatrical frippery: short bouncy fru-fru skirts in bunches of red, yellow and pink net, long silken golden stockings, fancy red satin suspender belts with little black

bows, tassled bras, plumes and feathers and spangles and swirls of shimmering confections, a whole jumble of tawdry attire, tumbling out and over each other on to the carpet. These were the things of her mother's past, the small, very proper, silvery-haired creature who occasionally knocked on the bedroom door with cups of tea and cake. I couldn't believe the woman. Not an eyelid flickered at the sight of our semi-nakedness, preening ourselves in the long wardrobe mirror. Her daughter treated her with scathing contempt, ordering her out of the room if she showed an inclination to loiter. I found her attitude very upsetting, but was powerless to remonstrate. No one argued with Bernadette.

It was in that sombre mountain room, way at the back of nowhere, shimmying and swaying in a web of see-through gossamer to a tin tune from the rackety old radio, scarlet lipstick across my mouth, that the first flame of raw lust shot through my belly and swamped my being with guilty heat. My parents had been right. This kind of company and behaviour were certainly not suitable for their rather naive convent-educated daughter. I was disgusted with myself and couldn't bear to think what Our Gang would say if they knew. Or how the guileless angelic face of Sister Gertrude would turn to stone, frozen at the horror, the unspeakable monstrosity, of my sin. Before I returned to the convent after that particular holiday, I took myself off to confession. To the old man.

'I've had bad thoughts,' *sotto voce.*

'Ah well,' he said. 'Well, well.'

There was a pause, and I hung on for dear life.

'Good,' he said. 'Now is there anything else . . .?'

And I was swung clear.

Somewhere around my fifteenth birthday, during a routine medical examination, it was discovered that I had a heart murmur. Nothing serious, they said, but just to be on the safe side certain precautions had to be taken. To begin with, I was not to take part in any more games for the rest of my time at school. I was delighted. Not only did I not have to try any more but I could glory in their sympathy for the times I *had* tried and had failed. I now, too, had an explanation for the breathlessness. However, it was also decided that to make doubly sure it would be preferable for the next couple of months for me to go to bed every day after school and rest. This was a blow. Nothing much was known about heart defects in those days. It was a grey area, with the notion of open-heart surgery yet to be conceived. So it was thought better to err on the side of caution.

The cramped dormitory times were finished. I was now in a room, one floor down, a lovely bright open room shared with Patsy and two others. But it was winter and darkness descended upon me and my books – I still had to study – as soon as I hit the bed. It was a period of acute loneliness, alleviated only by the brief appearance of Patsy with the supper tray. The silence was palpable. I hated it. In the distant depths of the house the nuns praying, on and on. Then the melancholy toll of the Angelus bell, the voices rising, strong, in unison . . . 'In the name of the Father, and of the Son, and of the Holy Ghost . . .' Kitchen sounds. The flat clomp of the girls' shoes on the path on their way back over to the school, their happy chatter, laughter. Fading.

I felt totally isolated and abandoned; the last sporadic chirrup of the birds getting themselves prettily fluffed up and comfortable and tucked in for the night, the fitful bursts of tweet and twitter finally vanishing into the gloaming. Then stillness. I was desolate.

Then one late afternoon, before the Angelus, I heard a new sound. It came from the river – a long, low cry which was neither animal nor human. I sat bolt-upright in the bed, listening. There it was again. Higher now, rising in a screaming wail like a demented baby. It lasted a few moments, then stopped. I was paralysed with fear, realizing exactly what it was.

All during my childhood years stories of fairies and leprechauns, pixies, elves and other ghostly beings had haunted the countryside. At wakes there was almost certain to be some old crone sitting in a corner, guaranteed to unfold a tale of such spine-chilling terror that we'd have to hold on to each other with the fright the whole way home. But the most scary stories we ever listened to were about the banshee. She was a ghost, a wailing woman, a spirit of the other world 'with a cry neither human nor animal' who could be heard in the trees, over the fields, around and about, by particular members of a family. When you heard the lamentation it meant only one thing: someone in the house was about to die. How I didn't die with fear myself, screwed up in my little bed, too frightened to call out – knowing I wouldn't be heard even if I did – was a wonder. I was sure it was me they were after.

That first time I heard it I told Patsy, but she had nothing to say, no comment one way or the other. There *was* nothing to say. Finally, after hearing it a few more times, I poured out the whole hysterical tale to Sister Gertrude.

The end of term was nigh. It was the year of the first of our two major exams, the equivalent of O Level. That and the general absurdity of the entire affair enabled the good woman to deem it appropriate that I recommence my normal routine forthwith, without the games, of course.

When my examination results came out that summer they were

good, perhaps even *very* good, but unfortunately not quite up to the scratch my father had anticipated, physics and chemistry being way down low. He recovered quickly.

'We'll just have to work harder, won't we?' he humoured me. 'We can do a bit of catching up in the holidays. Okay?'

I had no intention of catching up. On anything pertaining to academia, that is. I was fifteen and a half. There were boys to be caught. *Boys*. They were everywhere – St Columb's boys, from Dungiven or the mountains, up to play some serious Gaelic football with my brothers in the fine new sports field behind the Parochial House. I couldn't *speak* to them or anything like that, but I could look, mostly from the sidelines, while they half-killed each other on the pitch. The general idea was that they should look back and with an eye to this I persuaded my mother to let me perm my hair. It was longer now, still thin and becoming mousy, so it was more than ready for an uplift. Toni Home Perms were in vogue that season, along with skirts an inch or two above the knee. My mother had already done her own hair and we had a goodly supply of the correct spindly curlers for the job. Together we created my new image, labouring through hours of wrapping the strands in the scraps of fine tissue, rolling them up tight – skin-tight – me dictating, contrary, obstreperous, she patient, capable. Then dabbing with the pungent perm lotion, the timing, the rinsing, the chill acrid dribbles into the ears and down the neck. And finally the big roll in the warmed towel. And there I was. A new girl. A woman. A *gorgeous* young woman. It stood out around my head in a fluffy cumulus of finely frizzed curls. A miracle! My mother too was pleased with her handiwork and announced that it might now be in order to powder my nose.

This we set to, applying the stuff sparingly from her small powder-box of palest peach.

'Not too much now. Not too much.' She dusted the soft puff over my big rosy cheeks and bright shiny nose. 'We don't want you to look ridiculous, do we?' Then the lipstick. Poppy or Cherry Red were the colours then. The only colours.

'Where does she think *she*'s going?' remarked one of the brothers, passing through the scullery.

'Never you mind,' she called after him.

I felt warm and wanted inside. We were all girls together now.

By then I too was using the scullery, door closed, in which to perform my ablutions, the Saturday bath nights long gone. I was also sleeping in the spare room, at last rendered habitable by my resourceful brother Joseph. He was a great go-getter and was already excelling at woodwork at St Columb's. He could plaster, hammer, saw, paint, point – skills that had of course been passed on from my *mother*'s side of the family, the much maligned Philistine lot.

That was the summer I was allowed to go on holiday for the first time. Patsy had wanted to invite me, but there were too many already in their household; they were probably even poorer than us. But Fedelma lived in a handsome house out the country. They were prosperous farmers and with the mother a school-teacher and an uncle a priest in my brothers' college, they were considered eminently respectable.

Fedelma had pale blond hair, newly permed like mine, and a most happy disposition. She was also the proud possessor of a mother-of-pearl powder compact and a Cherry Red lipstick. But best of all she had an older brother, Joe. Joe of the fair hair and the fair words, of the gentle voice and the thinly fine hands, hands which heaved me up up up on to the back of their enormous cart horse and led us round the yard one sparkling summer's morning. I had never been on a horse before, had never even touched one, and the very magnitude of this particular specimen terrified me even from afar. But Joe showed me how to stroke him, draw my hand slowly down the long velvet neck, make eye contact with the wise brown orb, speak to him in a language he could understand.

What I knew of farm animals in general was slight, the farmers round our way being mostly crop-growers – corn, hay, turnips, flax. There were a few cows on a small farm past the crossroads from us, from where we fetched the milk morning and evening, still frothy and warm, in the tin can. Sometimes we watched the cows being milked. But politely, at a distance, they being of Protestant stock.

But at Fedelma's they had calves too. And pigs. And geese and turkeys and ducks and byres and outhouses with machinery and endless fields. Dogs and cats and a lot of commotion and a great slough of a puddle as big as a lake in the middle of it across the yard for everyone to fall into.

It was a happy time. I gave my heart to Joe that summer when I was fifteen. But Joe, like his ecclesiastical uncle before him, was already spoken for.

My next year at the convent was very special. I was at last allowed to drop physics and chemistry, both of which had given me a really big headache in the exams. In their place, I took up art, taught in the assembly hall by Molly, a new and quite startling young lay teacher. Small, intense, with wild black hair and blackberry eyes, she was a pretty, sparky, sexy piece of Bohemia, a hippy of her time, instantly popular with the girls but under woeful suspicion by the nuns. How she managed to be taken on by them we could hardly fathom, except that she came from a family who, although regarded as highly eccentric, had nevertheless achieved outstanding success in the fields of literature and art, Molly herself being top of the list.

It was impossible to tell if she was a good teacher, so overwhelming was her flamboyance, the reckless swing of the short skirt, the teetery heels, the flourish with which she brandished the loaded paintbrush across an easel, encouraging us to do likewise with no regard to the walls, each other, or the polished parquet underfoot. She smoked profusely, in the classroom, from

a long jade cigarette holder, waving that around in the air too, creating marvellous random swirls of lingering smoke-rings, all the while opening our eyes and lifting our sensibilities on to another plateau – a world of glorious colour, fantasy and escapism.

We revelled in this ocean of liberation. Not so the nuns. When Molly asked if there was some way of increasing the heat in the room so as to make it more comfortable for the life-drawing classes she was proposing to have, for the first time in the history of the school, they stamped their collective polished feet down. Hard. Nobody minded. Nobody was about to strip off and expose herself to the rest of the class anyway.

That was the age we were at; the age we were in.

I gave up a few other disagreeable subjects like Irish and history, although the latter I might have found interesting had we not been put upon to memorize dates – a peculiarity I found it difficult to come to terms with. Instead I took up domestic science and, as with art, discovered another pursuit which fired my imagination and creativity. Our teacher was Sister Gertrude and I flowered under her superb tuition, her calm steady ways, her absolute fairness in everything, singling no one out, giving every one of us – with infinite patience – an equal chance. I loved her more than ever.

Then there was my music, fervently encouraged every note of the way by the irrepressible Imelda. In singing I had passed every one of my exams with top marks, was performing solo in the chapel choir and had begun rehearsing the *Mikado*, the first operetta ever to be presented by our convent. I had been given the part of Yum-Yum, of the Three Little Maids, and Imelda was in her element driving us and herself absolutely berserk with the practising. My Japanese lover, Nanki-poo, was played by Anne, a day pupil in her final year and Head Girl of the school. Anne was a unique individual. Her pedigree was exemplary – moneyed, refined, multifariously talented – she herself a tall graceful girl with kind and giving ways, emanating a chic self-confidence that left the rest of us spellbound. Half the school had a crush on her, and I wasn't without the odd flutter myself when we sang into each other's eyes!

Every moment of our recreational time was taken up with rehearsing. We also had to make our own costumes and Sister Gertrude helped us work out the patterns, cut, sew, bind, edge, match colours – the while serenely guiding, directing and supervising everything in her usual imperturbable manner.

Molly, of course, took over the scenery aspect of the proceedings. Imelda was obliged to restrain her constantly, it being in Molly's nature to go right over the top, down the other side and back over the top again. Nevertheless she produced some blindingly ingenious backdrops, with skies full of silver stars and funny fat furry clouds and cardboard trees and bright tissue-paper flowers and side-effects of light and shade, using materials and methods that for sure had never before been thought of in the world of art and design.

End of term, summer term, was the Big Day. During the week we'd had a dress rehearsal for the pupils, and then on the Saturday afternoon the Grand Performance. The guest of honour, the *distinguished* guest of honour, the one that all the fuss was about, all the gorgeous tea things laid out for in the reception parlour, was none other than His Eminence, the Right Reverend the *Bishop* himself. The excitement was acute, the nuns taut, on edge; the actors in the show all of a tizzy, flapping around, complaining of sudden sore throats, forgetting their lines, generally falling apart.

His Lordship arrived in his purple, a small squat man, smiley, waving at everyone, full of his own pomposity, in his wake an entourage of some of his most senior parish priests looking miserable, hesitant, out of their depth in these unfamiliar and intimidating surroundings.

At the school entrance the line of nuns bent, genuflecting in turn, to kiss the great man's ring – a chunk of ink rock set upon the limp white hand. Parents were there, including mine, some ex-pupils and a variety of the girls' brothers from St Columb's. It was unbearably nerve-wrecking.

The show rollicked along magnificently . . .

'Three little maids from school are we/Pert as a schoolgirl well can be/Filled to the brim with girlish glee-eee!/Three little maids from school . . .'

Afterwards when we took our bows, me centre-stage hand in hand with Anne, the riotous applause seemed to go on for an eternity. They wouldn't stop. Without a doubt, it seemed that between us we had produced an unmitigated triumph.

But for me it was more than that. As I stood there smiling, my slit-eye make-up beginning to melt and drip under the lights and the little tear that fell, I suddenly knew that from that moment my life would never be the same again. I had been seduced – mesmerized for evermore – by the rarefied aroma of the grease-paint, the magnetism of the footlights, the irrevocable desire for the benediction of applause.

Nothing and no one was ever to succeed in quenching that flame.

'Brazen hussy,' said my mother in a loud and terrible whisper.

Sunday morning, summer again, and we were in the choir, herself and myself kneeling up front on the long wooden bench, leaning over the edge to see what was what. The choir box overlooked the men's side, on the right. Nothing much there except bald pates and unkempt mountain farmers' fuzz, and the younger ones, country clodhoppers, holding no interest whatsoever for me. On the left were the women, *always* of interest, particularly from the general adornment point of view.

The congregation for the most part took their places from the unpretentious side aisles, slipping in quietly, bashfully almost. The centre aisle was the one you went up in order to receive Communion. People were invariably self-conscious about the centre aisle, desirous of not drawing untoward attention to themselves. When the Host was received, it was held between the roof of the mouth and the tongue, being careful not to let it touch the teeth – chewing it was forbidden – until it melted or was nudged away, down the throat. The return journey was made down the side aisle, mouth clammed shut, head bowed down so low and so humble you could study your shoes meticulously, hands joined to tip your nose.

So apart from strays, like a visiting relative, few had the temerity to march up the centre aisle in order to accommodate themselves right or left at the beginning of Mass.

Until *her*. This ordinary Sunday morning, while we were calmly waiting for himself to come wandering out on to the altar steps for the purpose of commencing the performance. This young girl. A stranger. Saucy hat perched bolt-upright on top of her head, court shoes going clippety, the wide swing of her bright red coat ending just above the ankles. You could hear the shock waves rumble through the chapel. The stranger was wearing the New Look!

We had heard about the New Look, but only just. There wasn't much of a mention of it in the general Irish press. However, from within the women's magazines in Bernadette's house, I had culled every single word written about the look to date, memorized every last drawing and photograph. It was stupendous. In New York, in Paris, and in its first tentative foray into Britain, it was all the rage. But it was also precipitating some fierce controversy.

The antithesis of the hard masculine look of the war years, with its butch uniforms and utility dressing, the New Look was created by Dior in the late 1940s, the idea being to bring back nostalgia on a grand scale. The waist was tiny, the shoulders and bust padded, and the full skirt *huge*, swirling to just above the ankle, symbolizing opulence and femininity. It was the actual cost of the amount of material needed for the making of the skirt that was getting them all going, the dissenting throngs.

In Paris women demonstrated: 'Forty thousand francs for a dress, and our children are starved of milk.' They lined themselves up in the streets of New York, in their knee-length trim skirts, brandishing placards. In Britain the President of the Board of Trade warned that the entire future of the British economy was in jeopardy since it would be impossible to manufacture the normal annual number of garments, and advised the designers to boycott the new length. Nevertheless by the following year, when I was seventeen, the whole world seemed to be flaunting the New Look, the more impoverished of us sewing an extra band of contrasting material on to the hem to achieve the additional length.

But for now, on a fine summer morning in the year of 'forty-nine, the sudden appearance of this vivid creature, shamelessly parading her grandeur up the middle aisle of our inoffensive little chapel, was almost too much to bear for the collective congregation. Even I was aghast at the daring of it.

The following Sunday, back from Mass and my mother cooking the breakfast, there was a knock on the front door.

'Ssh,' she squashed us. Whipping off the apron. 'Quiet. *Qui-et.*'

Only the Schools' Inspector ever came to the front door; even the parish priest came round the back. My father went to answer it and the rest of us stood silent, waiting.

In she came, stepping daintily across the kitchen threshold, Mary Carton, the New Look girl dolled-up to the nines in her finery, here to enquire about my boarding school.

'Sit down, sit down,' said my mother, immediately fussing, patting the arm of the best armchair, my father's.

'Mary, china cup and saucer. And the cake tin,' in an undertone. To me.

I went out to the scullery and brought them in, laying them nicely on the table. This was wonderful!

For a whole week our visitor had been the talk of the parish. Minnie Mohan had been up no less than three times to convene over the situation, and in fact only yesterday had brought with her a catalogue she'd received from her niece in America, a whole section of which was devoted to the new fashion.

The family now sat around terribly politely and listened while she told us a few details about herself, and then addressed intelligent questions about the convent to my parents and me.

She was back from America, a particularity half the country already knew by now, the accent having been a dead giveaway in a shopping trip she'd made during the week to McGuigan's. Her parents had gone to live in the States when she was very young and now, at seventeen, she'd come back to stay with her grandmother.

We'd never heard of the granny, but there she was, and there she had been these long years, roosting in a neat little thatched cottage up our lane – way up at the very far end – a belated lonely place engulfed in brambles, into which none of us had ever dared venture. It was, we discovered now, the point at which the lane met with the road.

Mary didn't go into any detail about why precisely she had returned. It certainly wasn't to look after granny, especially as the plan was to go off to boarding school for the next year. Perhaps her parents wanted to round off her education with some of the refinements and flavour of the Old Country – rumour had it that they weren't so hot on education over there in America. Whatever the reason, we didn't ask.

Mary sat there on the edge of my father's armchair, serene and collected, looking a picture. The felt hat was the very latest – I knew from the catalogue. Called 'off the face', it had a big twirly brim and a bow to one side, the fringe of her shoulder-length brown hair falling in a 'bang' over her forehead. She wasn't very pretty, but it didn't matter. Her face was powdered, the lipstick matched exactly the shiny red of her nails, the small genteel hands folded formally upon the lap of the lovely red coat.

I couldn't stop staring at her. Neither could the boys, speechless for once, agawk at this resplendent vision sitting in their midst and conversing in the most astonishing American accent with just the hint of a charming lisp. I foresaw straightaway that, for weeks to come, the house would be resounding with pathetic imitations of her voice. I was, of course, quite correct.

Obviously, with her up the lane and me down the lane, and her nearly alone in the world as it were, it was inevitable that Mary and I should become acquainted. Not *great* friends, like I was with Our Gang – she was too aloof, too snobby, too different – but good enough for her to bring down some of her swanky clothes for me to try on.

It was a warm Sunday afternoon and the entire household was off to the parish sports day at Claudy, another village five miles out on the road to the city. Sports days were family days, held by the Church on Sundays during the summertime in villages throughout the countryside, incorporating football, egg-and-spoon races, sack races, donkey rides, tug-o'-war and much more, with lashings of tea and buns and sandwiches for the massed gathering.

My father had acted as master of ceremonies at these events for as long as I could remember, organizing everything and everyone, including the curates, judging the competitions, calling out directions and conveying messages on the dreadful multi-echoed tannoy system from the back of a bedecked lorry.

'We have found wee Willy. Don't worry. He's all right. He's here on the lorry. Would his mammy please come and get him?'

He was superb at the job and very popular, as was his back-up and first lady – 'the Master's wife' as she was known to everyone – supporting, advising, coordinating, in her magnificent hats and trim turn of ankle.

On this particular Sunday I didn't go to the sports. I had told my mother Mary was coming to see me with a selection of her clothes and there had been no real objection. In fact, upon studying Minnie's catalogue, she had remarked only recently, 'You know, that New Look isn't all that bad. Not bad at all.' Adding with a slight wag of the head, 'Especially if you're nice and thin.' (She herself was pure hourglass!) She had taken to doing odd, squiggly drawings of wide cuffs and big collars and fancy hats with veils falling down. I knew we were nearly there.

I tried on Mary's New Look dresses and coat and hat and court shoes, and titivated my face with her powder and paint. But the garment that really took my fancy was a pair of navy slacks. I had never had a pair of trousers. None of the women we knew would be seen dead in trousers. These were wool, wide, with turn-ups, and were to my adoring eyes the epitome of high fashion. This may not have been the case in other parts of the world, perhaps even in other parts of Ireland, but up our lane on that Sunday afternoon they were the most spectacular apparition ever to be sighted.

She let me keep them on and away we went, me in the turn-ups, her in her long billowing skirt, out and about around the roads on a couple of old bikes we had in the coalshed. I wanted to show them off, hoping to be seen, be admired, but there was no one around. The whole world was at the sports. Nevertheless, it was a glorious feeling on the bike, free-wheeling along, elegant-trousered legs stuck straight out on either side, screaming and yelling and yodelling at the tops of our voices as we flashed along.

Back home, the trousers still on, I was making the tea when my father and mother walked in. Far too early. I could see there was something wrong. She didn't stop for breath.

'Out running round the countryside in that New Look.' Somebody *had* seen us. 'Screaming like a lunatic . . . making an exhibition of yourself . . . disgracing us.' She was screaming herself, trembling with anger.

'He told us in front of everybody, right out loud, so everybody could hear. And everybody looking at us . . . in the middle of the field . . . in front of the priests. And the teachers too, everybody listening – not missing a thing. Our own daughter, a slut . . . scum . . . putting us to shame like that.'

I butted in. Shouting back.

'But I wasn't wearing it. Honest to God. I *wasn't*. I was wearing these. These . . .'

She went on, 'And we had to leave. Up and leave everything. With red faces. Your father about to make the speech. Disgraced. In front of everybody. Had to get John to take us home . . .' She changed direction suddenly, staring at my legs. 'Get those things, those terrible *things*, off you. This *minute*.' It was a shriek.

Mary and I scuttled upstairs to my room. There was nothing to laugh at any more. I dragged the trousers off, shaking, and put on my usual old skirt, my *best* skirt, a blue pinafore, handmade, let-down, ugly. I was embarrassed in front of Mary. We talked quietly for a while and I cried a bit with pity for myself, then we slipped downstairs and I let her out of the front door. I went back to my room, got into the bed and stayed there.

The following morning I had an appointment with the dentist in Derry. Few words were said as my mother, stony-faced, gave me some money for the fare, a cup of tea and a bun, and a pound extra just in case.

'Don't go buying any rubbish,' she cautioned. 'Not a thing. I want every single penny back, here, in my hand. And no hanging around either.'

I couldn't speak. My eyes were swollen with crying. I didn't even want any breakfast.

'Are you listening?' she said.

'Yes, yes, I heard,' I answered. 'No rubbish.'

'Well, then. Mind you don't miss the bus.'

She meant the bus home. There were only two buses in the day, each way. I'd have to catch the afternoon one back. I had been allowed to travel to and from the city for the past year. There was a new café just opened there, Fiorintini's, a bright, glitzy, fast, ice-cream sort of establishment, and the day we'd broken up for the holidays this time Our Gang had sauntered in there, feeling very important and adult. We'd been so occupied with primping ourselves and eyeing up the likely lads, most of whom had been let loose the same day from St Columb's, that we quite forgot about the time and Patsy's eldest brother had to be prevailed upon to come and rescue us.

I walked to the village and caught the bus. The journey was fifteen miles, and as I sat looking out at the hedges passing, and the fields beyond and the trees, and the houses with washing out and flowers blooming in the gardens, I got to thinking what a sad life I had. If I couldn't wear a pair of trousers when girls everywhere else in the world had been wearing them for years, or add a swatch of nice contrasting material to the tail of my best coat in order to bring it more up to date, then really life wasn't much worth living.

I was simmering with frustration and anger against the unjustness of my predicament. My mother was a tyrant, a silly woman who kept contradicting herself more times than most, my father so damned hamstrung and mindless he let her get away with murder, the priests and neighbours and Minnie Mohan and everybody a thousand years behind the times. I wished the whole lot of them dead.

By the time I reached the city, I had also arrived at a momentous decision. I would run away.

I was sixteen, I'd get work at *something*. It would have to be menial, which was a terrible waste of a good convent education, but that couldn't be helped. Hadn't I been doing little else but menial work my life long? And not a penny for it. Not even a word of appreciation. Financially I wouldn't need that much to survive. There were live-in jobs in hotels and I'd have a bed and food. Hotels. There were a few hotels in Derry, although I'd never been in one. Down by the railway I'd noticed the

Commercial Hotel, a fine-looking edifice presumably catering for commercial travellers. I liked the idea of commercial travellers – all that travelling. I could do worse.

On the other hand, it was too risky. Derry was too near home. Too full of relations. Somebody would be bound to see me.

There was one other town I had been to a few times. It was called Buncrana, a small seaside town up on the north coast, a pretty place as I remembered it. It belonged to another life. A time years ago, when Patrick and Joseph and I were small, they would take us up there, the three of us, in the summer, for a picnic and a paddle in the sea.

It hadn't happened often, but the sweetness of those lightsome days, the excitement of the train journey, the running in and out of the freezing waves at the sea's edge trying to catch them on the turn, the squeals of delight when we did. The raspberry ice creams. The pleasure of my parents as they held hands and smiled at each other – so happy – remained with me in a very special part of my memories.

I would go to Buncrana. They had hotels there. Nobody would find me. And serve them right for treating me like a child!

On the way to the station I had a sandwich and a cup of tea, perfectly calm now my mind was made up and a plan of action in hand. I bought a single ticket – there wasn't enough money left for a return even if I'd wanted one – and caught a train almost immediately.

It was a delightful day. The sun was shining, and already I was beginning to cheer up. This was an adventure, this was living. Too long had I been wasting my time, day-dreaming up our lane, bored, waiting. Waiting for what? For things to happen, that's what. Like the coming of the New Look. Like hanging around for a whole afternoon hoping my brothers would decide to go to the pictures in Dungiven, it not being acceptable for me to go on my own. Waiting. Always waiting. For other people to make the important decisions in my life instead of treating me like a grown-up and an intelligent human being.

The sea was warmer than I remembered it. I sat on the sand and watched it, watched it for a very long time. I didn't feel any inclination as yet to go looking for a job. The hotels were behind me. I kept turning round to look at them, but somehow I hadn't the courage to enter any of them, get my suddenly timid self past their frighteningly imperious façades. Not yet anyway. I realized I was hungry, but I had spent the remainder of the money on chocolate so there was nothing left for food.

Then to my horror, I began to cry. Darkness was falling. The bus from Derry would have long gone. My parents would be frantic, the boys sent out on the bikes to look for me. McGuigan's had recently had a phone installed. They'd be down there, ringing the dentist, ringing the relations, maybe even the police.

And here I was, sitting on a beach in the middle of nowhere, no money, no food, not even the fare home. Perhaps I should ring McGuigan's myself, let them know I wasn't dead at least. Not a penny. Best go to the police . . . Better still – and the idea struck me like a shaft of sunlight – go to the parish priest.

The housekeeper took me in, a sweet, kindly soul, and fed me. And listened to my tale of the New Look and laughed her head off and got the priest, a keen, lively spirited young man who was delighted to be of assistance and got everything organized straight away.

In a couple of hours there was a knock on the door and my parents were there. I couldn't move. The priest and his house-keeper both went to answer it and there was a murmur of voices. Then they came in, and one look at their streaming faces told me all. I was in their arms, rocked, held, safe.

'Didn't you know we love you, girl?' sobbed my father.

It was the first time in the whole of my sixteen years that this soft and reticent man had ever used the word 'love' to me. It was also to be the last, but that was never to matter, never to be of any consequence in the years to come. On this night, when I was sixteen, it had been said. That was enough.

Although the teachers had elected me as Second Prefect of my class when I first started at the convent, I rapidly learnt that the position held no significance whatsoever when it came to decision-making or matters of discipline within the group. The clique, the rich spoilt demagogue set, had straightaway decreed that as a minority boarder I had never been entitled to the honour and right from the beginning had chilled me out. Surprisingly, I didn't mind. Indeed I thought they were probably right, which is why at the start of the second year, when the girls chose the prefects themselves and I had to step down, I wasn't in the slightest bit put out. It was a blessed deliverance.

Elizabeth, the girl who at the beginning of each autumn term had been consistently elected Head Prefect of our class became finally, in our fifth year, Head Girl of the whole school. I didn't like her. I never had. Way back in that first year, I had made several attempts at reconciling our differences, whatever they were supposed to be, whatever *she* considered them to be, but she had remained hostile, aloof, shutting me out – as indeed did the whole troupe of her devoted flunkies. I accepted the situation then and got on with the life I had within the convent, amongst the boarders, amongst my own small band of friends.

I wasn't the only one to run foul of Elizabeth and her crowd. Although generally agreed amongst the staff to be possibly the brightest bunch of young ladies ever to have illuminated the hallowed environs of our school, they were also universally considered to be the most disruptive.

Three of the staff were lay teachers, ancient spinsters, an awkward cantankerous trio, hopeless at their jobs and giving a good impression of teaching under sufferance as they patiently awaited retirement day. Our class, right from the outset, succeeded in making their meagre lives a misery. In very subtle ways, Elizabeth's lot tested the women's knowledge of their given subjects, jumping in with a venomous kill at the slighest vacillation, arguing, firing ludicrous questions to which there were no straightforward answers. The three teachers complained periodically to Sister Eucharia, our School Principal, about the overall insolence and flouting of authority, resulting in interminable rows and disputations. I kept myself well out of it.

At the beginning of the spring term in this our fifth and final year, a meeting between the full staff and our class was called by the Principal. We piled into our classroom and chairs were lined up in front, facing us, for the teachers. I already knew what was coming, having been called into the cubby-hole the evening before by Sister Gertrude. I felt quite sick with apprehension.

A prayer was said by Sister Eucharia, expressing the desire that we be guided in this most difficult hour ahead, to which we responded 'Amen' and took our seats. In the silence which followed Sister Eucharia proceeded to talk, to reiterate that which had been said so often before.

We were intelligent girls, the best any school could ever hope for. Exceptional girls who everyone agreed would go far. Good girls, too, she was sure about that. No harm, no real malice in any of us.

It was just that, for some reason known only to Our Blessed Lord Himself, things weren't working out. Things had gone very wrong, in fact. In this our final year when we, the most senior class, should be setting an example to the rest of the school, demonstrating the most exemplary behaviour as well as being wholly concentrated on studying for our Leaving Certificate, some of us – not all, just some of us – had let the side down. Consequently the time had come to relinquish the past. Start afresh. Even at this late date . . .

It had been agreed, therefore, among the teachers, a vote had been taken, the result unanimous, that a new Head Girl be elected, and that Head Girl be Mary Kerr.

In the ensuing silence I sat in my desk, staring down hard at the grainy scored wood. I could feel the shock coming at me from every side. Then with a scraping of chairs as the teachers rose to retire from the scenario of annihilation they had just effected, a great hullabaloo broke out. Some of the girls came over to congratulate me, the nice ones. Elizabeth and her crew remained apart. Nothing would ever change. It was simply a continuation of a schism that could never be redressed, and as such was best ignored from now on.

There was one other difficulty which had yet to be resolved. The boarders always had their own Head Girl and this year it was Patricia. Since acquiring this new status, our friend had become extraordinarily bossy, even with us – or so we thought – nearly succeeding in causing a rift between us and the rapid disintegration of Our Gang. Now she had to contend with this unexpected débâcle of a boarder, and me at that, for the first time ever, becoming Head Girl of the whole school. She made it obvious that she wasn't in the slightest bit happy about the new turn of events – a perfectly normal reaction, I suppose – and I took myself off to the cubby-hole again. As always I had superlative advice. Low profile on home ground was Gertrude's cautious council. 'You may be Head Girl of the school, but within the convent you are just one of the girls. Here Patricia is in charge. It's not an easy adjustment to make, I know. It will require a good deal of humility. But you are strong . . . you can do it. Pray, my dear. Pray.'

So I prayed.

I was praying a considerable amount these days, and had been since our last retreat. Retreats were held every September, a time of prayer, of silence and contemplation and the considering of how best to make one's way of life more acceptable to the Lord. During this, our final retreat, Fedelma, Patsy and I, the three of us, with no mutual consultation whatsoever, had come to the decision that the good Lord would be well pleased were we to devote our lives entirely to His holy work, become brides of Christ, enter the Convent of the Sisters of Mercy.

From that time on we became preoccupied with prayer, slipping into the chapel at every opportunity, sending each other meticulously penned sweetly pious notes on the backs of Holy Pictures.

'To dear Mary . . . in rem. of our Senior Year and of our "Great Joy". God bless you. Love.'

Beautiful coloured pictures, which I still have. An assortment of saints, like my old champion Francis, a bird in his hand and a few around his feet. The Virgin in profile, a slender ring of gold encircling the lowly bent head, nursing a bunch of pristine lilies in her crossed arms. Symbolizing purity. We knew about that. No more bad thoughts.

We spoke of a transformation having taken place deep within us, a sensation of moving in another stratosphere, floating in an ethereal chrysalis of dazzling lightness. The light of God.

Had this glorious euphoria encouraged me to start concentrating on my studies, in order to obtain the top marks in Leaving

Certificate that the rest of the class were surely aiming for, or indeed could be deemed advantageous when being considered for acceptance by the noviciate come September, God could have been forgiven for blinding me. Instead I indulged myself in the things I really enjoyed – art, singing and domestic science – allowing the more exacting subjects of mathematics and languages to lag behind.

In trigonometry – 'Branch of mathematics dealing with relations of sides and angles of triangle, and with relevant functions of any angles' (Pocket Oxford) – right from the very first lesson the essential foundations, the simple basics required for further progress, any progress, in this most abstruse of subjects somehow eluded my powers of comprehension. I couldn't understand a thing, and very quickly found myself in trouble.

I thought of seeking help, knowing my confusion could only get deeper the further into it I floundered.

It was taught by Sister Eucharia, a good, good woman but a truly abysmal teacher. Most of the lesson was spent at the blackboard with her back to the class, the shorn bony head nervously twitching under the thin veil, pausing suddenly in mid-sentence to gather the beads into her fingers and murmur an expeditious prayer. Instead of using the duster, she applied copious amounts of spittle to the board, erasing an unsatisfactory line or curve with a wet forefinger, going over it again with the stick of chalk – hard – on the damp surface. Then pause for another hurried prayer, spit and rub again. It drove us mental.

In the end, having no choice in the matter, I gracefully allowed trigonometry to pass me by.

I took my position as Head Girl very seriously, too seriously. I looked after the welfare and problems of the younger girls, wrote and gave pep talks, settled disputes, reorganized timetables, introduced innovations which I considered to be for the betterment of the school. I was busy, busy every moment of the day, evenings too, leaving no time for myself or my studies, but I didn't care. With God on my side and a happiness within me that I had never dared dream of, I was on a joy-ride to heaven.

I couldn't know it then, nor was anybody about to enlighten

me or point the finger at my foolishness, but I was riding the merry-go-round to disaster. Total disaster.

Between grandiose attempts at trying to run the school single-handedly, I was concentrating on my three favourite subjects. In art and domestic science I had two projects in hand, both very difficult pieces, exacting, challenging, requiring months of meticulous eye-bending work. From my music I took the score of 'Who is Silyia?'* and illustrated it in the style of the sixteenth century, on parchment, in calligraphic script, with miniature depictions of nymphs and druids, and birds and butterflies and feathery flowers and bunches of grapes with trailing vine leaves. In the midst of it Sylvia herself reclining in the manner of a chaise longue, surrounded by an assortment of her adoring swains. Peacocks too, and the odd faun peeping out, the whole illuminated in gilt and the most glorious colours, found for me specially by the accommodating and delighted Molly. Each capital was a tapestry in itself, a picture within a picture, elaborate portrayals of countryside scenes, but executed in diminutive cameo. I spent hours and hours working on it, loving every moment, like a creature possessed.

In domestic science we had the whole year to work on our project, presided over and patiently guided by the steady and ever-composed presence of Gertrude. We were required to make a slip, a plain, short petticoat in our own size, but it had to be very finely hand-stitched, embroidered, every raw edge hand-scalloped. Gertrude gave us some advice on the choice of material: 'Not satin. And not white. They're both impossible to work with.' But when my mother took me into the draper's shop in Derry to choose, I saw only the bale of rich creamy white satin. I had to have it. It wasn't that I was deliberately creating a challenge for myself. It was simply that I preferred it to anything else in the shop. To complement it, I picked out a clear sapphire-blue silk embroidery thread. The colours of the Virgin!

---

* Who is Silvia? What is she,
  That all our swains commend her?
  Holy, fair, and wise is she;
  The heavens such grace did lend her,
  That adorèd she might be.

Gertrude said nothing, and we set to work. She was right, of course. The material kept slipping and fraying and I had to wash my hands constantly whilst handling it, as the slightest smudge on the immaculate white would have been lethal. I outlined, freehand and in pen – so I couldn't afford a single mistake – scallops so tiny along the straps and bottom edge that Gertrude herself couldn't bear to watch. They were smaller in size than the tip of my little finger nail. The subsequent buttonhole embroidery took many weeks.

As with my Sylvia painting, and indeed reminiscent of all those years ago when I had devised the most complicated Fair Isle patterns for my dolls' clothes, I discovered in myself a strange quirk, a contradiction almost, which would remain with me for ever. I found I was capable of exercising an extraordinary degree of patience, a surprisingly dogged perseverance, which I could apply to any artistic endeavour – indeed *any* endeavour – providing it was so complicated and demanding that it was almost impossible to achieve.

As for my music, it gave me, along with my commitment to my Master, the greatest happiness of all. The voice, after five years of exacting training, had developed into a classical coloratura with an almost four-octave range. Halfway through my final term, I took the examination, the *big* one, of the London Trinity College of Music, wherein I sang 'The Trout'. Before he left, the examiner told Imelda and myself that he was recommending me for a scholarship to study opera in Milan and there was not the slightest doubt that I would get it. I had passed everything – voice-production, control, pitch – with flying colours.

'Sylvia' also took full honours, being selected for exhibition by a Belfast art gallery. I was the youngest exhibitor, reported Molly proudly, they'd ever had. I never saw 'Sylvia' again. Rumour was that Imelda had grabbed her upon her return to the convent for the adornment of the music room. I was rather sad to have lost her, but I would never have asked to have her back. In fairness, I could hardly begrudge her this most appropriate of final resting places.

In practical needlework, as part of my Leaving Certificate, the slip too won first prize. I couldn't believe my good fortune:

three honeyed accolades to launch me on my way. I should have been overjoyed, I really should have been. Everyone else was congratulating me, Imelda saying how I was her star pupil and how I was going to become a great opera singer and put Derry on the map, Molly asking me to teach her 'Who is Sylvia?', even Patricia becoming my friend again. Only Gertrude was silent. Only Gertrude guessed the truth. I had scooped the only honours I was going to scoop.

The three pursuits which had for a few brief, sweet months kindled in me a passion and intensity fierce enough to set fire to my whole world had collapsed in a holocaust around me.

I was back again in the real world, the world of solid, dour academia, struggling with examination papers, cursing Sylvia and sapphire-blue silk embroidery thread and the myriads of silver trout swimming in brooklets clear throughout the land. Unable to cope with questions I *could* have answered had I worked that tiny bit harder. Had I worked at all.

Truth was that even in these last few weeks, when I could have 'crammed' – me who was so versed in such matters – I had been otherwise occupied. The farewell concert was coming up, His Lordship again in attendance. Not only was I singing both duet and solo, plus playing Hamlet, I was helping organize the entire operation with Imelda. The fare-thee-well speech, the last impassioned adieu, had to be written, practised and learnt. As Head Girl the honour was mine. There was no time to cram.

I stood at the bus stop on the road by the convent wall, surrounded by my bags, tears flowing freely. Behind me, back in the trees, the great stone building rose through the dejected leaves in a sombre shroud of pitiless summer rain. I didn't know if I would ever see it again.

The night before Gertrude had said to wait.

'Give it a year,' she'd advised. In the cubby-hole for the last time. 'Go out into the world. Go to a dance.'

'But I don't want to go to a dance,' I cried. 'I want only to be with Him. I'm as sure as I'll ever be. I will never, *never* change my mind. And anyway, what about the others? Are you telling them to wait too?'

'The others are different.' She was gentle. 'They're older than you for a start.'

'Only six months or so,' I interrupted. 'That's nothing.'

'I know, I know,' she said. 'But they're older in *every* way. They're more worldly. They're better qualified to make the choice. Just wait. A year may seem a long time, but it'll fly – you'll see. And then you'll know for sure. In the meantime, I shall pray very hard for you. And you say a wee prayer for me sometimes too.'

PART TWO

The summer rolled along harmlessly enough. My parents were relieved that I wasn't entering the convent – not yet, anyway. I couldn't understand their reaction to my news. My mother was anxious, like most Irish mothers, to have one of her sons, at *least* one, elect to become a priest. She couldn't wait for the day when she'd be kneeling down there in her dangly earrings and him giving her the first blessing. I thought she'd be as happy, well, *nearly* as happy, to have her only daughter a nun. To me it didn't add up.

They were more interested in finding me a man.

My brother Patrick, barely nineteen and just finished his first year at a teacher training college in Belfast, had already met the girl of his dreams, a nice Belfast girl from a good family, the girl he was later to marry. It was anticipated that I would follow suit.

The Ireland of the early fifties expected girls to marry young. A career was acceptable, but only for a time. Become a teacher or a bank clerk or a shorthand-typist, and get it out of the way. Then the serious job could start: the bringing up of a good Irish Catholic family. If you weren't married by the age of twenty-two or so, then you were definitely on the shelf.

Patrick had a great friend in Dungiven, also studying to become a teacher. His name was Sean and he spent whole days in our house. The main topic of conversation and of action was the Gaelic football. I took somewhat of a shine to Sean. He was a big, bright, handsome country lad, with rumpled fair hair and an easy smile all over his face. Safe. My mother liked him too. And proceeded to set about the baking with a new artistic vigour, livening up the tired old fairy cakes with a glutinous membrane of slippy white icing laid with slow deliberation across their corpulent tops.

'Mary baked these,' she would say. Off-hand. Proudly placing a huge plateful on the table for tea. Sean either didn't hear her or wasn't impressed, although he always managed to wolf them down with alarming voracity. He regarded me as one of the lads. So far . . .

There was a smashing dance coming up in Dungiven the opening night of a new dance hall – the only dance hall – calling itself 'The Castle'; it was in fact the ground-floor area of a real castle, derelict for centuries. Our Gang were all going, and even though Patricia too had now decided to become a nun, the three of them were hell-bent on having a good time. A perfectly innocent good time, of course, but certainly incorporating a kiss and a cuddle, in this, their last months of freedom.

Sean was going to be there, which provided some agreeable hours of anticipation for me.

Patrick, Joseph and I set off on the bikes in the warm glow of the evening sun. It had been a trying afternoon. The boys had kept changing their minds. One minute they were going, the next not. I wasn't allowed to go unless they were there to look after me. I had been standing around in the scullery, walking out and about the back yard, checking the bicycle tyres, in . . . out . . . Ready. For hours.

Mother had made me a sky-blue taffeta dress, with cap sleeves and a sweetheart neckline, a pinched-in waist and lots of layers of crisp pink and blue net petticoat flouncing out from under the flared skirt. It was a dream of a dress. On my feet were her new platform sandals, wine-red, peep-toed, wedge-heeled and ankle-strapped. Over my shoulders we casually draped her fuzzy powder-blue cardigan. I was the very embodiment of high fashion.

Patsy, Patricia and Fedelma were already there, standing by the wall on the girls' side, dressed in almost identical outfits and, like me, powdered and painted to kill. I joined them and immediately looked across to the boys' side for Sean. He was there, but he wasn't looking for me. And he never did look for me. The whole evening. We jiggered and swung and twirled through the quickstep and foxtrot and rumba and samba and tango, the girls partnering the girls, hoping for a tap on the shoulder, the excuse-me from one of the boys.

The boys, however, weren't very forthcoming. They stood

bunched on their side of the hall in their fawn and wine corduroys, a dollop of lurid tie hung loose across the pullover, lighting up their Sweet Aftons, eyeing the girls and shoving each other, shiftless.

As second choice I quite liked the drummer in the band. It was the start of a life-long groupie fascination for musicians – fat or thin, ugly or handsome, jazz, rock or classical – which has never left me, even to this day. He bought me a sarsaparilla in the interval and asked what I was doing afterwards.

It was mortifying to have to admit to being chaperoned, that my every hope or strategy hinged around the whim of an older brother, a brother who was at this very moment whingeing away over there in the corner about the dark and the five-mile bike ride

home. I knew he was only thinking of himself and what his girlfriend, safely tucked up in her Belfast bed, would say when she heard he'd been to a dance without her.

We were gone before the dance ended, me pedalling away behind them as hard as I could to keep up, no lights anywhere, the dark trees full of ghosts closing in around, the streely night air chilling to the bone through the layers of cardigan and taffeta. And the under-layer. The brand-new pointed boned flattening cinching uplifting all-in-one latex brassière and corset, otherwise known as the corselette.

A strange incident occurred that July which put the fear of God in me, or rather it took the fear of God *out* of me. We were invited on holiday, Patrick, Joseph, Sean and I, to a Capuchin monastery situated in grand isolation on the farthest extremity of the Aards Peninsula in County Donegal. My Uncle Pat was in charge of the place, the Father Abbot, and he figured us young ones would benefit from a gulp of invigorating Atlantic air down our lungs. It was a noble thought. We knew little of the sea, not having been there, apart from my brief escapade, since we were youngsters. I couldn't swim a stroke and my brothers only slightly, the only practice we'd had being in the deeper still pool pockets of the perishing cold mountain streams, where the fish dived into hiding when they saw us coming. It was going to be capital.

We liked Father Pat . . . *every*body liked Father Pat. He wasn't really an uncle, but the very young brother of our paternal grandfather, so young he was more like an uncle. We'd met him only infrequently, at the occasional family burial in the city and once at a truly spectacular ceremony down the country, when his first cousin, Cardinal McGrory, Primate of Ireland, was put to rest. That was the time my mother, being indirectly related as it were, borrowed the fur coat – a rare sighting in those parts – and stole the show, cardinal or not.

Pat was a jovial individual, plump and hearty and very good-looking, with wild tonsured red hair and an everywhere beard, given to thumping you on the back with a 'How's it going, then?' He was nobody's enemy.

The monastery was very old and stood in acres of woodland by the edge of the ocean. It was a heavenly place. I, being female, was not allowed to sleep there but stayed instead with an old couple in the gate lodge. I had told Father Pat about my desire to become a nun and he assigned one of the young priests, Father Bernard, newly ordained and on holiday there before commencing his ministry in the foreign mission fields, to look after me for the duration of my stay. He would spend time with me, talk to me about my vocation, and generally provide spiritual guidance. It was, I thought, an odd thing to do, but as nobody else seemed to think it was in any way peculiar and neither of us had any say in the matter, I silently acquiesced.

The boys played football and table tennis and swam and larked about the live-long day. I read, wrote poetry and painted, but most of the time I spent in the company of Father Bernard. He was a long thin man, humble of stature, with doleful eyes, a slow smile and a quiet mind, utterly devoted to God. We walked in the woods, rain or shine. And talked. For many hours. Theirs was an exacting training, fifteen years of study before ordination. The superiors of the Order left little to chance. He'd been put through his baptism of fire and brimstone and now he was ready for his Pastoral, fully prepared to go out and bear witness, hold the Cross high, carry it fearlessly across the mountains of Peru or Africa or to whatever un-Christian land they were banishing him.

On our last days together we both knew that we had become very close. Dangerously close. It was difficult to part, but part we did.

I was filled with a tremendous sadness when I went into the study to say goodbye to Uncle Pat. The car was waiting at the door. I wondered if he knew. I wondered if he realized what he'd done, the pain he had caused two hapless innocent souls. He was sitting by the table waiting for me.

'So you're going, then,' he said. 'Did you enjoy yourself?' The eyes twinkled and I wondered too for an instant if he was simply a wicked old man. May God forgive me.

'Oh yes,' I said. 'It was wonderful. Wonderful . . . thank you.'

He had taken my hand to shake it, when suddenly he pulled me towards him. I was on his knee, the scratchy beard scraping across my face, stinging into my skin, the wet horrible sloppy mouth slavering over mine. He was grabbing at my breasts, hurting them, muttering, muttering, in my face, in my hair, 'My darling. My love, my little girl, my beautiful little girl . . .'

It was the first time a man had touched me there. I tore myself away, sickened, and ran to the car.

'What's the matter?' asked one of the boys, alarmed at the state of me.

'Nothing, nothing,' I cried. 'Nothing. I'm only sad, that's all. It's the leaving, it's nothing.' I was sobbing my heart out.

And that's the way it stayed. Nothing. There was no one I could tell, no one I could turn to. No one to believe me.

I had unwittingly received my first resounding slap of disillusionment from the Catholic Church.

It had been decided that, convent or not, I would become a teacher. Teaching was in the family. Joseph, in his final year at St Columb's, was set on becoming one too. It was a pleasant enough career. I couldn't go far wrong. Where the plan *could* go wrong, however, was in my exam results. If they weren't high enough academically I wouldn't be accepted for teacher training. That is precisely what happened. I didn't fail my Leaving Certificate, but my marks were so low the bit of paper wouldn't get me anywhere. My parents fumed and roared for a day, thankfully blaming the nuns, then they settled down. There were a few alternatives, not that many – having failed maths, the bank was out for a start – but enough. Da was in his element, writing for application forms, filling them in, constructing letters, making phone calls from McGuigan's. If anybody could get me a job, he could.

In retrospect, I now wonder why no one thought of art or music. There must have been colleges in Belfast specializing in these, even technical colleges. But there was no mention of such possibilities. In our house, in our community, in our mentality, art was a pretty picture to hang on the kitchen wall. Singing was for chapel every Sunday, morning Mass and evening Devotions, and in the parlour to entertain various important persons. Singing was fine for men like John McCormack and Joseph Locke, but a woman on the stage was a scallywag, on a par with the ladies of the night . . . of whom we knew nothing, of course, but one got the general gist.

I was accepted for nursing by the Mater Hospital in Belfast, then turned down on medical grounds. The heart might not be strong enough to lift dead bodies. This was a blow. I thought I might have liked nursing. It was a profession to be proud of – all that caring. Besides, lots of nuns were nurses, although I was beginning to have my doubts about the feasibility of my entering a convent. The poverty and obedience I could handle – hadn't I been living with them all my life? – but the chastity aspect of the vows had begun to niggle me. I still liked Sean.

The problem was solved by a curate from another parish remarking that his brother, who owned a chemist's shop the far side of Derry, was in need of an assistant. Immediately my father leapt in, made the necessary enquiries about a career in pharmaceut-icals, met the nephew and sealed the appointment. I was not required to appear. Suffice that my father's reputation precluded any possibility of his daughter's unsuitability for the job. I would start on the Monday.

It was a three-year apprenticeship, minimal pennies of course, during which time I would also be expected to attend technical college in the city twice a week, to study the specified subjects for my new profession. At the end of that time, at the age of twenty, God willing, and a half, I would be a qualified chemist. My parents were delighted. A second one on the road to prosperity and respectability.

There was little point, I knew, in attempting to remind them that any hope of passing the exams I'd have to take in the required subjects went out the window a long time ago – two years ago, in fact, when I had changed subjects for my Leaving Certificate. Besides zoology and botany, which I knew I wouldn't mind, back into my life again loomed the two nightmares: physics and chemistry.

Still, there was one encouraging factor on the horizon, a sound justification for a rosy glimmer of hope in my life, a gleam in the eye. A gleam in my mother's eye too, a fresh fillip to the baking hand.

My father had taken on a new junior assistant. Another Sean.

A lad from a town miles away. Therefore lonely, socially in need of a gentle helping hand. And, without a doubt, the most gorgeous young man I had ever clapped my eyes upon.

I presented myself off the bus at the premises of one Jim Fallon on a cheerless Monday morning at eight-thirty sharp. The place was closed. Although still summer, it was raining fitfully, pitching chill snappish splots of wet down upon the footpath. I huddled in the doorway. My father had been asked to have me there early so I could familiarize myself with my surroundings before the onslaught of clientele when the door opened at nine o'clock. I looked up and down the main street. A garage opposite, closed. A café, closed. A pub, a few houses, another pub, a drapery shop. On this side, a long row of single-storeyed square houses, pebble-dashed, small windows sparkling in ruched lace and efflorescent finery, lying low a step or two down from the path. Jim Fallon's pharmacy was situated in the middle of them, the front full glass displaying a midnight-blue window arrangement of Evening of Paris perfume – small bottles, medium bottles, large ones – all prettily nestled into the pleats and tucks of a sea of dark velvet with, centre-stage, the slender soaring pyramid of the Eiffel Tower.

Down the street two children came out of a house and wandered off round the corner to the school dragging their satchels. A small dog, tail to the wind, trotted along, stopped at a telegraph pole, peed, trotted on. Cars passed on their way to work in the city. Otherwise, nothing. A terrible feeling of isolation crept up on me. I wanted to run away, but there was nowhere to run to.

Then Jim arrived, jumping out of his bright red car, full of apology.

'Sorry, sorry', he said. 'You're Mary, yes? Good. Have you been waiting long?'

We shook hands and he led the way through the dark shop, switching on the lights as we went, and into the back room, the dispensary.

'When do you start technical college?' he asked.

'Next Monday,' I said. 'Mondays and Wednesdays are the days.'

'Fine, fine,' he said, rubbing his hands together with cordial relish, a habit of his I was to become most accustomed to in the months that followed. He was a medium-height man, stocky, my father's age. The head was large, the hair black, heavily oiled and combed straight back from the shiny forehead in coarse symmetrical furrows, rather like a ploughed field. The slippy sloe eyes, close-set under the thick dark brows, twinkled merrily out – but crafty, shrewd – from a sallow, cunning face chinned in Bluebeard shadow round a thin-lipped mouth. I took an instant dislike to him.

'Tea,' he said, rubbing his hands again. 'Now that's where you come in,' laughing. He handed me a not-too-clean white coat from the back of the door. 'Here,' he said, 'put this on. Mustn't dirty that pretty frock.'

I had dressed in my best Sunday clothes, as befitted my new position as assistant to a priest's brother. His eyes glanced across my breasts. I blushed wildly, covering myself with the coat. It buttoned from the right. So I hadn't been the *first* girl to work here!

I made the tea and handed it to him.

'Eugene's late,' he observed, glancing at the big watch on his arm. His arms were covered with swarming black hairs. Although I knew little of men, I did know that I hated hairy ones.

'Eugene?' I enquired.

'Yes.' He nodded. 'Eugene's the messenger boy. Nice kid. He's been with me for ages, a good lad. Good as gold. Like a son, really.'

Oh Lord, I could have done without a son of the same. Still, it might be healthy to have a third party around. I was a little bit afraid of this man.

He gave me a guided tour of the place. There wasn't much of an expanse to stake out. One room, really: the shop. Along three walls, shelves climbed high the whole way up to the ceiling, spaces which were packed to capacity with every conceivable pharmaceutical requirement: fruit salts, health salts, laxatives, foot powders, knee powders, bandages, sanitary requirements, headache pills, ear pills, mouth pills, stomach pills, hair restorers, hair colours, combs, pins, curlers, make-up. Hundreds of things crammed in together in impossible disarrangement.

'I like everything to be tidy,' he declared, sweeping his arm across the battlefield. 'Everything in order. Then we know where everything is, don't we? Makes for speedy service . . . give the customer what he wants, I always say. No hanging around having to pass the time of day if he's in a hurry.'

I acquiesced, speechless with sorrow and despair. Already loathing the place and its sickening stink of chemicals with the self-same ferocity I had felt for the science laboratory during those cringeing first two years at the convent. Only now it was different. There would be no let-up, no escape. I was duty-bound to stick with it. My parents had already paid the college fees for the whole of the first year. Worse still – and this was the ghastly, irrevocable, deciding factor – in Catholic schools, government-controlled though they were, it was the Church, with all her priests, who ruled. So Jim's brother was, in a way, one of my father's bosses. I was well and truly trapped.

Unless, that is, I met the boy of my dreams! This was the perfect solution to my dilemma. If I put my mind to it, *seriously* put my mind to it, insisted on going to the dances alone – now that I was working I could be considered responsible – in no time I'd meet someone who'd put a ring on my finger and my problems would be solved.

My appearance had improved somewhat in the past few months. What my mother had been generously dismissing as puppy fat for the past ten years had gradually frittered itself away, so that my general all-over outline was now quite acceptable. I was halfway to becoming fairly presentable. I had added mascara to my nearly full sponge bag of facial ornamentation and the white albino eyelashes which had long plagued me were now sweeping fans of flirtatious comeliness. When I became somewhat more confident in the shop, I would start experimenting with the powders and paint and perfumes. I'd get acquainted with the commercial travellers, persuade them to bring me in a few choice samples. There was no end to what I could get up to in this job. All in good time, however. Right now it would not be advantageous to appear too forward.

I was having trouble with the shelves. He had provided me with a feather duster, the purpose of which was to carefully agitate the fluff around and upon the myriad of goods on display, the while memorizing their exact whereabouts in the general arrangement of things. This was my work for the first week, during which he also showed me how to operate the till. Then on my second Tuesday morning, white coat having been lashed by rains and wind on the weekend back line, followed by a loving starch and ironing *tour de force* by Mother, restoring it to its original pristine magnificence, I took up my servile position behind the counter. It was catastrophic.

I couldn't for the life of me *find* anything. I would stand with my back to the customer, leaning casually against the counter, and stare up at the rows and rows of merchandise. Hard. And see nothing. Behind me I would become aware of a slight impatience starting up, a restrained cough, the tapping of fingertips – testy – on the glass counter top.

'It's here,' I'd assure them. 'I know it's here, I saw it a minute ago ... can't quite put my hand on it. I *know* it's here, though.' The sweat breaking out, the embarrassment, gritting my teeth at my own asinine dim-wittedness, my eyes glazing over with the hopelessness of my predicament. 'I'm new, you know,' and laugh. Inevitably I'd have to call Jim out from his dispensing in the back room. Instantly he'd locate it, deftly wrap it up in brown paper, chatting away the while so as to alleviate any annoyance which might perchance have been accumulating.

'How's your mother? How's yourself? All well are they, then?' And so on, whilst I stood there like the idiot I most certainly was and made a firm note of where that particular article could be found next time.

Except next time I had forgotten again.

'And I thought you were a bright girl,' he said then. Slightly sardonic, but still prepared to humour me.

'Jesus Christ, where *did* they get you from?' he exploded angrily, after a few episodes like this. I knew then – an overwhelming wash of despondency engulfing my whole being – that we had hit nadir.

The situation was not helped by Eugene. Eugene had not made an appearance during the first two weeks of my employment, choosing instead to indulge himself in a fit of pique over the hiring of another apprentice, and moreover another *female* apprentice. I could hear Jim out back on the phone to him as I explored the shelves out front, cajoling, wheedling, the voice low – swearing how the place wouldn't be the same without him, how indeed his presence was crucial to the smooth functioning of the operation. I could hear whisperings, and I knew what he was saying . . .

'She's no good. She's thick. *Thick*. Don't worry, she won't last long.'

I burned with the shame of it. And when he came back into the shop, grinning all over himself and rubbing his hands with the satisfaction of a job expertly accomplished, I could have spat in his hypocritical face.

When Eugene finally did appear, he was treated like the prodigal son – as indeed he was, the son Jim wanted and never had. Eugene had been an orphan in Barnardo's for years until a local couple took him on and spoilt him rotten. I had been prepared to like him, already feeling sorry for him, and assure him that his position would in no way be jeopardized by my appointment, that I was only doing the job because my father wanted it, nothing more. I wasn't here to usurp his role.

But from the moment I laid eyes on his crafty smirking face, albeit a handsome face, with the same close black eyes as Jim's, I knew that any attempts at friendliness on my part were doomed. He looked what I presumed could be Italian – at least in his general resemblance to the Fiorintini Café lot – and had a pronounced hooked nose with a perpetual sniff to it, not unlike Danny of the whin bush episode when I was six. When he spoke, a cocky smart-arse with a stutter, his upper lip curled into a kind of snarl. I found him an altogether unpleasant snivelling little cur.

Jim, I soon discovered, had a predilection for the horses. And the dogs. Anything, in fact, that moved. And wherever Jim was, Eugene was right behind. If there were a couple of flies taking a perfectly innocuous ramble up the wall, the pair of them would go into a paroxysm of unbridled speculation about the outcome. Around lunchtime one or other of them would take a stroll out to the pub or the bookie's, or both, and lay wagers on whatever was running. This could have been one of the reasons why another pharmacist, or at least someone aspiring to that state, had been required on the premises. Jim needed his freedom.

Nevertheless he did allow Eugene to make up prescriptions, going to great lengths to explain the whys and wherefores of each draught or pill, the benefits, the side-effects, the dangers. I soon discovered that Eugene, lacking though he may have been in the rudiments of literacy, had a bright mind, an intuitive capacity for soaking up information instantly and putting it to good use. I had to admit, begrudgingly, that he was and always would be better at playing chemists than me.

'Let's have a go at the prescriptions, then,' Jim announced one morning, when I'd completed my first month in service and my progress thereat was manifesting some slight indication of improvement. I was pleased. The only enjoyment I experienced out front was in assisting the ladies in their choice of make-up or perfumes, nail varnish or sweet-smelling talcum powders. I delighted in creating pretty displays for the enticement of the female population of the village and its surrounds. But the possibilities were limited, what with the local farmers' wives being more preoccupied with their feet than their faces. Corn and bunion cures and suchlike afforded me little gratification. In short, I was bored.

However, I found dispensing very agreeable and actively enjoyed learning from the book about the various constituents in the medicines we made up. Jim was a good teacher, methodical, calm.

'Looks like there's hope for you after all,' he murmured one day, smiling affably. I was chuffed. Eugene sniggered. Eugene always sniggered when there was the slightest intimation of my incompetence. I tried hard to like him, I really did, but the softness, the warmth, the pity which sometimes swelled up in me when I considered his wretched childhood – or what I presumed to be a wretched childhood – was invariably squashed by another diatribe from his sarcastic, twisted, insolent little mouth. I found it difficult to take.

Sitting sipping my coffee in the local café, waiting for the bus home one blustery autumn evening a couple of months into the job, I spied a fine splash of an advertisement in the *Derry Journal*, our weekly paper. It was the dancing silhouettes which caught my attention, an enchanting tableau – him in his bow tie, her in the long flowing gown – going waltzy-waltzy across the page. It was the announcement of a Hallowe'en ball, a night of frolics and delight to be held in the city, the purpose of which was to celebrate the official opening of the Palais, the gorgeous new ball-room Bernadette had told me about the other day, when we'd bumped into each other at the bus stop, the one with the sparkly crystal ball rotating from the ceiling and coloured lights and shady corners and a proper orchestra. And a proper cloakroom, too, where you handed in your coat and they gave you a ticket, pink for the girls, blue for the boys, not like the Castle, where you threw everything on a chair any old how, or if you were friendly with the band, piled it up in the corner of the stage.

I couldn't wait to get hold of Bernadette. I hadn't been seeing that much of her over the past few years, not that there was anything unusual in that. Apart from my parents' surly disapproval of her Protestant policeman father, she and I had sustained an on-and-off sort of attachment; I knew she'd always found me too childish, and she herself was way ahead of her years and given to flights of high hauteur and an inordinate deal of snotty head-tossing. Still, when it suited her, she could be most accommodating and, there I'd be, once again, cap in hand, delighted to fall under her spell. At the moment, we were the best of friends. She'd told me about her boyfriend, but the whole country already knew she was going steady anyway. He was the dentist for whom she worked, and, strangely enough, my parents had begun to change their opinion of her. She'd suddenly come up in the world, entered the realms of respectability. He was a good solid Catholic, and besides, doctors and dentists were regarded with awe. Like priests, they commanded a superlative respect within the community. They were the ones who were university-educated, the paragons of uprightness, the breed apart who always resided in 'the Big House', peerless. And a splendid catch for any girl. The best.

'It's a pity Mary couldn't get herself a nice dentist then,' I'd overheard Minnie mumble in the kitchen when she'd come visiting for the purpose of imparting the news of the first inkling of a courtship between the pair.

'Naw, naw,' my mother remonstrated. 'Mary doesn't need a dentist. Mary'll be okay as she is. No need going above your station in this life, I always say. No need at all. A teacher will do her fine. Just fine.'

The two Seans were still around for the taking . . .

Benardette offered to tuck me under her wing for the ball. We'd be a threesome, but that bothered me not a jot. Nor did it bother her. She wouldn't mind sharing her John with me for the odd dance or so, should the situation arise whereby I was relegated to the disconcerting status of wallflower in the event of there being only couples in attendance. She was also going to lend me a suitable dress.

'What would you be doing going to a ball at *your* age, then?' from Mother. Like as if she would say anything different.

'But I'm nearly eighteen,' I cried. Like she knew I would.

'Eighteen nuthin,' she said. 'And anyway Bernadette is older than you.'

'Only a year or two.'

'So? A year or two makes a big difference, a *big* difference. And sure as well, what would you want to be playing gooseberry to the pair of *them* for. Bernadette will have John. You'll have nobody.'

'Yes, and I'll go on having nobody at this rate. Who am I ever going to meet around here? Or the Castle? Tell me that! The only half-decent chance I have of meeting *any*body is in Derry. I'll be stuck here for the rest of my life.'

'You're too young. Too young. Far too young.' She shook her head sadly and took herself to the scullery.

'Too young. Too young for *every*thing. I'm working, amn't I? Am I too young for *that*?'

'Calm down.'

'I *am* calmed down. Far too calm. So calm, in fact, I'll go mad in this Godforsaken place.'

'Don't you dare take Our Lord's name in vain,' she yelled.

And I slammed up the stairs to my flowery room, on to the bed, flump, and had a good cry.

'Anyway, what would you wear?' she enquired nicely. A while afterwards. Over the tea things.

'What's that?' said my father.

'Nothing,' she said sharply, giving me a look.

My heart leapt. She was softening, softening.

'So what colour's this dress then?' she asked when we were washing up in the scullery. I had told her about the proposed loan.

'Oh, Mammy, Bernardette says it's gorgeous. Really *gorgeous*. Pink. Softish pink, you know. Full length, a proper evening dress. Sweetheart neckline. Puffed sleeves. My white shoes would be fine with it – you won't see them anyway, Bernardette says – and we can clip a pink flower on the front. And she has a little lacy pink bag. Oh, please, *please* can I go?'

'Can Mary go to a dance in Derry, Dad?' she called to him, in his chair by the fire reading the paper.

'What?' he said.

'There's a big swanky dance in the new Palais in Derry. Very posh. Can Mary go? It'll be decent people there.'

We could hear him scratching the dead tobacco around in the pipe bowl, knocking it out on the range.

'Mmmm. Thought there was something funny going on.' He'd be digging the bowl into the pouch of Erinmore now, filling it up. 'Never far wrong, am I? Never far wrong.' We waited. He lit up.

'So how's she proposing to get home from this place then? Will she be able to catch the last bus? I take it she's not going to walk round the streets the whole night long?'

'Oh, no. She'd be going with Bernadette and her dentist, in their car. They've invited her, actually. So they'd be looking after her, see she comes to no harm.'

There was a silence. I could hear him puffing on his pipe, deliberating. He was making little sucking noises, a sure indication of inner turmoil.

'So where's she getting the money for this "do" then?' he said. 'Are *they* paying, I mean, seeing as they've asked her? How much is it anyway?'

'Oh, it's not much,' I cried, excited now, coming back into the kitchen. 'Not much. Honestly. You'd be surprised. Anyway, I've got plenty. Well, I mean I've got enough. Nearly.'

My father was both anxious and embarrassed by the subject of money. In conversation he avoided it whenever possible, preferring to skirt around the topic and leave that kind of business to the woman of the house. On the odd occasion when we went to Fiorintini's and the waitress handed him the bill, he would immediately slide it across the table-top to Mother, nervously glancing around the café, his face flaming with the ignominy of it.

When it came to Mother's clothes and hats and jewellery, nothing was too good for her, but towards the rest of us and the world in general his attitude was one of extreme parsimoniousness. It bothered him greatly to think that anyone should toss his hard-earned salary heedlessly hither and thither, and our teenage years especially were blighted by his tight-fistedness, particularly in the matters of pocket money and shoes. He had been mending our shoes himself for as long as any of us could remember, hammering away on the big iron last of an evening, doing his best but, in his usual slip-shod fashion, getting it wrong. It was fine when we were small and didn't know any better, but when I started getting opinions about myself and caring about how my feet – especially my potential *dancing* feet – presented themselves in the general appearance of things, he couldn't understand why thin slivers of rubber sole sticking out at random around the edges were really no longer acceptable.

'It was good enough for my father, and good enough for his father before him.'

Fortunately for us, my mother was generous in the extreme so any monetary arguments invariably culminated in her dropping us a shilling or two on the side with the admonition, 'Don't let on to your father.'

We both knew his decision on the dance would be more favourable were we to assure him that his pocket would be in no way affected.

'She's got the dress and that,' my mother called in to him.

'Yes, I've got the dress, so it'll cost nothing really. Hardly anything. Not even the bus fare,' I chipped in for good measure.

There was another silence, another brief interlude of sucking, whilst he weighed up the pros and cons. We both waited, me hardly daring to breathe.

'Whatever you think, then,' he said. His final word on the affair. Uttered to nobody in particular.

Jim gave me an extra pound in my wages to add to the dance kitty, which we naturally considered very generous. He threw in some of the slightly used or faded samples as well, so both Mother and myself had enough varnish and paint to last us a year. The anticipation heightened. I tried to lighten my hair – lift it out of the middle-of-the-road mousiness – but it didn't work very well. I was obliged to go easy on the stuff in case my father noticed, artificially coloured tresses being tartish and no two ways about it. My mother kept getting carried away with the preparations, every now and then lapsing into reminiscences of the old days.

'In my day we did this,' or 'In my day we didn't have that.'

It seemed that in her day they had very little. I felt sorry for them, and for her, caught up as she was in too early a marriage and mothering. Now she was playing at being a young girl again, and when she tried on the sugar-pink dress and twirled around in front of her dressing-table mirror, she looked such a trim slip of a thing and so beautiful, my eyes rushed with tears.

'You will behave yourself, won't you?' she kept saying. 'You won't let us down?'

'Of course not,' I assured her. 'I'll be so well-mannered you won't realize I'm there.'

'Ha! That'll be the day! You know, it's very good of your father to let you go. You do appreciate that, don't you?'

'Yes, yes. I appreciate everything. Stop worrying. I'll be fine, in good hands. You'll see. Safe as houses.'

'I wonder if he's serious about her,' she mused. 'I mean John. With Bernadette.'

'He's a bit long in the tooth,' I ventured. We both laughed. Comfortable together. It was times like this I felt I truly loved her. And she me.

We were extremely impressed by the car. We hadn't the slightest notion what kind of car it was, just that it was a nice satiny bottle-green, not too loud or pretentious like Jim Fallon's Spitfire. This one looked quiet somehow, with smooth classy curves.

John was very punctilious, like a proper gentleman, holding the door, helping me into the back seat, waiting until I could arrange the skirt satisfactorily around me. Bernadette was sitting up very straight in the front seat, in her correct place beside her young man. He really wasn't at all young – in fact he was quite old. More like a father. But kindly. I wondered, not for the first time, if she was sleeping with him. She looked very grown-up, her lovely thick wavy chestnut hair piled high and dotted with small daisies. The green of her dress reminded me of an ice-cream soda in Fiorintini's – palest lime, frothy, cool. Her neck and shoulders were snuggled into a sleak furry cape exactly the colour of her hair. The powder and eyeliner and lipstick were discreet. She hadn't tried to hide the freckles as I did, but then on her they looked absolutely right, fetchingly feminine. Her perfume filled the car. I couldn't quite place it, but I recognized it from the shop. Expensive.

I stuck my chin in my chest, the better to check the bouquet of my own Blue Grass. I had puffed the talc down into my bra and inserted a lump of scent-impregnated cotton wool into the cleavage. It was too much, too overpowering. But then Blue Grass soon wore off.

I was using roll-on deodorant now, too. My mother and I both used it, but we couldn't persuade the boys to change from the talcum powder they slapped on in fierce floury clouds into the depths of their great hairy oxters. Sissy, they said. As for my father, he would never, ever be prevailed upon to apply anything other than the faintest pat of Tweed, and that on his chest and then only on Sundays and Holy Days.

'Leave him be,' my mother would say when I complained of a not-too-pleasant whiff. She never tried to change him, not in the tiniest way. Nor him her. They accepted and adored each other without question.

As John turned the car round in the lane, Bernadette reached back with a packet of cigarettes in her hand.

'Smoke?' she said.

'In a minute.' I glanced nervously out at them, my parents and the two youngest brothers, waving in the front doorway, standing in a bunch, apprehensive, looking for all the world as though they were waiting to have their picture taken. There was a lump in my throat, a lump of guilt. Of anticipated guilt. They had such a look of innocence, of trust written all over them, but I knew that before the night was out I'd be lying to them. Only tiny lies, maybe, but one way or the other, however you looked at it, lies.

I had already started smoking, the odd one, and they knew it but couldn't make up their minds whether to forbid it or yield without demur to the inevitable. Patrick was already smoking openly, so with me too it was only a matter of time. They always kept their cigarettes and matches on the mantelpiece over the range, hers and his, the Sweet Afton and the Players. For the past week I had been helping myself to one or two a day from each packet, a thievery they would never detect, being such prodigious smokers themselves. I had a goodly supply now, tucked in beside the lipstick and powder compact in the side purse of the little lacy bag on my lap.

In the cloakroom the young ladies were powdering and painting and primping and giggling and prattling away forty to the dozen. I had never seen such goings-on, or so much style. Some of them were wearing strapless dresses, the bosoms pushed up by and nearly falling out of what I presumed to be the latest boned brassières. My father would have been horrified, and would have dragged me out of there had he known I'd be participating in such wickedness. I wished I could have paraded my own bosoms so blatantly, but I was shy. When the rest of me had stopped growing they seemed to go on and on, getting bigger and bigger. I was ashamed of them and had recently taken to wearing big baggy jumpers. These days, whether standing or sitting, I would position my arms vaguely across my chest in a slightly hunched-over-into-myself sort of way.

'Take that hump off your back,' my mother would nag. Incessantly, day and night. 'Stand up straight, for goodness' sake. You'll be an old woman before your time.'

Naturally there was no way I could tell her what was wrong.

John had reserved a table for us right at the front, in the corner to the left of the stage. It was the perfect position, for me anyway, with an unobstructed view of the band. And what a band! I counted them. Fifteen musicians, old and young, fat and thin, dark and fair, and a gingery reckless-looking drummer at the back. They were superbly decked out in the most splendidly dapper uniforms, bright royal-blue blazers with silvery buttons, white trousers, frilly shirts and a saucy scarlet dickie-bow under the chin. They were a handsome lot.

The most handsome of all was the lead singer, tall, dark-haired with a voice guaranteed to splinter any girl's heart. We caught each other's eye as I sat down, spreading my skirt around me like a fan in the fashion of a princess sitting down to dinner at the Palace Ball. I *felt* like a princess, straight out of a fairy tale. The only accessory required now to complete the picture was Prince Charming. I hadn't long to wait.

In through the doors, in a tumultuous surge of noisy joviality and lively chatter, there arrived upon the scene a party of boisterous rollicking American sailors. In uniform. In *glorious* uniform.

'Oh, I forgot to tell you,' remarked Bernadette. 'There's a boat in. It's your lucky night.'

We laughed and John nodded sagely. 'Yeah, yeah. All the girls love a sailor.' He smiled. He really was a nice man.

They arranged themselves at the tables by the wall behind us, ordering drinks, looking around. Looking for girls. For a special girl, a girl who was free, who was sitting here just next to them in her pink puffed sleeves and sweetheart neckline – a bit covered up, but no matter – and her mother's best glittery paste at her throat and earlobes and the smell of Blue Grass rising out of her like a blast of country meadow in high summer. A girl with no partner. A *friendly* girl dying to dance.

I had my first drink of alcohol, the very first time I had ever sampled the stuff. Harmless enough. But for me it was to be my introduction to a whole new way of living, a removal of self from reality – at times the *only* reality – the beginning of a journey down the long lonely road of self-destruction, a journey that would transport me to the greatest heights and simultaneously drag me down to the very depths of hell. And then heave me back up again. To start afresh. A journey that would last for well nigh on forty years.

At Bernadette's suggestion I had vodka and orange, on the presumption that vodka is odourless on the breath for the walking back in our front door again. I poured a full bottle of orange squash into the glass with the fear of losing control of my senses. And when I tasted it, so gingerly you'd think it was about to blow up in my face, all I got was unadulterated orange. What a let-down! Next time round, however, I went easy on the orange and sat there supping my drink, relishing the slightly numbing effect it was having on my limbs, the feeling of well-being permeating my body. And my soul.

When one of the sailors came over and requested the pleasure of my dancing company, I felt I would surely *float* around the hall, so carried away had I become by the romance of it – the glowing lights, the scintillating diamond reflections of the crystal ball flickering over the walls and ceiling, round and round, the glitz, the laughter, the conviviality.

And the singer. My lovely singer, his long fingers cupped

effortlessly around the microphone, gently serenading us with a mesmerizing rendition of 'Sweet Sixteen'.

'I loved you as I'd never loved before
When first I met you on the village green . . .'

God, if it were only *his* arms that were around me. Unfortunately, I soon came to the realization that my partner was not in step with me – neither would he ever be. He was in step of a sort, presumably his own American step, but it was doggedly at odds with mine. After a while one of his friends interrupted so I had a new partner, but with the same odd off-beat sense of tempo. It cramped my style. I could only hope the singer would realize what was going on and not think I had two left feet. It seemed every time I happened to glance stagewards he was looking at me, and once or twice he smiled. I knew he was singing for me and I couldn't wait for the interval. In the meantime, I managed to side-step the invitations from the sailor lads to join them, just in case. Happily for me, the minute the band stopped for the break down he came, directly to our table. He introduced himself – his name was Garry – and joined us. He ordered drinks all round and then . . . 'Would you like to dance?' he asked me. There was a nice slow number coming from some record player. We didn't have long together, but it didn't matter. The Blue Grass was doing its stuff. He told me he had to see me again. I agreed. Then with the promise of organizing something during the next break, he leapt back up on the stage. And I was in love!

The problem with musicians is that when the job is done they have to start packing up the instruments and equipment. Even the vocalists are obliged to lend a hand. I couldn't hang around, as John had to take both Bernadette and myself home. In those days fifteen miles always seemed quite a distance and it was already after one in the morning. There was also no way I could dare risk arriving up our lane in a stranger's car. I wasn't sure if they'd be waiting up, or wake up, or what. So we arranged to meet a couple of days later, on the Monday afternoon, off the bus. He was free. I would skip my physics class. Easy. He kissed the back of my hand goodbye as he saw me into the car. I nearly collapsed with the chivalry of it. On the journey home, I couldn't stop humming:

> 'Come to me e'er my dreams of love are o'er,
> I love you as I loved you
> When you were sweet, when you were sweet sixteen.'

The kitchen light was on, but nobody was up. I let myself in the back door – it was always open – in through the scullery and kitchen and up the stairs. Their bedroom door had been left ajar, and I had to go through there to get into my room. Even though I'd been assured the vodka was foolproof I couldn't take any chances, so I gulped a deep breath in and held it. The place was in darkness, except for the palest gleam of moonlight through the curtains, lighting my way around the bottom of the bed and across to my room door. Nearly there.

And suddenly she rose up. Like a phoenix. In the damned bed.

'I can smell alcohol,' she muttered. Low. 'I can smell alcohol in this house.' Louder. He began to stir.

Quick as a flash I whispered, almost a hiss through the dark, 'It's okay, Mammy. Go to sleep. It's nothing. Some eejit spilt his drink on my cardigan. Thought I'd washed it off, obviously not enough. Sorry I woke you . . . night-night.'

'Did you have a nice time?' she grunted, and fell down again.

Inside my room I giggled. A near miss. I'd have to be more careful in future. In fact under the present sleeping arrangements I couldn't risk drinking at all. Pity. I'd enjoyed it, the happy silly way it had made me feel, the freedom. I hugged myself to sleep, seeing his face, the way his hands caressed the microphone, the silky voice curling and bending round the notes, the control. I couldn't wait till Monday.

'You'd think we were going somewhere, the style of it,' was Ma's comment as I scoffed down a hasty breakfast on Monday morning. 'Aaah! *I* know.' She smiled. 'Well, well, there's a boy in the class at college, isn't there? Own up, now. Out with . . .' Hopefully.

I smiled too, rushing around, high heels peppering the linoleum, making sure I had everything – the books for the look of it, the Blue Grass for the seduction, the flats for a romantic walk in the moonlight.

'Wouldn't you all like to know,' I called out happily as I took myself out the door and away to the bus.

On college days I worked only mornings, and then it was off to the city and classes, followed by Fiorintini's and sometimes the pictures. As long as I caught the last bus home, nobody worried about me. So today I had ample time to rendezvous and talk and walk and romance, and not a care in the world.

'You look great,' he said, kissing my hand again.

'So do you,' I laughed. Feeling stupid. Blushing. Suddenly with nothing to say. But he did look great, although different. Somehow I'd expected to see him in his band uniform, but here he was in a beige duffel coat and stripy college scarf, so dashing, so gallant, tucking my arm in his and leading me to the car.

'I thought we'd go to tea in the country,' he suggested. His accent was quite posh. I hadn't noticed it in the general commotion of the ballroom. 'Would you like that?'

'Oh, yes,' I breathed.

If he had proposed taking me off to the Fair Day in Ballyjames-duff and wandering through the cow clap all day long, I'd have breathed, 'Oh, yes,' in precisely the same simpleton way. I was utterly smitten.

We drove out of the city, along the banks of the Foyle, a journey I had taken so often before. On the way, we passed the convent and with a fleeting stab of guilt, I wondered how the nuns were getting along. I hadn't been in touch. I hadn't even scribbled a line to the other girls in Our Gang. I no longer knew what to say to them. They'd stepped into another world, a world so far removed from the reality of mine. Patsy, Patricia and Fedelma, my dear dear friends, had indeed entered the convent and were now spending their novitiate in the Mother House in the city, getting up in the grey dawn, praying, fasting, struggling along with this almighty business of salvation – theirs and the rest of humankind's, sinners like me. My own vocation had lessened considerably over the past few months; Mother Gertrude would have been proud of my achievements in the worldliness department. Even so, I was still heavily into praying and had just finished a novena, the sole purpose of which was to provide spiritual guidance. But I was no better off at the end of it, still in a quandary, still doubting.

The café he took me to was by the sea and we stuffed ourselves with currant buns and raspberry jam and cream, talking and smiling and delighting in each other's company. Every now and then he'd reach across and place his hand over mine, hardly touching me, sending delicious little stirrings rippling through my body. It was already dark when I donned my flat shoes and we set off across the strand, clutching hands, bracing ourselves against the ferocious Atlantic gales, breaking away from each other, running, laughing, singing.

'You've got one helluva voice,' he called to me through the wind.

'That makes two of us,' I yelled back.

'But seriously,' he said, stopping, no longer laughing.

We faced each other, shivering in the bitter cold, the collapsing waves a great slough in our ears. The low sombre clouds heaved mutinously across the night sky. A bright moon, wanton, flitted effortlessly in and out, illuminating in stark moments the waiting earth. Soon it would rain.

'You know, you are absolutely lovely,' he whispered. And kissed me.

I had been kissed before, a couple of times. And held. But clumsily, gropingly, in the back seat of a car behind the Castle. The experience hadn't been too pleasant, more of an experiment really – on my part. When the hands had strayed, within minutes of slamming the car door shut, aiming for a direct hit to the breast, I had pushed them away, furious. I wasn't ready for that kind of thing yet.

But with Garry it was different. If he touched me there I wouldn't object. I could feel the excitement in my stomach, the heat, the lust. But he drew away.

'Come on,' he said, grabbing my hand, 'race you to the car.' And the danger had passed.

He had a radio in the car and we sang along at the tops of our voices, sometimes in harmony, as he drove us back to the city.

'You know, you should do something about that voice,' he kept saying. 'You're wasted . . . a chemist. I can't understand.'

I tried to explain the situation and as we passed the convent again I said, 'That's where I learnt singing. That's my old school – left this summer past. Great place. I was a boarder.'

'Oh,' was all he said.

And I knew then, suddenly, like somebody had slapped me across the face, that he was a Protestant. I couldn't understand how I had been so stupid not to have guessed before now. Why I hadn't had even the slightest inkling. He must have realized I was a Catholic, with my gabbling on about the curate's brother and how I spent my half-days arranging the flowers on the chapel altar. But he'd said not a word.

'And what school did *you* go to?' I asked lamely. Hating myself. I sounded like my father. Da never asked anyone directly about his 'colour' on the odd occasion that a stranger came into our midst. It was always, 'What school was it you went to, then?', schools being either Catholic or Protestant, never, ever mixed. He would sit there innocently puffing away, calm as you like, but waiting for the reply – depending on which he would be either overly polite or excessively friendly and almost backslapping.

Garry now mentioned a school I'd never heard of, so I was none the wiser. But then: 'Afterwards I went to Trinity for a while. Left in my final year to join the band. My parents were furious – still are.'

Oh, God! Oh, the stupidity of it. The catastrophe. Trinity College in Dublin had as yet never allowed a Catholic student to darken its hallowed halls. Garry *was* a bloody Protestant. How could I have been so witless? Right from the start I had been aware that there was something different about him. That's what had attracted me to him in the first place. Protestants had a special look, slightly hooded, though not unpleasant – just strangely withdrawn, over-mannerly.

I sat in the car and heard him talking about dinner, about the pictures, about lovely plans for the evening. And I heard not the slightest thing. The rain had started, thumping the windscreen senseless. He had the wipers swinging at full speed and I thought, It's raining in my heart . . . my poor sorrowful heart.

I loved the boy already, or at least had loved him until now. Now all was changed. Hard as I wanted to, I could never, *never* find it in my heart to love a Protestant.

'What's wrong?' he asked after a while, drawing into the side of the road and stopping the car. And as I told him, the tears fell, great big tears running down my face trailing rivulets of mascara. I didn't care. He held me, rocked me. And I cried and cried. For him. For me. For the trap we were both caught in, the unfairness of it, the idiocy, the terrible sense of loss.

'I've thought about it too,' he said. 'And was wondering about it. I was afraid to say anything . . . about how you'd feel. Like the situation with your parents – all that.'

'Forget it,' I sobbed. 'You know as well as I do it would never work. Even casually. My parents don't even accept converts, for God's sake. They're the most bigoted lot you could possibly imagine. My father's so conscious of his position as well. And it's only a tiny village. You have no *idea*. I could never take you home and introduce you, even as a friend. My father would have a heart attack.'

'So would mine,' he said.

My mother's jaw dropped when she saw the state of my face.

'What on earth's the matter?' Full of concern.

'Nothing,' I answered, hurtling straight through the kitchen and up the stairs. 'It's just this country,' I yelled back, so the whole house – and the whole neighbourhood for all I cared – could hear. 'This bloody, damned, Godforsaken country. I hope to God it bloody well rots in hell.'

There was no reply. No comment. No sound from anyone.

The long winter drawled laboriously on. I soon forgot Garry, which made me consider the possibility that I might be fickle in my affections, and was now concentrating on Sean – the JAM Sean – the Junior Assistant Master in my father's school. The other Sean had turned out to be a real dead duck. After all this time and the not inconsiderable effort put into the cake and biscuit-making by my long-suffering mother, he still considered me one of the lads or, worse still, that silly little sister of his pals, the extraneous hanger-on, the one who was forever stood there, forever dressed-up with an expectant look on her face waiting to be taken to the football matches or the Castle or the pictures. To *any*where, really.

On 8 December, my eighteenth birthday, the Feast of the Immaculate Conception and a Holy Day – therefore everything closed, and us all there in the house gorging apple tart and jam sponge – I finally advised my mother, forget it. Sean would never want me, and even if he did it was too late. I didn't want him. Leave him be for someone else.

I had decided that the JAM Sean was by far the better bet. He had a lot going for him. For a start he was always, every single day, in our house. Because he boarded with an old couple way up by the deserted quarry in one of the townlands, a pretty depressing locality with only a few worn-out individuals in their dotage and chickens and pigs for company, my father got into the habit of bringing him into the house for tea after school. He was invariably still there when I got back from work, the two of them comfortably installed in the corner, conversing happily in Irish. Sean, being from the West of Ireland, was a native speaker. It was an absolute joy for my father, who'd had little or no opportunity until now to indulge this particular obsession of his. It had become the highlight of his day.

I could idle around in and out of the kitchen, passing the occasional intelligent remark, watching Sean covertly. And covetously!

There was no doubt that he was beautiful. He possessed those very special looks whose rightful and proper place in life is on the big screen: the height, the courtliness, the rich black wavy hair, the cobalt blue eyes which, when he turned them upon you, would dissolve a lead weight. He could have played the hero in any Hollywood romance, putting Valentino well and truly in the shade. He also happened to be a champion Gaelic footballer, with a reputation for brilliance on the field before he'd landed in our midst. When he wasn't in our house he was out there on the pitch with the lads, through the frost, snow, rain, mud, forever in training, and amongst those who knew about these things it was rumoured he had the promise of becoming an all-Ireland professional.

But Sean was timid. He hadn't the flamboyance to carry it off and never would. Nor did he desire fame. There wasn't an ounce of vanity in him and, apart from my father, it was difficult for anyone to have a conversation with him. He would clam up and go into lengthy silences, which other people would have to handle as best they could. Most gave up. I didn't. I found him a challenge. I would chat away to him and ask questions about nothing in particular, until eventually he'd be forced to look at me. And speak. My mother in fact believed we got on well, or as well as could be expected. So did I. He didn't smoke nor did he go to dances – the latter an insurmountable drawback in the getting of us together socially. The dances at the Castle were a regular occurrence now and I was a regular participant. Sometimes Bernadette came with me when she'd had a row with John, and sometimes my brother Joseph who had become a day boy in his final year at St Columb's. But often I went alone and teemed up with a bunch of girls from Dungiven, one of whom, Eileen, became a good friend. She was working in the town's pharmacy and was in love with her boss. It was nice to have a really close friend again, although she did witter on rather a lot about *him*. However I, in turn, went on and on about Sean so I suppose we were well matched. It was a comfortable and comforting friendship.

During the autumn of that year, the parish priest had had a brainstorm and decided that he would do up the old church hall in time for Christmas, with the intention of holding whist drives and sales of work and dances and other jolly festivities in order to raise money for the fixing of the chapel roof. The hall had sat untouched for centuries, in the middle of a mouldy old lump of no-man's-land up a side lane from the village. There were holes in the roof, no glass in the windows, stringy lichen and clumps of grass hanging on to and sticking out of every pore and crevice, the heavy door riven from its hinges. But the men of the parish, in one powerful philanthropic heave, had the place expurgated, fumigated, ventilated and decontaminated, never mind rebuilt, within a couple of months.

Everybody became involved and life could have taken on a fresh enhancement were it not for the fact that neighbourhood participation hardly stretched to a radius of five miles, and did not even include the town of Dungiven. The dances were a disaster, with the music of a couple of fiddles and an accordion, the three instruments out of tune and out of sync with each other, hardly conducive to the satisfactory performance of the latest Swing. Then with a fair sprinkling of the relations, never mind the parish priest himself, in attendance and watching every move, and big bald bright lights shining down over the whole scene, there wasn't a hope of anyone having what you might call a private conversation let alone a furtive smooch. Not that I was interested in having anything to do with that lot, but Sean was always there, as behoved his position as Junior Assistant Master in the community, conscientiously doing his stuff. However he still wouldn't dance, absolutely couldn't, he said, the once I ventured to ask him in a ladies' excuse-me. So that was that. I stopped going.

Work was becoming more and more trying. Jim and Eugene had begun to play a new game together, a game of teasing, of teasing *me*. About matters sexual. Some time during the afternoon, most afternoons, when the prescriptions had been made up and there was a lull in trading and I was occupied with making the tea, they'd start relating dirty anecdotes to each other, loudly, so I couldn't miss hearing, afterwards trying to draw me into discussion on various aspects of sex. What position did I think women enjoyed most? Did I believe men preferred big breasts? Or saying to each other, 'Do you think Mary does that?' They even went so far one day as to speculate out loud about the possibility of my still being a virgin.

'She's never,' Eugene tittered.

'She could be,' said Jim. 'You know these convent girls. Tight little lot. They keep their legs crossed a lot longer than most. Mind you, having said that, they can be pretty wild once they get going . . . there's no stopping them.'

I burst into tears and ran out of the shop into the street.

It didn't stop them, though. A week later, gradually, they started up again. It was torture. I don't know why I couldn't brush it off and laugh. I had undoubtedly a mouth on me, and a temper. But it was so insidiously done, so slimy, so full of innuendoes and so deliberately hurting – added to the certainty that I would never tell my father – that I simply couldn't handle it. Pathetically, part of me also agreed with them. I knew I was too prissy, too puritanical. It was time I had some of the convent goody-goodiness knocked out of me. It was time I parted those knees. Except that I couldn't. Not yet. In the meantime, the only thing I wanted now was to get out. Get the hell out of this job, this preposterous career. I was never going to make the grade anyway. Jim knew it. We all knew it. It was just a question of *how*. I started another novena, this time to Saint Jude, the patron of hopeless cases.

On a rotten February afternoon, when I'd been in the job six months, I was poking about in the shop when a young policeman came in. I loved uniforms, and this one was no exception. Immediately the day took on a lift.

'Hi,' I smiled. My brightest. 'Can I help you?' He was a fine specimen of policeman.

'Yes,' he said. 'You could. I'd like to speak to Mr Fallon.'

'I'll get him for you.' I smiled again. My sweetest. Going into the back and fetching Jim.

'Well, good afternoon to you,' grinned Jim, extending the hand. 'Not often our premises are honoured by the presence of a member of the constabulary. What can I do for you?'

'I wonder, sir,' said the young man, 'if I could have a word with you, in private I mean. Where we won't be disturbed.'

Eugene, hovering in the doorway, looked over at me. Immediately my face blazed. But I hadn't done anything, hadn't stolen anything. It was just that recently I had been thinking of helping myself to a few bits – just out of spite. Anyway, this would have nothing to do with that. This had something to do with Jim. Maybe *he* had done something wrong – that was more like it. He'd be put in jail. What a pleasant thought! The pharmacy would have to close and I'd be free.

Jim and the policeman went into the dispensary and the door was shut. In my six months there I had never once seen that door shut. There was something serious afoot. We could hear the voices and once Jim's was raised for a moment in a small expostulation. I was sick in the stomach with the uncertainty and the thought of the various possibilities.

When the door finally opened, it was Jim. His face was grey.

'Can you close the shop, Mary?' he said. 'Put the sign up and both of you come in.' Immediately I burst into tears.

'Now, now, now,' he said, 'don't panic.' He was trying his best to be his usual breezy self, rubbing his hands together, but this time so tightly you'd think he was grinding corn. 'The officer here has brought some, well, not too good news.'

It seemed a farmer, living alone somewhere way out in the wilds, had been found dead on the road a few days beforehand. Nothing unusual in that. People were frequently dropping here and there around the place – the population was fairly aged. Except that this one hadn't been particularly old and he'd been as fit as a fiddle up until now, apart from a bad leg he'd recently developed – nothing untoward – for which the doctor had pre-scribed some rub-on embrocation. Having ruled out a possible heart attack, they had been obliged to hold an inquest, the results of which had just come through. The man had been poisoned, and the opinion of those concerned was that the wretched creature had done it himself. Not deliberately. Inadvertently, he had taken his own life. Being somewhat feeble-minded, he'd presumably forgotten what the doctor advised him to do. Not being able to read either, he was unable to follow the written instructions on the medicine bottle and had gulped the liniment down. A natural enough mistake, but in this case, a most fatal one.

As the story was unfolding, I had only been half listening. My eyes were riveted on a medicine bottle, one of the dark brown poison ones with the ribbed glass, sitting on its own like a time-bomb on the dispensing bench. The writing on the label was as plain as anything. Very neat, precise handwriting. Mine. I was in a state of deepest shock.

'It's all right.' The policeman smiled over at me. 'Yes, that's the bottle. We know you made up the mixture, but everything is in order. No blame attached, no blame at all. The bottle is the right type, the instructions are correct – absolutely correct and accurately stated. And Mr Fallon here supervised the dispensing.' He was wrong there. 'Everyone is in the clear. It's just one of those unfortunate things. Very unfortunate.'

I was aware of the look on Eugene's face. For once he wasn't smirking. He looked really shaken, ashen. He knew as well as I did that had *he* been the one to make up the prescription – as could easily have been the case – faultless though it had been, Jim would have been in very hot water indeed. The lad should never have been allowed near the prescriptions. Legally that is. He was the messenger boy, nothing more. Only bona fide apprentices were allowed to dispense and that under the strictest supervision. It was a near shave. We were very quiet when the policeman left. Jim made the tea. He had decided to leave the shop closed for the rest of the day, perhaps the rest of the week.

'It'll be plastered right across the front pages tomorrow.' His hand trembled as he poured the milk. 'Everywhere. It'll be the scandal of the century. 'I've certainly never heard of anything like this happening before. Of course the sodding eejits will think it's *our* fault. People are so thick. They'll blame *me*. The only damned thing they'll see is POISONED in big letters, they only read the headlines, they can't see further than their noses.' He was in a frightful state. 'Christ!' He banged the bench, hard. 'It'll ruin our business, you can be sure of that.'

I cringed. This was the end. I should have been relieved. Singing for joy. If only it could have come about another way.

'You'd better take a while off, Mary.' He turned to me. Kindly. 'Your name will of necessity be in the papers, I suppose. We can't help that. Best you keep a low profile for the moment. We'll see how things go. After a few weeks maybe.'

I went out of the door, head down to the freezing February wind. We knew, all three of us, that I would never return.

I didn't get off the bus at the village stop. Instead I travelled on for a further five miles, to Dungiven. I had to see my friend Eileen. She was the only person I knew who could be depended upon to introduce some order into this rather unfortunate muddle I'd got myself into. She was indeed the ideal person, being in the pharmacy business herself, with family circumstances similar to mine, but older than me and with a lot more common sense. Plus a marked absence of any hysterical tendencies.

She and Pat, her boss, were sitting happily out the back in their shop, having a smoke and a Guinness and a chat. I knew immediately he had proposed to her since we'd last met a couple of days ago. The lovey-doveyness was slopped like a thick syrup over everything in sight – across the boxes of pills, the bottles, the jars, the odious apothecaritic effluvium – and the pair of them sat there like two twittery tweetie-birds in a kind of stupefied trance, enough to make you sick. I felt a violent stab of resentment rise up in me. How could she be so damned lucky? She had everything. She was almost fully qualified, in a career she loved, would marry her boss and together they would run their nice flourishing business contentedly hand in hand in a town they really cared for, with never a desire to move, wanting and needing nothing further from life. And have lots and lots of beautiful children.

Except that Eileen had a club-foot.

I suddenly remembered. And just as suddenly, the envy left me and there I was with my arms around them both and crying and wishing them bags and bags, ton-loads, of happiness for ever and ever and ever. And meaning every word.

They made coffee for me and then . . .

'I've poisoned a man,' I blurted out, the tears starting again. 'I killed him. He's dead. Dead as a doornail.'

The back room froze. They both stood, transfixed, disbelieving.

'It's true,' I wept. 'He was a farmer. Way up miles away. He should have rubbed the stuff on his bad leg, but he couldn't read. So he drank it and died. And I was the one who made up the bloody mixture.'

'Oh God, oh God!' Eileen was holding me, crying too. Pat went out and closed the shop.

'Right,' he said. 'Give us the whole story. Every single thing that happened, right from the beginning.'

I told them everything, starting with the job in general and how nobody seemed to recognize the fact that I was totally misplaced in it, possessing as I did the kind of aptitudes which were the very antithesis of all that alchemy balderdash – with apologies to present company! I then progressed to the kind of treatment that had been meted out to me by Jim and Eugene, the subtle hints, the blatant speculations about my sexual activities, the pernicious degradation. Eileen knew most of this already, but it was heartening for us both to share it with a third party, moreover someone who was a senior and respected member of the profession and had himself met Jim several times.

'The bastard,' Pat said. 'Who'd have believed it of him, all that smarm and charm?'

'That's exactly what I mean,' I cried. 'Who'll believe me? They'll think I'm making it up, some kind of excuse or something. Anyway, what am I talking about, who am I kidding? Can you see me telling them that? The word "sex" has never been mentioned in our house. *Never*. I couldn't get the words out. They'd stick in my gullet. *No*, absolutely out of the question. I couldn't look at them, even—'

'No, but I can,' said Pat.

'Me too,' added Eileen. 'Come on. Let's get ourselves organized. Pat and I will take you home . . . No arguments,' when I started to protest, 'that's what friends are for. You can sit outside in the car and we'll explain everything. Your parents are intelligent people. They'll understand, they'll understand that the whole thing was a mistake, right from the start. You should never have been in that dump in the first place. Don't worry. Here,' taking me over to the sink, 'splash some cold water on that face of yours, you look a sight. Put a bit of paint on. No more crying, okay? Then we'll be off.'

I hugged them both. How could I ever thank them enough?

I sat outside in the lane in their car, and waited. My mind was empty, my body cold. The whole episode was out of my hands, and although in the very capable hands of Eileen and Pat I was still monstrously afraid. I tried to be calm. Eileen knew my parents and could handle them with her eyes closed. Pat spoke the Gaelic. Together they constituted a most formidable intermediary team for this particularly delicate exigency. I had nothing to worry about.

In a while, a very long while it seemed, but what was probably in reality only about ten minutes, I saw my mother coming out of the back door and across to the car.

'What are you doing sitting in there on your own?' she called through the car window. 'Silly girl! Come on into the house out of that. Come on, you'll catch your death of cold.'

Her make-up seemed slightly distressed around the eyes, but apart from that she was perfectly cheerful. Inside in the kitchen there was high action, tea on the go, what looked like tinned salmon sandwiches, cake and biscuit tins on the sideboard, cigarettes lit up. Sean sitting in the middle of it chatting merrily away, a whole different person. The three men were in full Irish parlance, my father sucking and lapping at his pipe, but peaceably, an easy agreeableness on his face, looking like he was having a wonderful time.

'There you are, then,' he said, as though I was just getting in from work. As though it was any average old evening. As though my whole world hadn't this very day collapsed in bits around me.

My parents had the grace never to refer to my pharmaceutical career again. Neither was the name of Jim Fallon ever mentioned as long as the pair of them lived.

My father straightaway set about finding me another job. One of the careers I had always fancied was that of an air hostess. Never having been on a plane I naturally had no comprehension of what the job entailed, but that was of little relevance. I had one lovely memory, from a film I had seen a few years back, of a pretty hostess in her stunningly glamorous uniform jouncing around in the cockpit with a personable young pilot. A fleeting memory, but enough to fire me up with a lasting and spirited enthusiasm for the lifestyle. To fly far away, through the sky, over the mountains, across seas, to new places, new people, new adventures. We all knew I had wandering feet, the entire world knew. It was a joke in our house. I was happy merely going down the road, even only as far as Minnie Mohan's for sweets. Any little trip would do. Just as long as I was going somewhere, on the move.

We applied to Aer Lingus – none other was deemed suitable, they being English or foreign in some way and therefore with possible Protestant connotations. Unfortunately, as with nursing, I was failed on medical grounds. The doctor stated that my heart murmur was now exceptionally loud. Nobody seemed to know how this could be so, or how serious the consideration given to the condition should be. And again, as with nursing, they insisted that it was a very common ailment and nothing to worry about. It was only that they thought they ought not to take a chance with me. Not where other people's lives were concerned, whatever that was supposed to mean. It wasn't as if I was going to be *driving* their stupid plane.

Next we set about applying for a selection of government posts advertised in the *Belfast Telegraph* – office-type work, which I knew I would hate, but would fill in the time until I met my future husband. I could put up with it for a while and indeed the potential for meeting someone would be heightened as I'd be working, if not in the city itself, then in a fair-sized town. No mention was made at this point of the possibility of my having to mix with Protestants, an unavoidable drawback. It was Desperadoes now.

However, notwithstanding my qualifications being more than adequate and glowingly augmented by a splendid reference from one of my father's colleagues, I didn't make it even as far as an interview with any of the jobs. We began to realize something was amiss. Then we had a reply from one of them which stated something like, 'Sorry but you have failed the interview,' and it suddenly dawned on my father what the trouble was. It was simply because I was a Catholic – indicated on the application form by the schools I had attended – and for no other reason that I was being failed. He was, of course, right. Jobs in government departments were reserved for 'their own kind', as my father put it, slamming off letters right, left and centre to newspapers and Members of Parliament and anyone else he could think of . . . possibly even the King of England.

The solution came about in the form of a visit from a Mr McNally, the self-same colleague of my father's who had provided the reference. He was principal of another two-teacher school some miles up the road into Mullaghash, a place we never much went to and knew nothing about. It seemed his assistant was taking maternity leave and he reckoned I would make a fine substitute, being as it were from excellent teaching stock and an ex-head girl into the bargain. Technically, within the primary school educational system, this was perfectly legitimate in those days. You could teach for a while under close supervision by the head and then, after a few months, along would come the School's Inspector for the purpose of assessing whether you were showing exceptional promise as a very junior JAM. And lo and behold, you could find yourself with a place in a teacher training college. Another way in, and amazingly a way my father had known nothing about. We were overjoyed. I had been given a second chance. Again I had been appointed on the strength of my father's reputation, the esteem in which my parents were held, far and wide. Wasn't I the lucky one to have such wonderful parents? This time, I wouldn't let them down.

There followed some of the happiest months of my life so far. Every morning I would set off on my bicycle, out the big back gate and away up the road, circling around the base of Mullaghash on my left for three or four miles, then up a brambly lane, off that a dirt track and there, standing in supreme isolation, was my school – my very own school. I loved it from the first moment I saw it. I cycled there on the Saturday afternoon before I started in order to time the journey, get my bearings and have a scout around. It was such a lonely place, not a house in sight, strangely lost, barren, the school and outhouses set against a background of stark louring winter trees affording but meagre protection against the bitter winter winds coming in over the bog. But it was a cosy building, tiny, like a doll's house, though sturdy, grey glinty stone under a thatched roof, the windows and doors painted a fragile blue.

I looked in through the windows. Two small rooms, the walls partly dark-wood-panelled, the top half painted a dubious yellowy cream, barely discernible under the haphazard farrago of children's paintings, elaborate montages, all-size maps, magazine pictures of exotic birds and fish, big cats and small cats and kangaroo types – a vivid hotchpotch of keen juvenile creativity. My room was the one with the more higgledy-piggledy pictures, the smaller desks, the bunched mélange of faded paper roses and dusty leaves and twiglets crammed into jam-jars on the window stills – the feminine touch of the departed mother-to-be. I'd make fresh paper roses. I'd get swags of blue and green and yellow crêpe from Woolworth's in the city, and I would fill the windows and every cupboard top with rich and colourific summer abandon.

In the corner was an old upright piano. I could get a decent choir going, train and accompany them myself. They'd have to sing in C, it being the only key in which I could vamp. Perhaps I should learn another. There was one with an F sharp and an A and something else, which wasn't too difficult. We'd see about that one. Children's voices were flexible, perhaps it wouldn't be necessary. Oh, the excitement, the brilliant ideas I had, the plans! I would be here only for a short time – I was determined to get my place, my *rightful* place, in teacher training – but when I had gone they'd remember me. I'd leave my mark on this darling of a school.

On the Monday morning my mother packed the egg sandwiches, wrapping them neatly in a white linen serviette and a
brown-paper sugar bag. She had taken the bus into Derry on the
Saturday and had bought me a new coat. It was a brickish-brown
tweed with flecks of red and green and was not the most flattering
colour in the world for me, but it was a beautiful coat nevertheless, very fashionable, tight-waisted and a full-gored skirt. Minnie
had contributed a nearly matching woolly pull-on hat with a
pom-pom on top, for the ears on the windy bicycle journey – a
terrible sight, but she'd meant well. I had to lump the coat skirt
all up together on my lap with a big old nappy pin to keep it out
of the spokes, but nobody would see me. Our back road wasn't
exactly the most likely *trottoir* on which to experience the delights
of a soul-stirring romantic encounter. The only diversions were a
few stray sheep guzzling in the hedges and further on a bit the
ditsy farmer, with soft cap and blackthorn stick and collie dog,
wandering along in the middle of the road, with not a care in the
world.

'Did ye happen to see me sheep anywhere in yer travels, then?'

I liked the headmaster. A kind quiet-spoken man, easy-moving.
And the children were a delight, ranging from the ages of four or
five up to about eight. In front of the open hearth, facing the
class, was the teacher's desk, and on that first morning, the
children in their seats silently staring up at me, the small round
faces, frightened, expectant, I took the sally-rod that was lying
across the top of the desk and I snapped it in two and threw the
pieces into the fire.

'There will be no caning in this classroom,' I stated. Very
firmly. Reminding myself for a giggly moment of Sister Gertrude.
'Not as long as I am teaching here, anyway.'

I smiled a nice bright smile, but they didn't smile back. Instead
they looked astonished. Perhaps they were in shock. Perhaps they
didn't believe me. Perhaps they thought I was a head case. It
didn't matter. I was sure I was going to love them anyway.

And I did. I knew already how to teach juniors, having had
lots of sporadic experience in my father's school. The female
assistant he'd had for years, ever since he'd taken over the school,
often took days off. She suffered from headaches, varicose veins,

indeterminate women's problems and minor disorders of the digestive system. Either my brother Patrick or myself would be obliged to take her classes, an obligation which afforded us much pleasure, being a respite from the daily grind of learning. The idea was simply to keep them quiet, maintain order and give them interesting passages to copy out from story books by way of improving their handwriting. But both Patrick and myself enjoyed teaching and could be quite bossy when placed in such a position of authority, so we took the opportunity always to practise on the luckless infants.

Now here I was, a *real* teacher, legitimate – near enough – and I was loving every moment of it. At the end of the first week, Master McNally came into my room as we were clearing up. As was the custom then in country schools, the teachers, with the children's help, did the cleaning themselves. We had moved the desks to one side and I was walking around with the kettle in my hand trickling out water in figure-eights over the old wooden floor, so as to settle the dust before sweeping.

'You're a good worker,' he said. 'Very good. The right attitude, too. And I can see the children like you as well. Excellent. I think we made an *excellent* choice, great.' He smiled bashfully.

My face flamed. I had to squeeze back the tears. Oh, dear Lord, dear, dear, Lord. Thank you for giving me such joy!

It didn't matter so much now that there'd be no choir. To my chagrin, I'd discovered that at least half the children were incapable of holding a note, if they ever found one, that is. Unfortunately this slight impediment in no way dampened their enthusiasm for vizualizing themselves as possible contestants in the Derry Feis, so when I took to the piano, with them lined up around me in lusty chorus, I hadn't the heart to squash them down or single out the good from the bad. They did that themselves anyway, the ones blessed with a dulcet ear nudging and nipping peevishly at the more spectacular of the caterwaulers.

It also obviated the necessity of me having to find any other key than my speciality. Not that even *that* mattered. Middle C, and most every other note along with it, black and white, had been on a steady downward slide for many years. Lack of tuning and the dampness and the thick turf smoke had done their demonic best to ravage the innards of the old upright. It was way beyond any hope of ever being restored to its former euphonic grandeur.

Mother and I made a dozen or so coloured roses and then got bored with the idea. By then, anyway, the daffodils were coming out, sudden shafts of vivid yellow rising out of the rippling swathes of sombre dark leaves, all down by the milk farm and behind the Parochial House. Clutches of pale creamy primroses and the finest gold of buttercups scrambled over the braes and around the ditches in the lane. The hedgerows along the back road began to thicken, tiny dots of young green sprinkling the scrawny winter branches, here and there a burst of starry white blossom shooting up in their midst. I threw out the dead leaves and filled my classroom with the dizzy radiance of the new spring. There was a lovely, lovely summer ahead.

I decided not to let either the thought or the sight of Sean bother me any more. I would stop, immediately, trying so hard to get his attention, prettying myself up and throwing myself at him every time he was in the vicinity. Soon I would be going to college, to a city much bigger than Derry, mixing with other students, being invited to parties, taking myself off to dances with my new friends in premises infinitely more galvanizing than the parish hall or the Castle, with loads of gorgeous boys to choose from. He'd lost his chance.

Or had he? Sometimes I forgot my good resolution when I'd be sitting quietly at the kitchen table, marking my exercise books, and I'd look over at him, at the magnificent chiselled features, the noble head, the rich black hair and the way the little curls turned lovingly around the cool sculpted ears. I wanted to reach out and touch those ears, stroke the alabaster skin, run my finger along his beautiful timorous mouth. Sometimes, sometimes, I ached for him. So bad . . .

But paradoxically, someone else began to yearn for me that springtime when I was eighteen. A creature so different from my fine and elegant Sean he could have come out of a comic book.

He was sitting ensconced in an armchair in the middle of the kitchen when I breezed in back from school, flushed with the cycling, happy, a fresh country girl aglow with the living and the shining innocence of youth. Immediately he stood up and his heels made an almost imperceptible clicking sound.

'This is our Mary,' my mother nodded, from her bread-slicing on the table, 'and, ah . . .'

'Paddy,' he boomed before she could get another word in edgeways. 'Paddy Loughlin. Pleased to meet you, ma'am.'

The hand-shake was as overpowering as himself, vigorous, weighty, violent enough to sever an arm at the elbow. Where the hell had he come from?

'Where on earth did *he* come from?' I whispered to my mother when she followed me out to the scullery.

'Ssh, don't. He'll hear you.'

'Yes, but who is he? He's American, isn't he? How come he's a "Paddy"?'

'He's a visitor. Well, I mean he's not really a visitor. He's from around these parts, born here. But he's been living in America nearly his whole life, he says. He's one of those Loughlins, up near Bernadette. You know that big old farm, well he's one of them. Actually, he's nice. Your dad and he are getting on great. Piles of money. *Piles* of it.' She shook her head in disbelief, whistling through her teeth at the presumed size of the pile.

I found him singularly distasteful. He gave me the creeps, merely looking at him. I guessed his age to be possibly in the region of forty. He was short and stout, with a surprised-looking, moon-shaped, ruddy freckled face, round gold-rimmed glasses with thick pebble lenses, whiskery bits down along his cheeks, the hair in strands of fading blondish ginger loping at random over the shiny erubescent pate. But what really stuck in my gullet was the sheer ostentation of his attire: the tartan jacket, the garish trousers, the flash outsized gold watch with the massive expanding solid bracelet on the furry wrist. There were glitteralia on his stubby little fingers – pudding fingers, with fastidiously manicured nails – the sparkle of a diamond tiepin on the broad magenta tie.

When I went back into the kitchen to sit myself down at the table for tea, he was talking volubly to my father about his plans for 'the old place', flailing the air with his porky hands. He would rebuild the house and the outhouses, modernize extensively, have an en suite bedroom for himself and his wife. En suite. I looked at my mother. He'd pronounced it 'N' suite. What a culchie! In fine sheep's clothing.

'You're married, then?' casually from my mother. 'Is your wife with you?'

'No, no,' he laughed. 'Goodness, no. I haven't got a wife. My wife died many years ago, God rest her soul. I'm a widower. But I'm *looking* for one. It's time I settled down again, now that I've got plenty to offer. I'll make a palace out of that old dump up the road. A palace. You'll see. It'll be the talk of the countryside. All I need now is a nice girl who'll appreciate it. A nice country girl, but with a bit of class. Style. You know the kind. A good worker, too. Like me. I've never had a kid,' and he looked over at me. I saw him through the corner of my eye, but I didn't look up, just went on eating. He was an obnoxious show-off, absolutely revolting . . . and *old*.

Unfortunately for me, my father took a great shine to him and began asking him over the whole time. He had never met anyone like him and could sit for hours listening to the man's tales, true or otherwise, of endless travels throughout the length and breadth of America, stories of towns and people and customs my father could only ever dream about – *had* dreamt about for years, through his collection of encyclopedias and musty old books on the history of the world. Every so often Father would interrupt, asking questions, seeking elaborations, refinements, and Paddy would laugh happily and patiently proceed to go into more detail, his accent swerving from American into countrified Irish and back into an affected mixture of both and not quite anything, so a stranger walking into the kitchen couldn't be rightly sure where he was from.

He'd made his fortune in cars, starting off as the lowest of the low, graduating to mechanic and saving through long hard years to buy his own garage. The rest was history. *His* history. Which I personally found unutterably boring. I had no interest in cars, except as a more agreeable method of conveyance to and from the Castle, but it was a history to which my parents, both parents now, began to nudge me into giving some attention. I had to admit grudgingly that he was what one might call a *decent* individual, a kind man, generous. He kept bringing things to the house, delicious sweetmeats, treasures, exotic chocolates that he'd found in Belfast, fresh salmon – *real* salmon – from a nostalgic trip to Donegal. He'd hand them to my mother, looking sheepish. 'Just a little extra something for the tea. You're always looking after me. I'll eat you out of house and home at this rate.' But he'd be staring over at me, the hang-dog devotion drooling out of his soppy eyes.

'I think Paddy has a wee notion of our Mary. What do *you* think then, Sean?' said father one day after Paddy had gone home, from the depths of his corner, by way of sounding Sean out on the subject. Da had no idea of my feelings for the lad. I pricked up my ears.

'She could do worse. A *lot* worse,' was Mother's crisp comment as she gathered up the expensive remains of yet another chunk of cool fat salmon. They'd make a tasty change for my sandwiches in the morning. Paddy knew this, which was why he was making a mighty lot of trips to Donegal of late, I thought – on the pretext of visiting some relatives. Did he take me for an idiot?

'Well, I can tell you that *I* haven't the slightest notion of *him*. And I never will have.' I spoke with grand finality. 'So you can get *that* idea out of your heads once and for all.'

'Oh, Mary, don't talk such rubbish!' Mother again. 'He's a good man. A kind, kind soul. Well-heeled, too. Many a girl would be glad to have him, give their right eye for him.'

'Oh, for heaven's sake! He's an old fogey,' I cried. In a temper now. '*Old, old* . . . enough to be my father.'

Sean said nothing. Sean always said nothing. I could have busted his stupid block in.

Spring drifted languidly into an early summer. The blossoms flew away off the trees in a flurry of snowflakes, the leaves gathered in sappy voluptuous clusters along the branches and the broad black crows sat and squawked against the sky. The air was alive with the twittering of small birds, fussing with nests, scooting and darting through the shafts of sun, the cry of the curlew in a lonesome skirl rising out of the new bracken across the veiled crags and soft misty hollows of Mullaghash. Soon it would be warm.

Over the ploughed fields the young corn sprouted a fine emerald thatch, enveloping the dry cinnamon earth, and couched along the low stone walls and ditches hummocks of spiky furze yielded their clutches of saffron capsules to the clear limpid day.

In no time at all, I'd be laying off the winter coat. Oh, if only I had a boy to take me walking through the meadows, wander hand in hand tra-la-la in the bluebell copse down by the stream, pick moonshine daisies over the braes, hold a buttercup under the chin: he loves me, he loves me not. Laugh with. Sing. Tantalize; in my new blue forget-me-not dress. I wore the dress the day the Schools' Inspector came for the purpose of assessing my prowess, my progress and my potential. It was the prettiest of dresses, the lightest cotton lawn, and it matched my eyes – *exactly*, Mother pronounced time and time again as she ran it through the sewing machine, whirr whirr, and stitched and picked and hummed, so happy with the successful turn my life had taken.

I had asked the children to behave, not to let me down, do their level best. Not to fidget. Not to forget a handkerchief for the runny nose, a clean one for preference. I'd explained the situation as simply as I could, even though most of them wouldn't understand, *couldn't* understand, that my life depended upon it.

'Yes, miss. We will, miss,' they chorused, looking up at me with a blast of such innocence and naïveté that my heart swelled. I was so lucky to have such a great bunch; I'd be sad to leave.

The Inspector and I got along right from the start. I told him I was nervous and instantly regretted it. Me and my big mouth. But he laughed.

'Don't worry,' he said. 'Don't worry. There's nothing to be nervous of. Anyway I've been hearing great things about you from Master McNally. You've got nothing to worry about. I'll just sit here at the back of the class for a while, and you carry on as normal. Good luck!' God, what a lovely man!

My anxiety vanished, and for the next hour I gave what I considered to be an exceptional performance. The Inspector then checked through the exercise books, asked the children some questions, drank the tea I offered him from a cup and saucer of the best china set in my mother's cupboard, and took himself off to the other classroom. After a time they both emerged, both grinning, and Master McNally stretched out his hand.

'Congratulations,' he said. 'You've passed. The Inspector here says you'll make a fine teacher. Well done.'

I had to cry, just a little. I couldn't help myself. It was the best bit of news I'd ever had. I couldn't wait to get back to tell the parents and sped free-wheeling down the back road, skirts flying, not a brake to hand.

Paddy Loughlin had brought an outsize box of Roses chocolates in anticipation. 'I *knew* you'd get in. I just *knew* it,' he effused, trembling a little, the jowls flushing turkey-cock, quite overcome with emotion.

'Thanks, Paddy,' I acknowledged. 'You're so kind.' I could afford to be kind myself. To him. This once.

But it ended there. I spent the rest of the school term trying to avoid him. Avoided having to look at Sean, too. His face. Day in day out, the sight of it, the remote implacable look every time his eyes risked meeting mine. With my new freedom, I took myself out and about all over the place, on my bicycle and on the bus. Bernadette and Eileen, in spite of being heavily involved with men, both managed to accommodate me for an hour or so of an evening. I was quite entertaining company myself at that moment, feeling as I did on top of the world. Bernadette had finally admitted to sleeping with John. She stayed over at his place most weekends. Her mother, it seemed, didn't mind, which, though you'd expect that kind of reaction from her, still astonished me. They were using French letters for protection. You could buy them from Protestant chemists. I'd known of their existence for some time and suspected that Jim Fallon was selling them under the counter. I'd never found out, and now who cared anyway?

Eileen was saving herself, keeping her virtue intact for the marriage bed. I was inclined to agree with her. Let them have their way with you, I said, and respect went out the window. Straight out the window. I hadn't the slightest intention of 'doing it', not for a long while anyway. And there certainly wasn't any danger of running into temptation with any of the lugheads I came across. It was different for Bernadette. John was a gentleman. Besides, he was old. Well . . . middle-aged. One supposed he'd done it before. One supposed. I didn't enquire.

Near the end of June – a particularly lovely June, sultry, the

haycocks safely stooked up in the meadows, a plethora of
fluttery dog roses, wild vetch and honeysuckle entwined in luxur-
iant concupiscence throughout the hedges – we had an unexpectedly inclement spell. On went the winter coat again. On too went
loads of turf on the fires to take the chill out of the damp
classrooms and save everybody from contracting pneumonia. It
lasted a week and I spent the evenings at home, reading or
correcting exercise books in my room. Neither Sean nor Paddy
was out and about either.

One early evening I happened to be looking out of my window
when I spied the parish priest and my father below, walking up
and down the yard, back and forth, back and forth, in dreadfully
serious discussion. It was something I had never seen them doing
before and I guessed there was trouble afoot.

'What are the PP and Daddy doing outside on a day like this?'
I came down the stairs to enquire of Mother, herself having a
peer out of the scullery window, making believe she was examining
the curtain.

'Don't know. Don't know,' she whispered. Like there was
somebody listening. 'He wouldn't come in, the PP. Wouldn't
even have a cup of tea. Muttered something about having a word
with your father. *In private*. Can you imagine!' She was ruffled.

'I hope it's got nothing to do with me,' I mumbled.

'Oh, go on with you,' she chided. 'What on earth could it have
to do with you, for goodness' sake? Sure, isn't everything grand?'
She poured some water into the basin and added, her eyes going
ceilingwards, 'Thanks be to God and His Blessed Mother. No, I
expect it's got something to do with the chapel or choir or
something. Yes, that's what it is. Something like that.'

She didn't sound too confident.

When my father came in he was alone.

'Where's the PP?' My mother asked as soon as he stepped in
the door.

'Gone,' he said. Oh God, his face was grey. 'Gone home. He'll
be back later. Maybe. Any tea wet, then?' He went over to the
range. 'Come and sit down, both of you. I've got something to
tell you.'

We sat, one each end of the table.

'It's your school, Mary.' He started to cry. My father, like the rest of us, cried easily. 'It's been burnt to the ground. To the ground. Every stick of it. The whole lot. Gone. Lock, stock and barrel.'

'Oh, Jesus, Mary and holy Saint Joseph!' cried my mother, adding, 'Pray for us all this night and day, pray for us all . . .' by way of modifying the precipitate mouthful of blasphemy.

She didn't burst into tears, but I did. They couldn't comfort me. No words, no pitter-pattings on the shoulder, no endless cups of tea and the best biscuits and cake from every tin in the house could help. I was disconsolate.

'Do they know how it started?' An intelligent question from my mother.

'No. No, not yet. The place was so isolated it was nearly gone by the time somebody saw it, so I suppose it would be difficult to tell. It's a mystery, though. I mean, how could it suddenly catch fire like that? And nobody near it. A mystery. The PP says there'll be an investigation. They have to have one, for what it's worth. The police are there now. They'll be going round the houses, asking the children.'

'They'll be questioning our Mary then, too, I suppose,' said Mother, practical now. 'Well, you'd better get your face washed, girl, and look respectable in case they come here. Yes. Yes, they will be coming here, for sure.'

I had started to bawl again.

'There, there,' she soothed. 'Don't go getting yourself in such a state. Here, you two,' she called to my youngest brothers, standing there open-mouthed and goggle-eyed at the botheration and the mention of the word 'police'. 'Run to McGuigan's and get us a loaf of sliced. And a tin of salmon when you're at it. Oh . . . and some more biscuits, too, chocolate ones. And make it sharp.'

She got them organized with money and a shopping bag and away they scampered over the braes, chattering excitedly about the latest turn of events. The news would be spilled in McGuigan's, and in no time it would have spread around the countryside like wildfire. Oh, God. Wildfire!

'Don't be crying any more.' My mother turned to me, intent upon taking me in hand. 'There's nothing to cry for anyway.

Sure, wouldn't you've been leaving there in a week or two when the school closed for the holidays? Finished, and on to bigger and better things. I know you loved the place but, well, anyway, just thank God you weren't in it when the fire started. Thanks be to God there was nobody in it. Nobody hurt. It's a blessing, really. A miracle.'

Some blessing! Some miracle!

It was only a matter of time. I wondered how long it would take. I sat at my little window upstairs and gazed out at Mulla-ghash, as I had so often done before, and let the tears fall quietly. I wanted to run away. Desperately. But I'd learnt the hard way that there was no place to run.

Looking back to only a few hours ago, I asked myself the question, what in God's name had brought about the inexplicable muddle-headedness of my afternoon? It was about an hour before going-home time and the children had started to moan about feeling cold. They were still wearing their light summer clothes in spite of the wintry weather. I piled on a great heap of turf and got a good fire blazing for them, thinking even the sight of it should be enough to cheer them up. And it was. So much so that without thinking I threw on another few clods. But by then it was half-past three and I thought, what am I doing leaving a great roaring fire and nobody here – wasting that turf when the school budget is so tight? So I took off the last lot of turf and put it back in the box with the rest of the dry stuff. A cardboard box. By the hearth.

'Miss! Miss! Look, miss! The box is on fire. Miss . . .

I looked. A thin tendril of smoke was rising up out of the box. Nothing dramatic. I poured water from the stroupe of the kettle over it. Done. And hoped Master McNally wouldn't find it too damp to light in the morning.

I had taught my pupils – amongst the other commandments, like thou shalt not kill and thou shalt not covet thy neighbour's wife – the one about lying, enjoining them to be honest, to be upright, never to lie whatever the circumstances. I had taught them well. Add to that the matter of their age. They were too young. Too young to be wily, too devoid of cunning to stand up to the questioning of the police. Besides, there were thirty of them. Some of them, at some stage, would tell.

And they did.

The Education Authority decreed, with formidable finality, that I be not allowed anywhere – and they meant *any*where – in the vicinity of any establishment *whatsoever* of scholastic inculcation in the Province of the Six Counties of Northern Ireland.

I was sent to stay with my Aunt Kathleen, a sister of my mother's, in Castlederg, a small town near the border in County Tyrone, where, it was ordained, I spend the rest of the summer. Aunty Kathleen was adorable, an easy-going rosy woman with a cascade of tumbling Titian curls and a smiling beautiful face. With two small children on the long summer holiday from school and a husband who hit the bottle in his spare time – plus the added complication of some 'women's problems', about which ones specifically I wasn't enlightened – she could do with a bit of help in the house.

I had never known my Aunt Kathleen, having seen her just once at a wedding and Castlederg being somewhat out of our way for the visiting, but now I got to know her. And I loved her. In a strange way we had something in common, her being considered by the family in general as rather irresponsible for having been foolish enough to marry someone who would turn out to be a drunken wastrel. But to me she was a woman in a million.

That summer I worked in the house, did the shopping, took the children for long walks by the river. There was no rush, no fuss. There was time for everything and time for anything. I had plenty of food, a pretty pink room with my very own radio, pocket money, and lots of freedom to come and go as I pleased. The town was bigger than Dungiven and had more of a buzz. Every Saturday night they had a dance in the parish hall, situated right in the centre of town so I could walk to it. *Walk!* Kathleen, like my mother, was a superb seamstress, and she went to the trouble of finding a dress pattern in the very latest fashion, helped me choose the material and presented me, almost overnight, with not one but *two* fabulous dresses.

I had a bit of romance, too. I met him at a dance and he took me to the pictures and afterwards for a stroll along the river and

kissed me under a dead apple tree. But I didn't love him. I couldn't love anybody ever again.

I wouldn't permit my mind to wander, wouldn't allow myself to think of those awful days after the fire. And Sean's face. So full of sadness. And sympathy. Sympathy for my parents. I had lost him for ever now. Whatever chance I might have had was gone. No boy in his right mind, especially one in the teaching profession, would be seen dead with such a dim-witted imbecile of a girl.

As for Paddy, I'd overheard him from the landing one evening where I stood poised for flight, listening. He was stuttering and pontificating and carrying on like a Bishop from a pulpit: 'What was she thinking of?' I heard it. Quite distinctly. What a sanctimonious mealy-mouthed hypocrite of an individual he was, even worse than I had suspected. I was well rid of the lot of them.

Here in Castlederg I was allowed to be myself, valued for it. Nobody to bother me either, to say, 'Why don't you . . .?'

I could have stayed for ever, but the idyllic interlude was not to last. In September the summons came. My father's letter stated that they had found me a job, a new career. My *last*, he hoped – manifesting a smidgen of the old humour. I was to become an assistant sub-postmistress in a lovely salmon-fishing town on the south-west coast of Donegal. There I would learn my trade and in time, perhaps two years, be promoted to the position of postmistress. A good job. A respectable job. One where I could hold my head up high . . . again!

I wondered how they'd found it. Donegal was in the Republic of Ireland. I'd be crossing the border, going to the other side. My aunt and I looked it up on the map. Nothing. We borrowed an atlas from the boy next door, and there it was. Ballyglass. The most infinitesimal mote of a landmark stuck away out on a promontory on the extreme south coast of Donegal, a jagged coast by the looks of it, right out in the middle of the bloody Atlantic.

I got the picture immediately: I was being banished. But perhaps that was unkind; they'd had a tough time with me. Furthermore, we all knew how difficult it was for a Catholic – any Catholic, but especially one with little or no qualifications plus a track record so catastrophic already it had hit the press twice – to get a job in the North. Nevertheless, if they'd tried they couldn't have found a spot further removed from the realms of civilization. Kathleen and I scrutinized the map looking for places of interest – like the nearest town. But there wasn't a nearest town, and don't anyone try to hoodwink me into imagining that that wee fishy pimple itself, hanging on for dear life to the very extremities of the universe, amounted to what one could call a 'town'.

God, you'd need Paddy Loughlin's glasses in order to make out the writing. It was a *village*, smaller even.

We tried hard to think of something good about it to cheer me up. Kathleen was distraught for me.

'There'll always be a bed for you here,' she promised. 'Always. No matter what. Come hell or high water, this is your home.'

We hugged and patted and cried.

There was one good thing about it. In fact, there were two good things. For a start, nobody would know me there, not a soul; not one tittle of my shady past would travel before me. I'd arrive as clean as a whistle, the recent tragic events in my life wiped cut. Obliterated. I could make a fresh start.

Then there was the freedom aspect of it, the exquisite freedom I would have to come and go as I pleased. Ballyglass was far too far away and too *out* of the way for them to come checking up on me every five minutes. And it wouldn't be convenient for me to go running home to Mullaghash, either, every time they felt the urge to make my reacquaintance. I'd just experienced the luxury of a summerful of emancipation and had developed quite a penchant for it. There was a lot to be said for being left in peace to conquer the world in whatever way I saw fit. It mightn't be much of a world. But it would be *my* world. All mine.

The more I thought about it, the more promising it began to look. I would fold away my soft summer dresses, pack the biggest and warmest and toughest winter woollies and stride forth, with a new zeal and a jaunty lilt to my step, to face the challenge of the broad Atlantic roll.

PART THREE

There are certain places laid fortuitously upon the face of this earth, a few rare pockets of perfection, superlative jewels in the diadem of creation. And when you happen upon them, all others are forever found wanting. For me, the County of Donegal in the far reaches of the north-west of Ireland was to become one such pearl.

Snuggled into the window of the bus, though, as it ground and bumped and undulated its tortuous way through the narrow twisting roads on that day in September, and me every bit of eighteen going on nineteen, I could think only of the life I had missed, of those bright lights and the wild city living on the streets of Belfast. Gone. Garrotted by one simple act, one thoughtless moment – one gesture of largess, indeed, albeit misguided: the taking out of two fecking lumps of turf from a fire. Nothing more. Not a single drop of wickedness in it. And here I was, exiled, ostracized, on my way to the ends of the earth. And to God knows what. I was indeed a sorry figure. The tears fell, flooded down my poor red face as I thought *what* a sorry figure.

I was missing them already. This departure was different. This time I wouldn't be seeing them for a long, long while. I'd miss the endless cups of tea with soda bread and strawberry jam, my father daydreaming away in the corner, his favourite pipe clamped between his teeth, my mother's rare moments of warmth when she swept up the whole wide earth in her beatific apron and everything was wonderful in our happy domain. I'd miss my comfortable room, too, up above at the back of the house, cocooned, the muted sounds from down below. The clink of china, the clatter of the range door as somebody poked in fresh turf, the dishes washed, dried, placed. Paddy's awful laugh. Out the back the subdued clucks and chirrups of the wilting hens. And the fanciful cock, in an unexpected blink of late sunlight, rearing his blue-blooded head to the sky crying, 'Cock-a-doooooo . . .'

Fading, stopping short in mid-gullet with the suspicion that it might be unduly early for another dawn. He too could make a mistake. Kicking a ball around down by the lavatories would be the boys. I could hear the odd shout, whoop, slurred oath, the dull thud of a boot landing on rock-hard leather. Whilst standing sentinel over all, steadfast, imperturbable, would be the enduring bastion that is Mullaghash.

Out of the window I could see new mountains. They looked much the same as our lot, but of course they weren't. These were the famous 'Hills of Donegal'. Ever since we were small we had been singing the song.

> All night and day I'm dreaming
> Of the hills of Donegal
> The heather on the hillside
> And the sunshine over all . . .

But there was no sun. Not today. The first chills of autumn had hit the air and blue-grey mists wreathed the low encircling hills in a shroud of ethereal stillness. Here and there were scrappy pockets of green, the odd small tree which stood low, bent against the harsh unpredictable winds that whipped up from the ocean and whinnied across this barren land. The heather was still a coppery purple, reaching down into the dull umber of the boglands around us, sweeping swards of punctured wilderness sliced into steppes by the peat-cutting, the small stacks of angled sods laid out across the moorland for the drying.

In the pits the water lay flat and calm and brown, sombre bogholes of unfathomable depths, capricious, unpredictable. This was the land of the banshee, of the weeping and the wailing and the long sad songs. A desolate land, forlorn, abandoned, full of lamentations. But a place, too, of enchantment, romance, of infinite tranquillity, where a soul could lay down her weary head and rest a while. I would be all right here. For the moment, anyway.

There were bus stops everywhere along the route, official ones in the villages and small towns, but we also stopped at telegraph poles or people's front gates or any old place really. All you had to do, it appeared, was to stick out your arm. This seemed a very friendly idea and took my mind off my worries for a bit. It amused me, until the day wore on and we seemed to be getting slower and slower and I began to get properly fed up with it. But there was no hurry. I wasn't going anywhere. Much. Everyone talked to everyone else, which I was used to, but here they seemed to be even more talkative than at home, more congenial. The accent was different, too. Only slightly, but it was noticeable. Less strident than ours, there was a silver-toned camber to it which harmonized agreeably with the surroundings. At the big main town we had a break for tea, and then into another bus, a desperate wreck and draughty too, for the last leg of the journey. I dozed.

It was dark when we arrived, but not so dark that I couldn't make out the size of the place. It was one street. No side streets, no interesting shoot-offs, no village square, nothing rambling on vaguely into obscurity round a corner. One street. Plain and simple.

The bus stop was the post office, so I was here already: one cardboard suitcase, one shopping bag with a pot of homemade jam for the family, one good warm tweed – Donegal tweed – coat, one woolly hat. And a soul that was half-paralysed with the fear.

Miss McNulty, my new boss, opened the side door to me. A dumpy woman, probably in her forties, the far end of them, she was smiling a welcome.

'Come in, Come in. You must be frozen. It's a terrible long journey. Come in. Here, Kitty,' turning round, 'take Mary's bag. There's a good girl.'

Kitty emerged from behind the flowery overall, a tiny child with huge frightened eyes and long curly dark hair, a thumb stuck firmly in her mouth. Without a word, she bent down and lifted the case with her free hand, turned and walked the length of the long dim hall and up the stairs.

'You know which is Mary's room, darlin', don't you?'

Kitty didn't answer.

Tea was ready for me, scrambled eggs, keeping warm in the oven. The massive range, set into the whole wall of a raw brick inglenook, was rusty, dusty even, not excessively black-leaded, I was pleased to note, and blasted out a heat that would knock you sideways. Obviously the kitchen was the place to be.

Her name was Margaret, I noticed from an envelope addressed to her on the table, but she didn't say I could call her that. Kitty was her niece, from down the country, she explained, living with her permanently by way of companionship. I never thought to question why a young child had been taken from her mother and whatever siblings she might have had and planted in a strange environment just to give an aunt, much loved or not, a bit of company. It was only many years later when I was talking to somebody about it that I suddenly thought, how odd!

By eight o'clock in the morning, I had already breakfasted and was in the post office ready to start my final career. I was well-rested, fit, prepared to give it a really good try. I'd make my parents proud of me yet! But I was cold.

The counter ran all around the room – a kind of wooden horseshoe, the surface scratched, ringed, scribbled upon, dug into, elbowed. At the top end of it, somewhat far removed from the main action area, was placed the only object of heat emission, a smelly old paraffin stove. The walls were panelled halfway up, also dented and kicked, and painted a mouldy chocolate-brown. The top half had once been papered, tiny spriggy flowers on a yellow background, or perhaps it was cream – white even – with scraps of the map of the world in damp patches here and there, time-worn, mellow, like fine old parchment. I liked it. It didn't bother me in the slightest that the whole establishment looked run-down, seedy, cobwebby, with a healthy layer of dust every-where. At least I wouldn't be expected to do any polishing. Blessed relief!

As well as stamps and postal orders and the usual parapher-nalia, the place also sold a smattering of everything on the side. We had shoelaces (black and brown only), nappies, safety-pins, Aspros, balls of wool, spools of thread (black and white only), rosary beads. A few other items of religious impedimenta – statues of Our Lady of Lourdes with Bernadette in attendance, the Sacred Heart, the Infant of Prague, Anthony, the Little Flower – all sorrowing away in the dust and grime. Under the counter I noticed we had a big box of those rectangular parcels, the ones that were invariably wrapped in smooth brown paper, which I knew to be sanitary towels. And beside them a smaller box containing the sanitary belts for anyone who could afford the luxury.

'Your main job is the office work,' Miss McNulty told me. 'We'll concentrate on that. Obviously if somebody wants something from the shop, you can sell it. Here's the cash box for that end of it,' showing me. 'Watch and don't get them mixed up, though. That's important. Anyway, we don't do that much trade in haberdashery, so don't go worrying your head about it. The main thing – and this is *very important* – is the switchboard. The town depends on us *absolutely*. We're like life and death to them. I can't emphasize that enough, but you'll learn for yourself anyway in time.'

I found the switchboard very difficult that first morning, understanding not one single word she was saying. I was also understanding that I was being a moron again, that the thing was simple enough if you had a mind to it. A bent. But again, like my father, a comprehension of anything that might necessitate some slight technical expertise was not one of my strong points. I was a poet, for God's sake.

Still, I *would* learn it. I knew I would. As the good woman had said, in time. All in good time . . .

The 'Board' was a square box attached to the wall near the window. If you stayed on the phone from morning till night you could look out at the whole neighbourhood passing by, see everything. Not that it was that easy to see out. There was a great iron grille in the way, to keep the thieves at bay I supposed. I couldn't imagine anyone thieving in this dozy back of beyond.

The phone was going already. Miss McNulty answered. God, she was bright for that time of the morning! She plugged them through to somewhere. Then another call. And another. For heaven's sake! Who in their right mind would be making calls at this time of the morning?

'They're late today,' she managed to get in during a moment's respite. 'Must be the storm last night.'

Storm? What storm? I hadn't heard a thing, snucked up as I

was in my sweet settle bed above the kitchen in a direct line with the heat.

'It's the salmon fishing, you see. It's huge business here. *Huge*. But desperately secretive. It's a question of who can get in first in the morning when I switch the phone on. God help us if we're late. They'd tear the eyes out of you – they do tear the eyes out of each other – terrible men, terrible altogether. I feel sorry for their poor wives, with tempers like that.'

I didn't know what in hell she was talking about, but I supposed it was something to do with selling and best prices being paid and serious trading and bartering. Miss McNulty was standing there for a whole hour, plugging in and pulling out and turning the handle birr-birr, like my mother's now-defunct pre-historic sewing machine. There were fifteen or so subscribers in total, plus a couple of exchanges in the big main towns, each of them represented by a small round window on the board face which dropped down every time that particular person required your assistance. You then plugged them into one of the holes, either local or an exchange, went birr-birr, had a bit of chat, pushed one of the levers on the desk-top part of the contraption, either backwards or forwards as the case may be, then everything should be in order – more or less. That's the way I saw it, anyway.

You could also listen in, by keeping the lever pushed back and not breathing. Miss McNulty let me do this. He was talking to London. *Roaring* down the line, like it was across the wide expanse of the Irish Sea. Which of course it was.

The catch was bad, he was saying, then something to the effect that the price was the same anyway whether he – the listening ear – liked it or not. I could have laughed, but naturally didn't.

It was interesting, though, very interesting. The danger was that at this time of the morning, and you still not properly awake, you might somehow inadvertently connect one salmon man to another. Worse still, if you didn't have your wits about you, you could easily plug them into each other's lines and God help you then. You were a dead man, as they would have said themselves. I realized very quickly that with the likes of me holding the reins, the possibility of this happening was indeed higher than average. I'd have to be careful.

I wondered, just in passing, how I could get through to McGuigan's – I mean, for free, to ask them to tell the folks back home that I was all right, arrived in one piece as it were. That kind of hookery would have to wait. And maybe wasn't even possible. Outgoing calls had to be detailed on a ticket and then speared on to a nail on the wall. Dodgy. What happened to them after that I never did learn. Madam dealt with them herself, alone, on a Sunday afternoon at the kitchen table: numerous bundles of tickets neatly stacked around her, numbered, elastic-banded, tucked away in a box. And much puffing and blowing.

We were on the go from eight in the morning until eight at night, when the switchboard was put out of its agony – and us, too – by connecting it for emergency calls only to the main exchange. Doors were open from nine until six except for a lunch-hour break, but even then someone could catch you with a tappety-tap on the window if you had been called to the telephone, which was connected to the kitchen by a warning bell. Sometimes I'd swear they were waiting for me. They'd stand there smiling in at you through the grille, only a foot away, tap tap, and you could hardly ignore them. Besides, there were some of them who we knew wouldn't be seen dead producing their pension books in public and the whole nosy world looking on. They'd rather starve first. So we had no option but to let them in. It was a friendly custom to which I was *never* to become resigned.

Every night we'd tot up the incomings and outgoings, and every Saturday we'd have the big count, starting about five to try and get it over and done with at a reasonable hour. Not that I was rushing off anywhere. I had decided, for the moment anyway, to concentrate entirely on getting to grips with this career. Time enough for fun and games later, if there were any fun and games, that is. There was a cinema, I knew that, but I had to be careful with my money. I had my full keep, bed and board, plenty to eat and drink. But my wages were only ten shillings a week. A body wouldn't get very far on that. And that ten shillings, madam informed me, would be severely docked were I to hand over too much change in my counter dealings, leaving us short at the end of the week. I nearly snapped, what about *her*? Did she not serve the customers as well? But I managed to control my tongue. I supposed that since she'd been running the business for thirty years, her arithmetic was beyond reproach. So I was careful to be most meticulous in my transactions. No matter how much of a hurry the customers were in, I always took my time. They could wait. It worked.

The first few weeks I spent my Sundays exploring. It was a lovely village, quaint, with friendly people, mostly oldish but a few young ones too, sons and daughters attending day-college in the town. At the top end, near the sea, was an enchanting stone chapel surrounded by an overgrown graveyard with falling-down tombstones. I knelt in the cold dim interior of the church and prayed. Prayed for my parents, who'd had such a disastrous time with me so far. Prayed for me so I could stop being such a disaster. And lit a candle at the feet of the Virgin by the side door, her face pale and unhappy with the numerous troubles that beset her, looking down on me and assuring me it was going to be all right. Things were going to get better any day now. The tide had turned, and there'd be a nice boyfriend for me too. He was just around the corner. Never mind how diminutive the place was. Weren't they going to be opening a big, a *massive* dance hall at the other end of the town in the New Year, St Mary's Hall, named after herself and myself? They'd be coming from far and wide. In their cars. *Big* cars. Bought with the money sent back from England and Scotland and America.

I'd been there a month when he walked in. Five past nine in the morning, and me just finished with the switchboard rush, I turned around and there he was, the first customer. My heart gave a little hop in my breast. He was as good-looking as Sean, every bit of it. But very different. In the two minutes it took him to purchase some stamps – he was in a hurry – I had his appearance nailed. Tall, thin, fair, with that very pale Irish skin which turns pink in the sun and covers itself with freckles. A halo of soft curly hair – halo was the only possible word to describe it – blond in parts with a hint of red. The nose was absolutely straight, the mouth absolutely perfect, the dimples perfectly placed. As for the eyes, which met mine for a split second only

and looked away again – well, what did I expect with not a drop
of make-up on? – his eyes were the shock of blue in the sky on a
hot summer's day with the birds singing and the bees humming
and fairies dancing in the long cool grass. In a minute he was
gone and I glanced through the grille, peeping, in time to see him
jumping into a dark-green van. On the side of it, in stylish red
and gold script, was written the name Paul Gallagher, and underneath 'Family Butcher'. A butcher? A bloody butcher, for God's
sake! I couldn't believe it.

'Who was that?' I asked Miss McNulty.

'Who? Oh, Paul. Paul Gallagher. The local vet's son. Lovely
lad. The whole family are lovely. Three sons, they have. A credit
to them, every one of them, a real credit. Paul's the eldest.
Twenty-three, I think.'

'What does he do?'

'He's a butcher, actually. You'd never believe it, would you? A
fancy one, of course. He studied it in Dublin, properly. Vitamins,
different bones, weird cuts and the like in some university or some
place. Got a degree in it. He has a great big shop in the town. His
father set him up, of course, but even so I hear he's doing well.
Fantastically well.'

I couldn't ask if he had a girlfriend. It would have been too
obvious.

'I suppose you're wondering if he has a girlfriend.' She smiled.
She was in a very good mood today, a terrific mood. It wasn't a
frequent occurrence. Often she'd get herself into a tizzy for no
discernible reason, throwing things around, banging, giving out
to everyone in sight and some who were *out* of sight – which was
a very enviable position to be in, especially if you were in the
firing-line, as *I* sometimes was. Or the poor child, sullen and
stroppy as she was, to whom she'd administer a quick clip round
the ear as soon as look at her. It was, I knew, 'the Change' and
she couldn't help herself, but I was sorely tempted oft times to
start shouting myself. By some miracle, I managed to desist,
giving back only the usual soupçon of mouth, which she was well
accustomed to receiving from Kitty and able to take in her stride.

'Paul's a strange lad,' she was saying now. Oh, yes? Do tell me
more. 'He works far too hard. Kills himself. I know he's only

trying to build up the business – he hasn't been going long – but he's there all hours of the day and night.' I felt like saying, what about us? 'He's too pale, far too thin, all skin and bones.' Get on with it, woman. Get to the point.

But the phone went. I ran a few oaths through my mind. And a customer came in, a gossipy one, so I'd missed my chance.

It came again, very soon and very often. Every time his father's little window, numbered six, fell down on the board I held back the lever and listened, but it was always horsy stuff. Or dogs. Or his treacle-voiced terribly refined mother. Or one of the brothers. Never, never him, for a whole week, not once him. And then it happened. The following Monday night their window went down and it was Paul. I'd recognize that golden mercurial voice any-where. He asked for a number in Dublin. I put him through, politely and efficiently, trembling slightly. And listened.

'Anne?' he asked. Feckin' Jesus bloody Christ, it was a girl.

Wouldn't you know! I couldn't breathe. Even if I *could* have, I wouldn't have been able to anyway. He was telling her he'd be down next weekend for the dress dance in the Shelbourne. He'd pick her up at eight. He wouldn't be late. Was that all right? Was there anything in particular she wanted, like a side of beef? They chuckled – so comfortably – together. She had a tinkly laugh. High, like a silly twittery bird. Her voice was so posh it was a really putrid pain in the arse. I had an urge to vomit. Like down the mouthpiece. Into her beautiful ear. They said goodbye. 'Saturday, then. At eight.' He didn't say darling or sweetie or I can't wait. Or I love you. Nothing like that. She was the one, if anything, who was making the play with that simpering come-to-bed voice of hers. *His* tone had been practical, as though he was talking to a supplier. Perhaps they were merely friends.

By now I was getting up earlier every morning in order to put a dollop of make-up on, and earrings. Fixing my hair nicely, having slept in curlers. Alternating my two favourite sweaters, a blue and a green, always one on, the other drying on the kitchen line, ensuring that the top half of me, as perceived from the other side of the counter, was a vision, absolutely breathtaking, one well worth loitering for.

It worked. Next time he came in, I was prepared. Was that a double-take he was doing, or was it my imagination? He didn't even ask for stamps.

'Well,' he said. '*You're* new, aren't you?' Good Lord, he hadn't recognized me! 'Are you from around these parts?' Shaking my hand. A good strong hand-shake.

'I'm from Derry,' I replied. Warmly. Giving him the full battery charge from the forget-me-not eyes. 'The *county*, not the city. I'm apprenticed here to be a postmistress.' What a prim thing to say.

'Aaah, a wee Northern girl, then.' He cocked his head on the side, in exaggerated mimicry of the accent. Jesus, he was beautiful. 'You'll find it a bit dull here after Derry, I suppose?'

'Well, yes. Not really, though. You see I'm not from Derry itself. I'm from the mountains, you know, a country girl.' We laughed.

'Well, you don't look much of a country girl to me,' he

grinned. Oh, the gleamy teeth, the mouth, the dimples! I could have put my finger into them!

'See you soon,' he tra-la-laed. And off he went.

Oh, the glorious saints and apostles and martyrs and holy Saint Joseph and the dear, *dear* Blessed Mother, be praised! He had noticed me. He had said I didn't look like a country girl. That was a compliment. Wasn't it? He was implying I looked townsy, sophisticated. Like a Dublin girl, perhaps? Oh, the bliss of it, the lightness, the sparkle in the dust, the mellifluous tring of the telephone bell, the beatific smiles upon the countenances of the statues that only this morning were crying their eyes out over there in the corner.

This was different. This wasn't like you know who, the one whose name would not be heard in utterance from these lips again, the one who had refused to look at me and had sat there drinking his tea and a face on him as long as a wet week. This one had allowed his eyes to rest upon me and, beholding to the full the ample bosoms (albeit engulfed in a great woolly), the entrancing curls, the sparkling forget-me-nots, had professed to being well pleased. I had to get that new Max Factor Panstick I'd seen advertised.

He was back again the next morning. 'I forgot the stamps,' he announced cheerfully. 'See what you did to me!'

'Oh, go on with you,' I countered. Blushing beautifully. And he was gone.

'Well,' she said, in a big W-E-L-L. 'What's this about, then?' She'd got out of the wrong side of the bed this morning. Already Kitty had had an earful. Oh, sweet Jesus, let her not flatten me down.

'Nothing,' I said. 'He came in yesterday and forgot to get his stamps. That's about the size of it.'

'That's about the size of it,' she imitated. But smiling now, thanks be to God. 'If you ask me, he likes you. Dear, oh dear,' shaking the head. 'Poor you. It's a broken heart you're in for.'

'If you're talking about the girl in Dublin . . .'

'Ah, you know about her already then? Good.'

I had to watch my step. I wasn't so sure she'd approve of my eavesdropping on *personal* conversations.

'What about her?' I asked. 'I mean, is it serious?'

'Aaah, so you *do* like him, then? Thought so. Well now, is it serious?' She put on a suitably serious expression. No telephone ringing. No customers. Her in a good mood, pleasingly disposed to the imparting of some vital information. Hurry, hurry.

'Nobody knows really, I suppose. It's been going on for years. *Years*. The families are friends, have been since Paul was a baby, even before, so they've grown up together as it were. The father's a famous judge down in the Curragh somewhere, so it would be a good match. Anne is going to some domestic science college – in Dublin, I think. She comes here sometimes. I've seen her once, a nice girl. A bit toffee-nosed, though.' The phone went. 'There, now,' she finished. 'Did I give you the low-down, or didn't I?'

So. There was no need to panic. They were like brother and sister. I had suspected it was thus when I'd been listening to him on the phone talking about the dance. It was her. *She* was the one reading more into it than there was. Silly tart. Girls were so hopeless, throwing themselves at men like that. No shame.

I wondered if he'd be going to the grand opening of St Mary's Hall, scheduled for New Year's Eve, music provided by the most acclaimed show band in the whole of Ireland and an awful lot of merrymaking and celebration. The place looked absolutely magnificent, a purpose-built hall situated at the bottom end of the village and, although ultra-modern, supremely elegant. I couldn't believe my good fortune. It was the time in the early fifties when dance halls were going up everywhere, the beginning of the Big Band boom, an exciting romantic socializing whirl of a time, providing the ideal situation for encountering the boy of your dreams. Why tiny Ballyglass was so blessed, I couldn't imagine. And for me, what a bonus! It was going to make such a difference in my life, a place like that right on my doorstep, visiting bands from everywhere including, reportedly, even from abroad. Think of the musicians . . . the *musicians*! I came to the conclusion, on my nineteenth birthday, well, this is the happiest birthday I've ever had. Mother had sent me a parcel, a gorgeous Fair Isle sweater and a Gor-ray skirt to match, soft misty heathery colours. I had spoken of Paul in one of my recent letters, omitting to mention the nature of his occupation but putting powerful emphasis on the veterinary aspect of the lineage. I'd also described the big house – *the* big house – and the land they had, and the horses. I found a crisp pound note in the pocket of the skirt. She was thinking about me! Straightaway, I ordered the Max Factor Panstick, medium shade, by post from Dublin. It should arrive in time for the dance.

I went home for Christmas. And missed him. He'd been coming in quite regularly and always stayed for a short chat. He was often flattering, flirty. Once he said what beautiful eyes I had. It's the make-up, I said, before I could stop myself. God, why couldn't I keep my stupid mouth shut? Why couldn't I just look up at him, bat the eyelashes and simper 'thank you' like any girl in her right mind would have done? Another time he noticed a change in my hairstyle, when I'd tied it up with a pretty ribbon.

'You know, I do believe Paul fancies you,' remarked Miss McNulty. I thrilled to her words. There had been no more calls to Dublin, although one imagined he'd have a phone in his butcher's shop so that didn't signify anything. I stood by the window every morning to catch a speeding glimpse of him in the window of his snazzy green van as he drove past, up the street, at a thousand miles an hour. It was the highlight of my day, the highlight of my life.

'Are you going to grace us with your inimitable presence at the big night, then?' I enquired two days beforehand. It was the talk of the countryside. The press were coming, all kinds of important people.

'You mean the new hall? I'm not sure really. Don't know what's happening. I'd like to, though. Are you going?'

'Oh, I expect so,' I replied. So casual. Like I hadn't carried my best dancing dress and shoes all the way back from Mullaghash, plus a loan of Bernadette's second-best evening cape. And like the new Panstick wasn't sitting upstairs in its cream and gold case, in pride of place on my dressing table, carefully poised and ready for the kill.

'Something I've been meaning to ask you,' he said then. 'Nothing to do with the dance. Do you happen to sing, by any chance? Forgive me for asking.' He suddenly looked shy. 'But, well, everybody knows that Derry's *the* place for singers. We're starting up our wee concert party, a kind of amateur dramatics society, again after the New Year. I was wondering if you'd be interested in joining. I mean, in *any* way, not necessarily singing . . .'

Oh, God! Here was my chance. Grab it!

'As it happens,' I heard the words drop out of my mouth, 'I actually studied singing,' brag brag, 'for five years. I'm a trained coloratura.'

His face was a picture. I would see it for ever, I was sure I would. The enormous blue eyes, the mouth fallen open like it could entrap a whole herd of elephants. 'I don't believe it,' he whispered. 'I *can't* believe it. What luck! That means we might be able to do a duet together – I mean if you're willing. I sing too. I know exactly the song for us. Oh, gosh, this is wonderful. Look, I have to run now, but can you come to the meeting at Gerry's Sunday week? You know Gerry? They have the garage. Three o'clock.'

It didn't matter that he hadn't come to the dance. Or that I had never looked better and it was wasted. I was danced off my feet anyway, whirling and twirling and spinning across the floor the whole night long. I met Gerry, too, a nice boy, friendly, studying engineering in the town. He took a slight shine to me and rather monopolized my time, making sure to be the one to kiss me Happy New Year at midnight. I didn't mind. I didn't mind anything. I had so, so much to look forward to.

Then, about ten minutes before the end, I got the shock of my life. There he was by the door, standing stock-still, staring straight at me. I caught sight of him in the instant of a turn, my head thrown back, laughing, in Gerry's arms. Our eyes hit for a second and neither of us smiled. I knew he was still standing there when I waltzed off on to the floor with Gerry for the last dance, the hold-me-close and never-let-me-go one. The one I had been dreaming night and day for weeks of having with *him*. But he was dancing too. I couldn't look. She was here. In this very hall with him. As tall as him, thin, a sensuous curve to the delicate gleam of the dress, the hair in a sleek brown coil. Damn my flouncy skirt and puffed sleeves. I was sick to my soul. The cow! But I laughed and laughed. I noticed he wasn't laughing. He wasn't holding her close either. They were drifting around like they were in the middle of a fight, scarcely speaking to each other. By dancing cheek-to-cheek with Gerry in the dimmed lighting, eyes half-closed like I was in seventh heaven, I was able safely to observe the pair of them. His face, the darling beautiful face of him, actually looked bored. Perhaps I had been mistaken. Perhaps they'd been having a family dinner and the two of them had popped in afterwards, like the old friends they were, to give the place the once-over.

So I was glad I was looking good, and I was glad I had nice Gerry to dance attendance on me. And I was exceptionally glad that *she* wasn't living in the village to muscle in on the prospective theatrical activities.

Sunday afternoon I was like a breath of Mullaghash, so heathery was I in my Fair Isle and Gor-ray and a fine ribbon through my hair. The Panstick was proving nothing short of a miracle. It had a smooth glabrous texture to it and possessed a phenomenal advantage over that stupid pulverizing powder stuff in that it covered everything. Everything. Every single spot, every would-be and has-been spot, every crater and dead-end. The result was the gleam of finest Connemara marble, sultry, the embodiment of heady sexual allure.

They were a wonderful bunch, warm and friendly, a variety of ages. Most of them I already knew – everyone had to come to the post office at some time or another – and of course Gerry was there running around after me, plying me with tea and buns. We had each of us contributed something in the victual line and a few of them had brought beer and wine. I had never tasted wine. I sat there in the middle of them with a cup of tea and a glass of red and I could have burst into song already with the joy that was in my heart. All that pharmacy business and the rather foolish school episode were long gone, forgotten; fanciful yarns I would relate to my children in years to come and have a great laugh about.

Paul was late and came flustering in with lots of apologies. I had decided to play it cool, but he immediately came over and squeezed in beside me on the sofa and the minute his arm rubbed against mine my good resolutions ran amok.

'You looked quite something the other night – at the dance,' he said, for openers. 'In fact,' stretching back and viewing me critically, 'I have to admit you look pretty good right now.' Oh, thanks be to God for Panstick. It was working, even better than I'd hoped for.

'Well you look pretty good yourself,' I returned smartly. Why in hell's name did I always have to say something inane? Why couldn't I have come up with something original, something clever – like a Dublin girl would. It was just that when he was around I had so many butterflies jittering away in my stomach, it was difficult to think.

It had been agreed that the Ballyglass Dramatic Society would present 'An Evening of Romance' in St Mary's Hall, to celebrate May Day. We would gather most Sunday afternoons before this and then in Gerry's kitchen to have discussions, general chat and socializing, plus some serious rehearsing. They were going to present an eighteenth-century love story in which, being a new-comer, I wouldn't have a part. Perhaps next time. However, with my partiality towards all things arty and my penchant for putting bits of material together and creating something interesting – though I have to admit not always wearable – I was put in charge of costumes and scenery and the overall appearance of everything and everybody.

Paul asked me to sing, there, on the spot, and I did – nervously at first as I hadn't uttered a note for such a long time, but gradually gathering strength as they all began to join in.

> Drink to me only with thine eyes,
> And I will pledge with mine;
> Or leave a kiss within the cup,
> And I'll not look for wine.

I couldn't look at Paul. I wanted to, the song was for him. But I couldn't. When I had finished and the applause broke out, he grabbed my hand.

'Wonderful!' The smile radiated across his face. 'Absolutely wonderful!' Then to everyone, 'Wasn't that wonderful, folks? Some voice, eh?' He released my hand. 'Who's the clever one for finding her, then?' They laughed good-naturedly. I looked at my hand. It should have been soaring up in flames from his touch, but it looked the same, sitting there white and fat on my Gor-ray lap. I wished it would not be necessary to wash it ever again. I wished I could have kissed it, every inch of it, there and then.

He sang a few lines of the proposed duet, another love song and the number that was going to close the show, in a splendid tenor voice. He was indeed a singer. I wasn't sure of the song so he would have to teach me. We would be obliged to practise it together, alone. I told him I was a slow learner, which was in fact the truth.

'No bother,' he said.

'But you're so busy with your work,' I started to object.

'Oh, work, work, work. My life has been nothing but work for years and years. Time I eased up a bit. For a while anyway.'

'Oh,' was the most I could say.

From then on, my life took an idyllic turn. I had found the man of my dreams, the man I would one day marry. There was no doubt in my mind about it, no uncertainty whatsoever. He was everything my yearning heart desired, and more. Everything my parents would desire too, possessing as he did a goodly supply of the necessary prerequisites for the role, not the least being his indubitable Catholic pedigree. The only thing left to do now was to catch him. I couldn't, in all honesty, see that that particular achievement would present any insurmountable difficulties. It was obvious to everyone that he liked me – even Gerry had backed off – and didn't madam herself say that she'd never seen so much of him through the twenty-odd years she'd known him before? Running in and out like a yo-yo, she said. *And*, she said, what in heaven's name is he doing with those loads of stamps? I cared not to allow my thoughts to dwell, even for a moment, on the Dublin association. It didn't concern me. How could you feel fierce passionate love for someone you'd known all your life, who was like a drink of tea to you? Impossible. And how in God's name could you flirt with a body and look at her in that special

way, holding her delightful blue forget-me-not eyes just that
second longer than was strictly necessary, if you didn't have a
great big hankering for her? You wouldn't stoop to that kind of
thing if you were in love with someone else, you just couldn't.
Not if you were a half-decent lad. And Paul was most definitely
that. So. There was no problem there.

They were going to hold the dances every other Saturday. In
practical terms, this meant that I would work really hard at the
accounts one Saturday night – sometimes until nine o'clock – so
as to make up for the following Saturday when I'd need to be out
of there real sharpish, allowing me heaps of time to get myself
ready. Madam was in agreement with this plan of action; whether
she would stick to it was another matter. But for the moment,
everything was fine.

I went to the first two dances and he wasn't there. I waited the
entire evening, dancing of course, but with only half a mind to it,
making frequent trips to the cloakroom to check the lipstick, the
eyeliner, the hair, so they'd be nice and perfect for him, keeping a
stealthy eye on the door, glued, my heart in a tizz hoping he'd
walk in. But he didn't. Was the local hall not good enough for
him, then? Was that what it was? Would he only frequent fancy
playgrounds like the Shelbourne, full of toffs and smart sophisticated Dublin ladies? He hadn't been at the first two rehearsals
either and had come running in for stamps – and that absolutely
flying – only once and hardly a word out of him. If it hadn't been
for the sight of him in his green van, whizzing up the street past
my window every morning, I would have presumed he'd gone on
holiday or was ill or something. I refused, I would not allow
myself, to consider the possibility that it might have anything to
do with that person down in Dublin. But there was the slightest
twinge of unhappiness, a small nagging inside me, that wiped the
edge of the smile off my face and somewhat eclipsed the glint in
my eye.

But at the third dance, in he came. Granted the night was
nearly over, but who cared? He was here. And this time he was
alone. I was hopping around with some idiot when I spotted him
and immediately excused myself to go to the ladies'. It was a
terribly impolite thing to do, I knew, but my partner was drunk

and wouldn't notice, and anyway why should I be wasting my time on somebody like that?

In the mirror I could see myself shaking. I was trying to re-do my lipstick and my hand was trembling. I must calm down, must get out of here, mustn't lose any time, out out quick, *get* him.

The last dance was being announced, the lights dimmed, and he was striding through the people towards me, tall, arrogant. It was me he was coming for, I knew for certain, with his chin in the air, smiling at me over their heads.

'Dance?' came a voice from behind me.

I swung round, on edge. 'No,' I snapped. 'Can't dance . . .'

'May I have the pleasure, dear lady?' He was here, by my side, my darling, bowing slightly, the hand reaching out for mine.

'Certainly, sir.' I dropped a perfect curtsy.

Of course he was a brilliant dancer. Of course our bodies were made for each other, folding in neatly together, his breath warm on my cheek, my mouth almost touching his delicious ear. I could have put my tongue out and licked it. I started to sing the song they were playing, sliding my voice just past the ear, pianissimo, so as not to hurt, and his hold on me tightened. Our cheeks touched and stayed and I closed my eyes and died. I saw nothing, I heard nothing. Only felt. His skin, his hands, his body all over mine.

The music finished and we stood for a moment, still holding on. He broke away.

'Can I drive you home?' His voice was low.

'But it's only up the road . . .' I began. Oh, God! You know there are times in my life, many, when I am utterly amazed at how excruciatingly devoid of grey matter my head can sometimes be. This was one of them.

However, he was not to be put off.

'That doesn't matter.' How self-confident he was, how cool. 'It's raining, you can't spoil your nice dress. Come on, get your coat. I'll be waiting at the door.'

The van was outside. He opened the passenger door and, lifting up the skirt of my coat, placed it neatly over my legs.

'There,' he said, patting my knees. 'Comfy?' Sweet Jesus . . .

'Fine. Fine, thanks.' My stomach was in a tumult. I hadn't had this sensation way down in my tummy button since that afternoon with Garry. Not even with you know who, the one who shall not be mentioned. But then he'd never touched me, never actually *touched* me, had he?

'Would you like to go for a wee run?' He cocked his head to the side as he turned the key in the ignition, giving me the quirky smile that I loved so much.

'I suppose . . . Yes, why not?' I was learning!

He drove up by the chapel and out along the coast road. The rain was lashing down on us, the few trees leaning out of the crumbling walls, bent and bowed low in the wind. He stopped the van on the cliff top, facing the sea. The rain had eased off.

'Shall I open the window, get the sea air? Would it be too cold for you?'

'No. Lovely,' I whispered, helpless.

We sat in silence for a while, smoking, looking down on the huge ocean as it came thundering towards us, gathering head in a powerful onslaught of foaming breakers until it crashed against the rocks and reared up into the air in an almighty monumental crescendo. I shivered. He turned to me.

'Cold?' Gently, taking both my hands in his.

And then he kissed me.

We rehearsed our song most Thursdays, Thursday supposedly being our mutual half-day but through which we both worked, him at his butchering, me on my switchboard. But it still meant a comparatively early evening for a get-together down at his house. There was a grand piano in the drawing room and on our first evening there we played around with keys and notes, experimenting with the resonance of our voices, marvelling at the way they blended. We were perfectly matched. That's what *he* said. I felt like adding, 'I could have told you that, weeks ago.' But I held my tongue.

His mother was in and out, around and about, a frail woman, terribly genteel with a slight air of abstraction about her. Perhaps she was worried that her eldest son, every Irish mother's pride and joy, was getting along so famously with some improbable little scallywag from the North, some painted and powdered wench, background unknown. She was a snob. A *gracious* snob, but a bloody snob nonetheless. And her supreme charm and friendliness and servility with the cosied teapot and hot buttered scones and what a really lovely jumper wonderful colours did you knit it yourself how clever, parleying, didn't cut the slightest sliver of ice with me. It was a worry, already, in the general plan of things. I couldn't see her and my mother hitting it off. This woman, with her long plain pontifical face and her fawn twinset and her brown spit-and-polished lace-up shoes and her air of aloof condescension would make mince-meat of my poor mother in her danglers and spindlies. As for my father, 'And what school did *you* go to, then?' Oh, God, there wasn't a hope. Class was class, no getting away from it.

His father, though, was quite different. He came in before I left, a fine cut-glass of whiskey in his hand and immediately offered me some.

'I'm just going,' I said.

'Rubbish. What would you be going for, sure isn't the night young yet? Paul, what's the matter with you? Get the girl a drink, for goodness' sake.'

'Well, just a small one then. *Tiny*.' I had a gin and tonic – naturally they had everything.

'Well, well, what have we here then? Practising, your mother says. What's the song?'

We sang the few lines that I had succeeded in learning so far.

'Ah,' he said. 'Beautiful. God, that doesn't half take me back. No songs like the old songs, I always say. Beautiful.'

There were tears in his eyes. I could see he'd had a drink or two. I could also see from which side of the family Paul had acquired his good looks. The man was wickedly handsome, vaguely rakish, voluble, given to swearing but, I surmised, also caring. A lot. I suspected, too, that he was a little bit of a womanizer; it occurred to me that perhaps his wife hadn't come by that long face for nothing. And I wondered in passing if his son took after him in that department as well. Paul may have had his father's looks, but he had his mother's finesse. And the father, despite his bluff ways, and his hearty divil-me-care attitude, his euphuistic use of risqué language, was still class. The whole house exuded it – out of every cranny, every Regency stripe and damask rose, every gilt-framed antediluvian landscape, the grand and the baby grand, the three red setters, the two horses and pony in the paddock. I would have to think about this, give the matter some serious consideration.

I could *not* see Mrs Gallagher tripping down our back yard to rest her fragile bum on the edge of the tin bucket of the 'Adults Only' privy – the one in the middle, with the cut-out squares of newspaper for the wiping hanging by a length of string from a nail on the wall. Nor even could I see her making out in the new house, the one they were proposing to give us when the bigger and better school was up and running, one of the brand-new council houses in the village, every single one of which had a bathroom. Plus a flush lavatory.

No, I couldn't see any of that.

As the day of the concert drew nearer, Paul and I saw hardly anything of each other. He had a part in the play, a 'young male lead' type part, of course, and I was swamped in materials and cardboard fireplaces. I still went to the dances, though. Sometimes he turned up, mostly he didn't. But when he was there, he took me home. I could have walked it in five minutes but these days such a suggestion would never have escaped my lips. He always parked in the back alley behind our house, and there we would kiss and cuddle and touch and stroke and have tentative feels. But no more. He too was a virgin and he too was afraid – afraid to go 'all the way'. I wanted him madly. For God's sake, I was nineteen going on twenty, and what the hell was I saving it for anyway? But I was scared of the consequences and of the mortal sin we would commit, one sin each – indeed, I wasn't too sure that we hadn't already committed a few as it was. What we were doing would come under the category of 'carnal knowledge'; the trouble was that the catechism didn't go into explicit detail about where precisely the line was drawn. One thing I *did* know: I couldn't look the statue of the Virgin in the face any more.

I wished Bernadette was around for first-hand information on French letters. Writing to each other on the subject wasn't a satisfactory method of probing the nitty-gritties, the snags, the actual practicalities of the issue. Paul often made business trips to the North and could easily have purchased the articles in question, but naturally I could never have come out with such a suggestion. That was up to him. So we fiddled and faddled, getting ourselves in a state, nearly getting there but not quite – so getting ourselves nowhere in the end.

I wished sometimes that he would take me out in daylight, so that the world could see he was my man, or at least *kind* of my man – as near as dammit. I wished he would take me to the pictures in the town, or to dinner in a posh restaurant with a candle on the table and a miniature vase with one simple perfect rose in it. And we could hold hands across the table and I would look ravishing in a low-cut slinky dress with the flickering light playing across my soft creamy bosom, his eyes melting with love as they gazed into mine. I knew exactly how it would happen. Hadn't I watched it often enough in the pictures?

But he never invited me. Right now there was no time, of

course, not with the big concert coming up and us both so involved. Plenty of time for that afterwards. I could wait.

The concert was an unmitigated success. It had been extensively advertised and people came from everywhere, as far south as Sligo and Galway and some even from the North. I was chief prompter and miscellaneous runabout, until my moment came, the Grand Finale. I had put together a new outfit for myself from a variety of the leftover materials we'd used for the scenery and costumes.

It wasn't exactly a dress, more of a drape really – several drapes – an interesting melodrama of indeterminate historic origin, perhaps somewhere in the region of Greek tragedy. During the theatrical part of the evening I'd kept my hair in a headscarf, but now I had taken out the rags – an old-fashioned trick my Aunt Kathleen had performed on my cousins' heads, the purpose of which was to create corkscrew ringlets, and the result was, as it were, in general, astounding. God, if he didn't want me now, he never would. Still, I was nervous. It wasn't exactly the most conventional of get-ups.

He was standing off-stage waiting for me, dressed to kill in a smart country-gentleman-type tweedy suit – so gallant – and gave a most gratifying gasp of astonishment at the sight of me.

'Like it?' I asked, fearful.

'Like it? Oh, God, it's the most beautiful thing I've ever laid my eyes on. *You* are the most beautiful thing I've ever laid my eyes on.'

I could have burst into tears.

We stood centre-stage, as I had done all those years ago with Anne in *The Mikado*, holding hands, singing our hearts out to each other.

> 'Darling, I am growing old,
> Silver threads among the gold,
> Shine upon my brow today,
> Life is fading fast away . . .'

We looked at each other and we meant every word. Never would

I forget these moments, these precious moments when we declared to one another, and to the whole world, our undying love.

'But, my darling, you will be
Always young and fair to me.
Yes, my darling, you will be
Always young and fair to me.'

On the final note of the final chorus, we soared up in harmony, way up into the air, his tenor and my soprano blending in ear-shattering resonance, finally bringing the audience to its feet. We bowed low. The lights came up.

And it was then that I saw her, sitting near the front in a bunch of people – his two brothers and his parents and an assortment of strangers, city folk – a noisy lot, busy chattering and laughing and applauding. I could have been sick on the spot, my stomach gave such a heave. But I bowed again and smiled – smiled at him, smiled at the people, smiled at the piano player, smiled my ravaged tortured guts out.

When the curtains went across for the last time, he grabbed me in a huge bear hug and planted a good solid kiss on my quivering mouth.

'Well done.' He was on top of the world, jumping with excitement. I *could* have been. We were surrounded by the cast, the helpers, some of the audience. I expected her to come through the stage door any minute, but she didn't. Weren't we good enough for her then, or did she simply regard us as a pack of country hicks? It was a relief anyway. I certainly would take no pleasure in meeting her.

But what was going to happen now? An after-the-show party had been arranged back-stage; I had been looking forward to it but now of course I had lost interest in it. I was standing in the middle of the ladies' dressing room doing nothing, wondering whether to keep on my garb or change, when he walked in. He was in a hurry – when was he not?

'I have to go,' he apologized. 'Sorry I can't stay for the party, but my parents' friends are here. My mother's cooked dinner. It's a combination birthday party, as well as the concert and stuff . . .

Afraid my father's a bit under the weather. I have to play host.
You know . . .'

I looked at him. Straight up. Into his big blue innocent eyes.
The bastard!

'I know.' I was quite calm but, if the truth be known, shattered.
'You go and do your duty. Go on, off you go. Don't keep
anybody waiting.' I turned to the dressing table. 'See you around.'

He hesitated. 'Go on,' I said, into the mirror, managing to give
a kind of laugh. 'Go on with you. See you soon.'

He turned and went out, slightly less cocky, unsure of my attitude towards him.

I got over it. He came bouncing into the post office the
following morning as large as life.

'It was wonderful, wasn't it? And weren't you just magnificent?'
– curly hair, broad grin and little-boy enthusiasm, catching at
my heart again.

The summer came and I took to going for lengthy walks along
the shore in the light evenings. It was beautiful. I had never known
the sea and now I sat for hours, up on the headland or amongst
the scalloped dunes, contemplating its elusive enchantment, its
ever-changing colours, the turn of the waves, the suck and flow of
them as they rushed in towards my feet, bubbled for a moment in
a froth of hissing globules and slavered back out again over the
rocks. I grew to love the sea, as I loved this powerful land of
Donegal with its harsh brown and purple bracken, the haunt of
moorhen and curlew, the unexpected jewelled spills of shining
emerald where the sheep roamed, the diaphanous mists lying low
and still or circling and shifting restlessly across the brooding
sapphire hills. This was a lost land, a sad land, a land of dreams
and dreaming. But no longer – as summer idled into autumn – the
land for me. Too long had I been dreaming, *day*-dreaming.
Nothing had changed. If anything, the situation had worsened.

He was as charming as ever, as flattering, still collecting me from
the dances, still getting himself in a state over my body. But the
long-awaited trip to the cinema and the romantic dinner by
candlelight were not materializing. I was beginning to feel used.

When his younger brother Kevin returned from university in Dublin for the summer holidays and started coming to the dances and making a shy play for me, I responded, if not in spirit then certainly in show.

He started borrowing his mother's car and taking me to the pictures on Saturday nights as an alternative to the dancing, and then one night, over an easy gentle meal, he bashfully explained how what he felt for me must be love. I liked him – you couldn't help liking him. He didn't have the looks of Paul nor the swash-buckling joviality, rather had he inherited his mother's thin aristo-cratic face, her courtly manner, her unpretentious circumspect ways. He was going to America soon, he told me, to complete his medical studies, but he would be back. Would I wait for him? Alternatively, I could come and join him there. He would pay for my ticket, look after me when I got there, no strings.

'You know I want to marry you, don't you?'

I started to cry. 'I don't know, Kevin. I don't know.'

How could I tell him about my feelings for his brother, how we had been mucking around in the back of the van for months? How disgustingly I had been behaving, but how it didn't matter; how, in fact, I had no thoughts for any man but Paul?

'Give me time,' I said. 'A bit more time. We'll write to each other, get to know each other first, I mean *really* know. I love writing letters, I promise I won't let you down. Anyway, it might be only a flash in the pan for you.' I laughed. 'You're only twenty, after all.'

As I said it, I suddenly thought of my brother Patrick, just turned twenty-one and already engaged to his Belfast lass and getting married next year.

'You're the first girl I've ever kissed,' he said. 'You're the only girl I'll ever love. I can wait.'

He bought me a wristwatch before he left, my first watch, a miniature of the one Paddy Loughlin had, with the gold expanding bracelet.

'It'll be the ring next,' commented my new friend Helen, Gerry's young sister. 'You mark my words.'

*

November descended upon us in an abrupt merciless blast of winter. The gentle Kevin had gone to his America and a letter arrived from him every week declaring his unceasing adoration for me and I was lonesome. Not for him, though. For his Rabelaisian brother.

'He's making use of you, you eejit,' muttered Helen darkly.

'I know,' was my lame reply.

'Well, why the hell don't you do something about it? Why do you have to be so wet? It's not like you. Tell you what, why don't you ask him what he does with his weekends?'

'He's working,' I shouted. 'Working. He works morning, noon and night.'

'Oh yeah . . .'

'What's that supposed to mean?'

'Nothing, nothing. Just ask him, that's all. See if he can give you a straight answer. It's a simple enough question.'

It got me to thinking. Perhaps I was making myself too available. He hadn't noticed that I'd been going out with Kevin, or if he had, he had never mentioned it. He was too sure of me, that's what it was – too damned sure of me; he had me exactly where he wanted me. It might be an idea to go away, somewhere, *any*where. Well, not America, nothing as dramatic as that. Besides, it wouldn't be fair on Kevin. But somewhere in Ireland, away from here, so he couldn't see me if and when he felt like it, would appreciate what he'd lost. The more I thought about it, the more appealing the idea seemed. I was bored with the job anyway. I'd been here over a year. I knew the lot, I was weary of it. Time to move on.

I began to study the 'Situations Vacant' column in the *Irish Press*, furtively, every day. The jobs were few, mostly cleaning, shop work, nannying. And then one evening I spied a beauty. It had been written with me, *exactly* me, in mind. 'Irish actress, young and energetic, wanted. To join English Repertory Company for comprehensive tour of Ireland. Wages eight pounds per week. Telephone . . .'

I cut it out carefully and threw the rest of the paper into the fire. Miss McNulty must suspect nothing. She had become very difficult of late.

'Dreaming, forever dreaming, your head stuck in the clouds all day.' She'd shaken her own head. 'I dunno. Girls these days.'

I knew about her past now. She'd been jilted, literally left standing at the altar in her full white regalia and him hounding it off across the Atlantic – the scoundrel – to America, and not hide nor hair of him from that day to this.

I kept looking at the advertisement, wondering if I should call. There'd be no harm in calling, after all, to find out more about the job, ask a few intelligent questions. The number was a Tipperary one, the exchange had told me that. Come Monday morning and not a sighting of him all weekend, I decided to do it today, in the afternoon; theatrical people probably wouldn't get up too early.

Then, just before nine, in the middle of the early-morning fishing verbiage, the exchange rang with a call from Dublin for Number Six. His mother answered. It was Anne, asking for Paul. He came on the line. I stood there, paralysed, not breathing, my fingers covering the lids of the three salmon men, effectively seizing them up so they couldn't get through to me.

'Darling,' she said. Oh, sweet Jesus . . .!

'Gosh, this is early.' He sounded sleepy. But pleasant. I could hear the smile on his silly face.

'Oh, darling,' mawkish, 'I couldn't wait to talk to you again, couldn't possibly wait till this evening.' Aaah . . . 'I've been awake for hours, just looking at it, kissing it. Oh I'm so happy. It's the most beautiful ring I've ever seen. I wanted to tell you—'

I shut them off, I could listen no longer, and like an automaton for the next few minutes handled the screeching fishermen and pushed them through to wherever they wanted. My mind was frozen, my entire world shot to smithereens.

I then switched the whole damned monster off – dead – she was out getting the messages and having her hair done, she wouldn't be back for hours. Kitty was at school so I had the whole house to myself. I made a cup of good strong cofee in the kitchen. My hands were trembling. I felt sick in the pit of my stomach and I was cold, even with the scorching range at my elbow. The switchboard was fluttering away when I returned. Number Six was finished.

I saw to everybody and then got myself through to the bus station in the town. By bus and train I could be at the village way down south by six o'clock tomorrow evening.

Then I rang the theatre company and spoke to some Scottish woman. I lied about my age, I lied about my experience, I said certainly I could come for an audition, I could be there tomorrow evening. Would they meet the train, please? And considering the distance, could they also put me up for the night? The arrangements were made, the deed accomplished.

I wrote to my parents and told them I was very, very sorry to let them down yet again, but I'd this minute heard that Paul was going to marry another and they may or may not have been aware of it but he was the supreme love of my life and so my heart was broken, which was why I was running away to Tipperary to a new job, a job that would pay me a salary of eight pounds a week – a sum not to be sneezed at, they would agree – a wonderful new career, the chance of a lifetime. I would be a renowned actress, maybe end up in the Abbey Theatre. Hadn't everyone always said I had it in me? One day, they would see, I would buy them a house. A big house. And they'd be so proud of me. And they were not to worry; above all they were not to worry. I was fine, I had enough money – surprisingly I had saved some – and I'd write as soon as I arrived. In the meantime, by separate post, I'd be sending home a parcel of some of my clothes – sorry to be a bother – but things like my best dance dress and items of that order I imagined I would not be requiring in the deep south.

I prepared a note for madam, resisting the temptation to tell her what I thought of her in case she put the police on to me. I'd write a letter, an extremely long letter, carefully worded so as to ease the hurt, to dear Kevin. That could wait. As could Helen. I couldn't risk the mouthful she'd give me, the criticism, the angry accusations of having finally gone round the bend.

All day long I kept myself busy, managing to wrap and stamp the parcel and get it into the big sack for the afternoon collection without madam seeing it. I didn't pay for the postage and I hadn't made a note of any of the calls. For a whole year she'd been having my life's blood, slave labour it had been, day after day, for the mere pittance of ten bob a week. To hell with her. To hell with every damned feckin' one of them.

At lunchtime I bought a loaf and a tin of spam for the journey. I'd borrow the butter from the larder and also one of her sharp knives, long-term as it were. Every penny was precious. I couldn't go throwing it around in cafés. I wouldn't be able to have breakfast in the morning, either, so I stuffed myself with the stew she had made and a huge pile of toast before bedtime.

I couldn't sleep. The case was packed – everything I possessed. Whatever happened down in Tipperary – I mean there was no guarantee I would get the job – I wasn't coming back. Or going back home either. I would scrub floors first. The morning bus left the town at seven thirty; I had to be out of the house by seven in case she caught me. Through the back door, along the alleyway – don't think of the millions of times we'd parked here, don't you *dare* think of it – and away up the road as fast as I could, lugging the old case, to the next bus stop, the one beyond the chapel.

It came lumbering along and I settled myself down, nodding at the two or three locals already seated from the post office stop.

'Going on holiday?' one of them enquired kindly.

'Yes,' I replied. 'Just a wee break before the winter. Not long.'

The same old bus, the same road, the same bog, the self-same hills. It was raining as usual, but it was nothing to the deluge that was threatening to submerge my heart. I wouldn't think about him. As far as I was concerned, he was as good as dead. I had made a terrible mistake, behaved in a very foolish way, cheapened myself beyond belief, been a complete idiot when everything was said and done. No matter, it was over now. Finished. On to better things. I would become a brilliant actress, acclaimed the length and breadth of this land. That would show him. Judge's daughter nothing. I'd outshine the lot of them, they'd count themselves lucky if I deigned to draw breath with them.

In the town I had a coffee and then took the train south, through Fermanagh, by the lovely Lough Erne – I wondered if this was the one that was created by the giant Finn when he scooped up the rock that landed on top of Mullaghash – then along the Shannon River. I had never seen anything of my own country before, had never suspected the vivid crystalline greenness of it. Even in the winter rain, it was stunning. But I kept falling asleep. It was cold in the train, damp. It only added to the misery, the unease, the downright terror of what lay ahead. What if they didn't want me? I was already beginning to regret my foolhardiness in running away. Because this time I *was* running. This was no passing tantrum, no feeble attempt at a day trip to the seaside, this was serious breakaway business. I was on my own now, really on my own.

In the post office, in spite of the freedom I should have had, there was always *her* there, watching, listening, suspicious, constantly getting herself thoroughly geared up to pounce. When I'd crept in late, up the back stairs in sock soles after the heavy alley necking sessions, I could almost *hear* her checking the time and going tut-tut. Sunday Mass, regular confession and Communion had also been unavoidable, the latter two having become increasingly painful of late, especially confession. It wasn't a case any longer of, 'I've had bad thoughts, Father.' Now it was the actual deeds, the actions, on top of the bad thoughts – a desperate load to have to confess, especially when the local priest was young and of impeccable hearing.

Living and mixing with English people should put a stop to that. They'd be Protestants, atheists, Communists, persons of that ilk.

Past Tipperary town and on to the village. It was dark already but at least the rain had stopped. The station was tiny. And deserted. Nobody got off, nobody got on, nobody was waiting. I checked my watch again. We were only ten minutes late.

'Did you happen to see anybody waiting to meet the train?' I asked the station master.

'Not a soul,' he said. 'Not a one. But sure they could be late. Come on in here and sit down by the fire and wait for them, get warmed up. You look frozen.'

I was. He had a big turf fire going and I sat there thawing out, feeling the heat sink into my bones. I offered him a cigarette and he in turn gave me a cup of tea and one or two chocolate digestives from a tin. I waited an hour and still nobody came.

'What do you think we should do?' he asked. By now he must have been worried he had a stray on his hands.

'Do you think we should call the police?' I ventured. 'See if they know anything about them?'

'Oh. You mean the Gardai. Yeah, why not?' Obviously relieved, he went into a side office.

'Can you come?' he called out to me after a minute or two. 'They say they've never heard of a theatrical company, but would it be that circus crowd that were around during the week and took themselves away off up the country somewhere this afternoon?'

Oh, God, the relief. 'Yes, that'll be them.'

He had another word with the police and turned again to me. 'They're going to make enquiries, they said, and come back to us.'

We had another cup of tea. He really was a kind man although far too curious about how I'd got myself into this state of affairs. To keep him happy, I painted a pretty picture for him which was more or less straight and above-board. There was no telling what move the police would make if they knew the truth. The phone rang again. It was the police to say they'd traced them to a town twenty miles away, and as it was so late and no transport they'd come and collect me and drive me there. Which is why I had an escort of two young coppers in a nice comfortable police car to deliver me into the care of the James Struan Robertson Theatrical Company.

The 'Company' were seated around a fine open fire in the sitting-room of a boarding house on the outskirts of the town, rehearsing their lines. They were delighted to see me, although nobody gave me an explanation as to why I wasn't met, and I was too afraid to ask. I was introduced to everyone and given a plate of scalding Irish stew, which I shovelled into me like it was the Last Supper. Then, with a cup of tea and a chunk of fruit cake in my hand, I joined them around the fire. Somebody handed me a school exercise book in which were written, scribbled cover to cover, my 'lines'.

James Struan Robertson was a short wiry gingery-headed Scot of volatile disposition, which manifested itself several times during the course of the evening. Fortunately his annoyance was not directed at me or I would have gone to pieces right there on the spot; I could only hope that any performance of mine would not, at some future date, incur such grievous displeasure. The word 'audition' was never mentioned. The ensemble consisted of himself and his sister, obviously the woman I'd spoken to on the phone, her English husband and their two children. Then there was Jane, a plump, pleasant English girl in her thirties, who kept wondering if I was all right. I was in excellent form, thank you, what with a decent meal inside me and the excitement of being in the middle of this wonderful theatricality. I was on top of the world.

There was a nice young Irish lad by the name of Brendan, stocky, full of chat, cheeky. He introduced himself as the juvenile lead. Immediately a second boy, the last of the bunch, also introduced himself as the juvenile lead, glowering at Brendan. He was John, very English, posh, tall, lanky. And supremely effete. I was curiously struck by his speech and mannerisms, and kept watching him covertly the whole evening.

I had never heard of the term 'heterosexual' – perhaps because of that word 'sex' lodged in the middle of it – never mind '*homo*sexual'. For me, to date, there had existed only two genders, the girls and the boys. I hadn't reckoned on the boys and the boys. Jane, with whom I was to share a room, explained the situation to me later. I was fascinated, delighted by this scene of intrigue and glamour. Gosh, hadn't I come a long way from Mullaghash!

I slept soundly and contentedly, having found a new confidante in Jane. It seemed business hadn't exactly been blooming since the company had moved to Ireland, only a month ago. The public weren't very interested in coming out of their cosy cottages into freezing church halls, not in the middle of winter anyway. Perhaps it would pick up in the spring. Spring? It was only November. A long time to wait. I didn't ask her about the money situation, how exactly that part of the business functioned. I didn't know her well enough.

The following morning we breakfasted early and were in the church hall setting up the scenery by eight o'clock. I discovered that we, the performers, travelled by lorry, along with the scenery and props. The director had a car, but it was a lorry for the rest of us. I stood and looked at it. To me, it resembled what I had considered all these years to be a cattle lorry; only now it was filled to capacity with cardboard wardrobes, sideboards, a cocktail cabinet, two fireplaces, chairs, standard lamps, side lamps, vases of paper roses, and huge wicker baskets full of musty old clothes and shoes and wigs and boxes of mucky greasepaint. It was wonderful! We got the greater part of it out and hauled it on to the stage, and for the next couple of hours we hammered and pushed and shuffled and pummelled and rammed and elbowed the lot into position. Oh, it was exciting! In the middle of it I thought, God, how had I stuck that bloody post office job for so long? This was Living, this was how life was meant to be. In the town, from one end to the other, I had seen the posters up, in shop windows, on telegraph poles, on stone walls. 'The James Struan Robertson Company presents . . .' Oooh, I couldn't wait to get on that stage.

Meanwhile I had to learn my lines. It wasn't much of a part, but it was a part. Vital to the smooth running of the show, Mr Robertson said. I was playing a parlourmaid. After lunch, it was down to some serious learning. But as with singing, I discovered I couldn't remember a thing, except that with singing I could make up the words as I went along. In the Derry Feis, when we sang in Irish, I was forever finding myself in trouble. I'd be coming to the end of a line and ahead of me, looming up in terrifying silence, would be an awful blank wall. It never deterred me. I simply carried on singing, smiling away through my teeth – '*war – ee – feel – i – oh – branning – oh*', or words to that effect – thinking, Jesus Mary and holy Saint Joseph take pity on us. Sometimes a judge's head would jerk up and stare at me, but nobody ever seemed to notice too much and I still almost always won anyway.

With the acting, though, things were not so straightforward. Other people stood there, hanging on to my every utterance, most especially my *last*. I couldn't go waffling on, delivering words which were not in the script or words which I thought would do just as well, better even. Himself finally lost his temper at the dress rehearsal.

'I thought I asked for an actress,' he accused me.

'Well . . . I *am* an actress. It's just that I'm a bit out of practice. I've been mostly singing of late. I suppose really I'm more of a singer. I've studied –'

'Studied, my foot!' he interpolated. 'If it's singing you wanted to do, why the hell didn't you join a variety act? Or,' he added laconically, 'the circus?'

'Don't listen to him,' consoled Jane, in the wings. 'He says those things to everybody.'

'But it's so much to learn,' I cried. 'Plus I have to know everybody else's lines as well, and this is only my first day.'

'I know, I know. Look, when we're free, I mean any time this week, I'll work on the part with you. It'll be fine, you'll see.'

I had always been under the impression that actors were born, not made. I was neither.

We stayed in the town for a week. The audience trooped in every night – about a half-dozen of them, take or leave the odd mangy dog as well. It was most demanding, trying to give everything, the heart and soul of you, your life's blood, as James Struan Robertson kept reminding us, to a virtually empty house. But I wasn't in the least disheartened. I was having a glorious time, learning my lines, going to the pub after the show, rehearsing, having long talks with Jane and long looks with Brendan. He was younger than me, but it didn't matter, we really liked each other. That is not to say that I had forgotten Paul. I would *never* forget Paul. It's just that he had hurt me so much I needed a *soupçon* of consolation, a small restoration job performed upon my bruised self-esteem.

The money situation was dire. The director paid for our keep in the boarding house and gave us two pounds a week for incidentals.

'It's all I can afford at the moment,' he told us. 'It'll be better in the next town.'

But the next town was no better. Or the next. We travelled around the entire southern counties, taking it in turns to ride up front out of the wind and rain, but most of the time we snuggled into the back of the lorry, wrapped in smelly old curtains, amongst the baskets and rickety swaying furniture. Sometimes when the snow came flurrying down, I'd climb into the copious cardboard wardrobe and Brendan would sit outside leaning his broad strong back against the door in a gallant effort to keep it closed for me. It was a strange sensation, rattling along in the darkness curled up inside a wardrobe. But nothing bothered me. This was living. This was the supreme adventure.

Early December now, and my twentieth birthday had come and gone. Jane had given me a pretty bracelet of hers that I'd admired, Brendan a bunch of flowers. They were the first flowers that anyone had ever given me, and it was significant, too, that it was the brave Brendan who, a few days later, took it upon himself finally to deflower me – by the soporific glow of the sitting-room fire, kind of sliding off the armchair, gravitating towards the hearthrug, neither of us particularly aware of what was going on, both of us stone-drunk. The quick stab of pain jolted me into sobriety, but it was too late. The thing was done. I didn't care. It was high time it had happened. It *should* have happened with Paul, but it hadn't. Brendan at least cared. And he had bought me flowers.

We were staying in a terrible tenth-rate hotel when the bombshell hit.

I came down to breakfast about eight as usual, surprised that Jane had already gone without me, even more surprised that she wasn't in the dining room when I got there. I sat down and waited, waited for someone to serve me, but nobody came. I got up and went over to the waitress. Before I could open my mouth she whispered apologetically, 'I can't serve you.'

'Why not?' I asked, thinking, what have I done now?

'It's got nothing to do with me . . . sorry, but it's orders from up top.'

I sought out the manager.

'They've gone,' he explained. 'Scarpered in the middle of the night. Off across the water on the boat, I suppose.'

'Who?' I asked, stupefied.

'Your boss. The whole damned lot of them. Did a midnight flit, they did. And not a penny he paid, not one single cent.'

I burst into tears.

'Sorry, darlin', but I have to pay my bills, too.' He studied me for a moment. 'You weren't one of them, then – a relation like?'

'God, no,' I said. 'He was no relation of mine. I was just some sucker that answered his ad for an actress. I came down here the whole way from Donegal, in good faith, thinking it was a great job. But we've been traipsing halfway round the country for weeks now, and he hasn't paid me, either. I haven't even got the fare home.'

He felt sorry for me, I could see.

'Tell you what,' he suggested, 'you can help in the kitchen if you like. I could do with an extra hand in there, what with Christmas coming up and everything. You can stay in the same room – they were the cheap ones anyway – no sense in changing, and have all your meals. I'll pay you two pounds a week. It's not much, I know, but it'll give you time to get on your feet, find a proper job. How do you feel about that, then?'

I was so grateful I nearly gave him him a whopping great hug. But I couldn't. He was now my new boss.

I walked into Brendan in the corridor, on his way home to mama. And upstairs, on the dressing table, I found a note from Jane, with profuse apologies and a contact address in England. So they were gone. Vamoosed. And here I was in the middle of nowhere on my own once more, with not a soul to know or care what happened to me. I could have cried again, but I didn't bother. Best be philosophical about the situation. If this was the price you had to pay for freedom, then so be it.

My new job was primarily as a patties-of-butter maker. The butter was from their own churns, plump brooding yellow slabs of it, oozing out in frog-spawn globules of bitter salty sweat. You cut off a knob the size of a walnut and pitter-patted it about between two small wooden bats, finely corrugated, so you ended up with lots of little corrugated tubular balls. Dozens of them, one after the other, hour after tedious hour, day after day. Sometimes as I stood at the table, pat-a-cake, pat-a-cake, baker's man, the tears would fall down splat on top of the lump of butter. I was past caring. Sure, what was another drop of salt water anyway? It was a far cry from the vision of my name up in bright lights across the front of the Abbey, or the pleasure I might have been able to indulge myself in with the purchase of that dream house for the parents. I had been writing to them regularly, and now at last I had a steady address to which they could reply. Immediately, by return post, I had the peremptory summons from Father: 'Come home at once, otherwise we'll come and get you.' I knew it was no idle threat. My brother Patrick had recently acquired a car, and they'd be delighted to have the excuse for a good long run in it. My father had always loved cars. They didn't have to be moving or anything; sitting in one was sufficient to transport him into a euphoric daze. If anyone arrived at the house in a car, he'd go out after a while to where it was parked in the lane and get in. He'd sit there in the passenger seat, sometimes in the freezing cold, as happy as Larry, gazing out, perhaps dreaming of where he *might* go. A while later you'd look out of the kitchen window and the inside of the car would be completely clouded up with the pipe smoke and his head hardly visible. We'd been making jokes about it for years.

In a panic I wrote back. Yes, I was on my way, it was only that I was waiting for my pay at the end of the week – no sense in losing that. And so sorry to be putting this terrible worry on you . . . no need . . . no need at all. I was absolutely fine. I didn't think it necessary to enlighten them as to the source of this particular pay-packet. A patties-of-butter maker could scarcely be considered a step up from 'that terrible travelling gypsy crowd', as they were now known in the Kerr household.

And then a miracle happened. It was the first of many miracles which would occur in my lifetime. Some people call it 'the luck of the Irish'. I prefer to think of it as some kind of guardian angel floating around in my aura, always there, watching over me. And when I'm at my lowest, this wonderful blessed creature picks me up and delivers me on to a safe path again, sometimes changing my life around, at other times lending a comforting hand – enough to get me through the next bit.

The hotel manager told me of a possible job going in Galway. And what a job! It was as lead singer, front man (except that they wanted a woman) in an all-male, nineteen-piece broadcasting Big Band, the Des Fretwell Orchestra. I rang them and they invited me to audition, so I collected my wages, accepted the good wishes of everybody, packed my cardboard case and took myself and it away off cross-country, hitching for the first time, to the wicked wild west of Connemara. I was getting used to travelling now and even though the excitement was tempered somewhat by trepidation, fear originating mainly from the lack of funds, I loved being on the move, the challenge of new scenes, the exhilaration of the unknown.

I got the job, and posted an instant missive to the home front with the joyous tidings, my new address, phone number, weighty emphasis on the twenty-five pounds a week salary, and a directive about returning the dancing dress and shoes which were once more urgently required. Plus anything else my mother could think of which might possibly be utilized for stage clothes, like the lovely old curtains in the parlour – the self-same drapes in which I'd cocooned myself during those childhood Christmases, so long ago. Now that they were shortly to be moving to choicer and very modern premises, I imagined that none of that old tat would any longer be appropriate. I added that, within a week or two, I'd be able to reimburse any postage incurred; right now, what with one thing or another, shoes and a new perm and that, I was a trifle low on funds. To keep them happy – I was terrified they'd come and drag me home, depriving me forever of this God-sent opportunity – I quickly chased the first letter with another one, a lengthy newsy epistle describing the delightful boarding house, the boys in the band, how charming and kind Des was . . . and of course how terribly, terribly famous. I described Galway city, what I'd seen of it, and the new ballroom known as the Seapoint, an astoundingly glamorous edifice, recently completed, perched on a rock overlooking the sea. Just wait till they saw it. They'd never been to Galway and hadn't they been singing 'Galway Bay' all their lives? Now here I was, actually *living* there. A great excuse to come and visit. Because – and here I chose my words carefully – very sorry, but I was afraid I wasn't going to be able to make it home for Christmas. The official opening of the Seapoint was on the twenty-seventh, and what with so much rehearsing – they should see the *piles* of stuff I had to learn – and having to put together a long black velvet dress, well, going all the way back to Mullaghash for the day was simply out of the question. They'd be able to understand that, I knew. Anyway, getting back to the visiting, couldn't they come soon after, so handy now with Patrick having the car and that? They'd enjoy the wee run and wouldn't the sea air do them a power of good?

I was still full of the audition, standing alone and terrified in the middle of the enormous stage, looking down and out over the most magnificent auditorium I could ever have dreamed of, in or out of picture houses, hearing my own voice fill the hallowed well of it and come bouncing back over me in a wave of soaring resonance. I had declined the use of a microphone, having never handled one before and possessing not the slightest notion of what to do with the thing and afraid to let on. Now, unbeknownst to myself, I was discovering the mystery of acoustics, a joy which remains with me to this day, as fresh and wondrous as that momentous afternoon when I sang my heart and soul out to the accompaniment of the same old Atlantic crashing itself to bits against the rocks outside. When I had finished, I heard Des speak deep from the belly of the house.

'Great voice, girl, great voice. Wonderful. Welcome to the band. It will be a pleasure to have you with us.'

With only a week to go before the opening, it was flat-out rehearsing now, work work work. Very quickly we made the discovery that my sense of tempo was weak, nay negligible. I had been used to free-wheeling my whole life, sitting on a note for hours if I felt like it or thought it sounded especially good. The odd pianoforte had had no difficulty in tinkling around me, pandering gracefully to my particular little whims, but I could hardly expect nineteen musicians, strong and true and of impeccable rhythmic accord, to so accommodate me. In the end we worked out a satisfactory compromise. The fast and slightly hip-hoppety numbers, which I wasn't much good at anyway, would be performed by the two other singers, musicians who doubled as singers (I was learning the language) and I would take the slow ones, the romantic, the easy to count-in ones, and I would follow the musicians rather than the other way round. The hits of the day were 'Three Coins in a Fountain', 'Vaya con Dios' and Secret Love', lovely sloppy old songs, every word of which I still remember. As it happened, words were no longer a problem. Now I had my own music stand with my own book of songs, the notes and words laid out for me. I was able to read music and as I was long-sighted the lyrics posed no difficulty. It was an altogether splendid arrangement.

The boys in the band, nineteen in total, were a pleasure to behold. Even the middle-aged ones, the short and the tubby, the old-timers, held for me a certain charisma, that indefinable emana-tion of mystique which, even though I was now one of them, had dimmed not a jot through the years. They sat in a two-tiered semi-circle, each behind his individual music-stand box with the initials DF printed on the front. My position was centre-stage, playing at being front woman, singing solo, harmonizing, going ooh-aah ump-itty-ump, swaying the hips, rattling the tambourine, rolling the maracas in the very strictest tempo – most of the time! Periodically, sections of the band would rise up, the easier to strut their stuff, the brass, the wind, the strings, interspersed with solo trumpet, solo double-base and, most electrifying of all, the drum solo. Aah, the drums! Soft at first, the brushes, an easy pitter-patter opiate on the senses, flowing over you, caressing. Then rising, louder, harder, the pulse quickening, faster, on . . . on . . . merciless staccato thundering through your head, no stopping it now, your insides screaming to be let out, up up, into the final tumultuous explosion as the whole orchestra came charging in with such an eruption of triumphant jubilation you wanted to leap into the air and go jumping out of your skin.

On the very first day Des had asked me if I required a sub, and with the two folded five-pound notes nestling contentedly in the pocket of my swinging new shoulder bag, I had taken myself out to reconnoitre the drapery possibilities of Galway. I had purchased a swathe of the finest, sleekest, glossiest black velvet for the dress for the opening night, the likes of which you'd be hard put to find the length and breadth of this fair land. With it went elegant suede court shoes, a glittering dia-manté cluster already affixed. No stick-on make-do efforts for this gig.

Christmas morning and there was a giant box of a parcel from home wrapped in brown paper, with holly leaves and 'greetings'

labels painstakingly glued over every inch of it. I couldn't get the string undone for the crying. She'd sent the curtains and the dress and the shoes, and a length of soft sea-green material and a pair of earrings. And my father's letter, saying how delighted they were, especially about my salary. It must be a decent job, must be a *very* respectable set-up indeed, to pay that kind of money. And yes, they would come to see me, were really looking forward to it and, like I'd said, to giving a rendition of 'Galway Bay' with their feet there, standing on the very edge of the bay itself. That would really be something. They couldn't wait. They'd see me soon, real soon. And God bless.

In the afternoon, a phone call came for me from McGuigan's, and I heard my father's voice, gruff, awkward, afraid of this new-fangled contrivance, beginning to shout, 'How are you, then? Good, good . . . just a minit now, a minit . . . here's your mother for you. All right then?'

My mother's voice, high, also nervous. 'Did you get the parcel? Did you like the earrings? I can change them if you —'

Then the brothers, one after the other, the two eldest experts now in the art of operating any telephonic eventuality, laughing, calling, 'Paddy's asking for you. You should see the house . . . fantastic . . . says he's coming to see you one of these days. He's threatening to come with us and pay for the petrol, ha, ha.' And me crying the while, sobbing my heart out, blubbering into the mouthpiece, hardly able to speak.

It was the drummer boy who wiped away my tears afterwards. A group of us had gathered in my house – about half a dozen of the band had rooms there, too, including him. Some of the boys had gone home to their families, the rest of us had decided to have Christmas dinner and party here. I liked the drummer and had come to know him well in that first week. He was a great blond ox of a man, Russian by birth, with fair Nordic looks and a prodigious beard and the timorous soul of a gentle fawn. He was the one who'd brought me coffee in the rehearsal breaks, who'd sorted out my music stand when it collapsed at my feet, who'd walked me home and sometimes took my hand in his big broad paw and put a little kiss in it. That Christmas night, when the partying was over and the fire burned down, he too was the one who took me into his soft, warm feather bed, laid me down and slowly, carefully, and with excruciating tenderness, made a woman out of me at last. A beautiful woman.

It was a hectic existence. We played three nights a week in the Seapoint, plus a further two or three in dance halls all over Ireland, travelling around in a gloriously comfy spongy coach with 'Des Fretwell and his Orchestra' inscribed across the side. Whatever time was left to us was taken up with rehearsing. Masses of it. New songs had to be learnt, fresh arrangements discussed, mistakes rectified and argued over, suggestions noted for further consideration – busy, busy, always busy. A mite in love too. And my head way up there in the clouds, flaming, frivolous pink ones with a bright yellow star on top.

I had decided that the name Mary had far too much of the plain-Jane ring about it and was not consistent with my new glamorous image as lead singer in a top orchestra, so I'd changed it to Mareena, dropping the surname. Now I experienced the exquisite thrill of seeing my name on posters throughout the city and in the towns we visited . . . 'featuring the lovely vocaliste Mareena'.

I found myself constantly astonished at the turn my life had taken, the incredible good fortune that had befallen me and didn't omit to dispatch the odd grateful prayer to the One up in the clouds for keeping them rosy for me. Sadly, it was about the height of the attention He was getting from me these days. I couldn't in complete honesty go to confession any longer, when I knew very well that a few hours later I'd be committing the self-same sin, and as for Sunday Mass, well, as I didn't get to bed until dawn and the birds singing, I could hardly be expected to get up for that any more.

In spite of the hard work, or perhaps because of it, or there again because it was simply the normal lifestyle of musicians anyway – anywhere – when the gig was finished we hit the pub every single night of the week. So it was that, at twenty years of age in the fine city of Galway, I learnt to drink with the boys. Serious drinking, I mean. Often I was plastered, out of it, but those lads looked after me and were supremely protective, caring for me as they would a wayward baby sister. And my drummer boy, silent, steadfast, imperturbable, was always there to pick up the pieces. Fortunately, I managed to escape the trap of pill-popping, having on the one occasion I'd tried it nearly blown my mind. We were playing a double bill down in the south of the country, a lot of travelling involved with no sleep whatsoever for two days and nights. It was a particularly tough one. When I was offered an 'upper' I took it. And couldn't sleep for a week. I got the shakes, became completely paranoid and very frightened. Small wonder I swore I'd never touch another pill again as long as I lived. Happily, I never have.

We would drink in the back room of public houses until four or five in the morning, talking, singing, making music. Sometimes other musicians would join us from local bands or from folk groups, and the jam session would go on for hours, getting louder and more carried away as the night progressed, the Guinness bottles piling up, the gin in pint glasses, ashtrays overflowing into the puddles of spilt beer. The Gardai would take it upon themselves every now and then to conduct systematic raids. One pub would alert the next, and the news would go rocketing down the telephone lines in a paroxysm of frenzied panic. In a trice, the lot of us would be bundled unceremoniously out the back door, through the chicken runs, up over the walls and fences – instruments and bags and bottles and us all falling and tumbling over each other and great hushes and swearing and strangled screams of drunken hysterical cackling. We were a wild bunch.

Seapoint Ballroom rapidly became established as a venue of some renown, and after a few months we had requests from some of the big English bands to come and 'double' with us. We played with Geraldo, Stanley Black, Joe Loss – famous names in the Big-Band circuit of the Fifties – and it was Geraldo himself who approached me with a view to joining his orchestra as lead singer. Had I been at all ambitious, had I not again been smitten with love and my head full of wistful woolly notions of a husband and babies and playing houses, had I not been anxious about being disloyal to the kindly Des . . . had I had one single damned ounce of ordinary common sense about me, I would have jumped at the chance. For it was indeed the chance of a lifetime, the kind of break any singer in her right mind would have killed for. Geraldo was big at the time and was to become even bigger, a world-wide celebrity, but in that mad summer of 1953 I turned him down.

I was to regret that decision, bitterly. Only a week later, after the Saturday-night gig, Des collected the band together and made the devastating announcement that he was quitting show business, for good. It appears there was something seriously the matter with his heart. Effectively, it meant the band was finished. No one else was capable of taking over the show, or indeed possessed the disposition to do so. We split up. Some of the boys returned to their own countries, a few went to London where there was plenty of work, as session men if nothing else, the rest of us took ourselves off on the train to Dublin. Almost immediately, my drummer boy dropped me. With a tear in his doleful eye and a quiver to the bearded lip, he laboriously explained how he thought he ought to give his marriage another go. His *marriage*! I looked at his earnest spineless face and could have spat in it – let fly the jaundiced saliva spluttering across the bland blond stolidity of it. How dare he! How feckin' dare he? To have led me on like that these weeks and months past, to have sworn his undying love to me time and time again and not once a mention of a feckin' bloody wife. No wonder he'd always had a lavish supply of French letters. Like the man said, a girl in every port. Or something along those peripatetic lines . . .

It was the first week in May. Warm. Things were abuzz in Dublin. It was a good time to be there. I felt I was right in the middle of things now, at the core of where it was all happening, or at least where it could happen, given half a chance. I had plenty of money, but with no job I'd have to watch it. No need to go mad. Nevertheless, it was the fancier end of the city, the south side, where I chose a girls' hostel, share-a-room, in which to lay down my rather disillusioned, slightly heartbroken body. Thirty bob a week and do your own cooking in the damp dreary kitchen way down low in the basement. It didn't take me long to realize that, in spite of the toffy address, the place was still a dump. I wouldn't let it bother me, though. I was central, safe, and the other girls seemed nice. It would do me fine – for the time being anyway. I had a lot going for me. Slim now, with hair that was a credit to the bottle, the bleach bottle that is, streaks of golden blond intermingled with the nondescript, catching the eye every time it caught the light. I had a bagful of clothes and another of stage frippery, a wonderful assortment of alluring garments that would take me anywhere. These days, too, I was right up to the minute on the latest developments in make-up, and how to present myself in a manner befitting an up-and-coming young star of stage and screen. With nearly six months' experience in fronting a top band, the very best in the country, and a superb collection of songs, my own arrangements, the correct keys – it should be easy enough to find a job as a singer. I wouldn't allow myself to consider the alternatives. The post office days, those hapless days of dreadful tedium and malcontent, were a thing of the past, not to be contemplated for a moment.

With regard to the parents, well, they would have to wait for the time being. Bad news could always wait. No rush in that department.

I took a few days to settle in, walk around the city, get my bearings and check out the various dance halls. The one I liked best, the Four Provinces, was right in the centre beside St Stephen's Green and within walking distance of my hostel, thus saving on fares and shoe leather if I could get a job there. My father would have been proud of my economy! I went along to a mid-week dance and noted with a certain amount of pleasure the glaring absence of a female singer. At the interval I approached the band leader, Pat Moran, a small mild man and extremely pleasant. When he heard that I'd worked with Des Fretwell, an old friend of his, he said he'd be delighted to have me in his band – he'd been looking for a suitable vocalist, male or female, for weeks. No need to audition, just come along to a short rehearsal tomorrow afternoon and start work in the evening. He introduced me to the musicians – 'our new vocaliste' – and I walked the whole way home, sailing along on my cloud, smiling at everyone. I was praying too, 'Thank you, Lord, for this, this wonderful miracle. Yet again. Oh, I'm so happy! And if only for that, I'll go to confession again, and this very Sunday You'll see me at Mass and Communion. I promise.'

The gig was excellent, only four nights a week, which suited me fine as it gave me ample opportunity to socialize. The money was good, the people respectable – altogether a decent place, as I explained in the long, long letter home. I asked them to write to me for the moment care of the ballroom, as I was going to look for a more suitable room and didn't know how long it would take. That should keep them quiet for a while. Again, the musicians were kind to me, patient with my minor tempo idiosyncrasies and making light of them, always helpful. This time it was the tenor sax who favoured me, and I him. Within a week he had me bedded, the good confession and its attendant trappings out the window. I was becoming a right trollop.

Meanwhile my landlady had taken a dislike to me. 'Going somewhere?' she would sneer, all hoity-toity, down her horrible hooky nose as I tried to escape out of the door in a flurry of perfume and finery and clickety high heels. She disapproved of my job, my drinking, my clothes and general appearance, taking great exception for some reason to my streaked hair, even though her own was dyed a bright carroty henna. The inevitable happened. She came up to my room one morning bright and early and me not long in bed, and requested me to leave. No reason given, no notice, no nothing.

I found another place immediately, off the South Circular Road, no better than the other but with a piano in the front parlour. A house with a piano in it had soul, and at least the landlady should have some understanding of the ways of an artiste. It would be better here. Again, of course, just for the time being. I was thinking now along the lines of trying to make a record, become a pop star, a *famous* pop star – no point in even trying if you weren't going to make it big. I would be massive. There weren't that many female singers around, none really apart from Ruby Murray, so the competition was minimal.

It was at this point that Nancy came into my life. Nancy from down the country, of the wild red hair and the innocent guileless look, belying the tight compact wiry mind within, a mind that was packed to capacity with unadulterated devilment and the kind of mischief that only a kindred spirit could appreciate. We hit it off straight away and thereafter proceeded to lead each other astray. So far astray, indeed, that those months in Dublin had, through the years, become something of a blurry memory to me until one morning, a couple of summers ago, I saw Nancy again in a Camden Town bus. I was sure it was her. The same short red hair, the same quick birdy movements, still tiny, thin, lithe, like a whippet.

'Are you Nancy?' I asked. She nodded, but didn't recognize me.

'We knew each other in Dublin over forty years ago,' I said. 'I was known as Mareena then. We shared a room.'

Thus was re-established a rare and wonderful friendship. We had lost touch, that time ago, both of us too reckless, too scattered, too hopelessly incapable of sustaining anything tangible between us. But she remembers that time well.

She was playing the piano in the parlour one afternoon when I returned to the hostel and, delighted, I started to sing. The daughter of a farmer, amongst whose acquaintances were a few greyhound trainers, Nancy had taken an avid interest in the animals from an early age, had acquired one of her own – it seemed you could buy one those days for a fiver – and become a trainer herself. But with not a lot of steady money to be garnered from such an occupation, she'd come to Dublin to try her luck in the big city. When I met her she was working in a factory, two pounds a week and if you clocked in five minutes late they'd dock a whole hour's money out of your wages. Straightaway we got her a job in the cloakroom of the Four Provinces. Nancy says that when she heard me singing the song 'Beautiful Dreamer', she knew it was time to sit up and get herself into gear, time for the nightly assault of garrulous females scrabbling over one another in an attempt to get in there quick for their coats and umbrellas and miscellaneous assorted impedimenta. I remember well the song, the last one of the night, the smooch, when I would look down and over the punters, going slow-motion, cheek-to-cheek around the polished floor, grinding into each other with turgid lust, broad hairy hands straying below the belt, tentatively feeling their way, scared of rebuff. And I'd turn around, in a breath between the lines, and I'd smile at my tenor sax.

'Beautiful dreamer, Prince of my song
List' while I woo thee with soft melody.'

It wasn't to last. After only a month, Pat gave me the terrible news. The Musicians' Union had ordered him to lay me off until I had become a member. I went to see them immediately, fee in hand, thinking it was simply a matter of routine. I was an established vocalist, already in a first-class job, I could see no problem. But there *was* a problem. In order to qualify as a potential member of the Union, one had to be resident in the Republic for three years, and as I was from the North, I was not eligible. But, I argued, I've lived in Donegal – that's the Rebublic. Prove it, they said. I couldn't. There was nobody up there I could turn to. By running away I had burnt my boats. Whether they were telling me the truth or not, I never found out for certain. But one thing I did discover: the head of the vocalists' section was himself a singer, a singularly nasty specimen who had auditioned for my job and had been turned down by Pat. When I heard this, I knew for sure I hadn't a hope in Hell. Pat, being the beautiful man that he was, defied them, saying, 'Now let's see what can be done here,' and nervously I took to the stage again. But not for long. A week later, suddenly one night, in mid-song, through the door at the far end of the hall marched four men, straight up the middle of the dancing couples, in a direct hit for the bandstand.

I knew, Pat knew, we all knew. This was the end. Without a word, they grabbed me by the arms and half-dragged, half-carried me off the stage and into the wings. Only then did one of them speak, hissing through his yellowed teeth.

'Don't you ever,' he said, '*ever*, sing on a stage in this country again. We'll fine any band that is stupid enough to hire you. Heavily. And I can tell you, girl, here and now, your life won't bloody well be worth living.'

The viciousness of the attack scared the wits out of me. It was the end of my singing career in Ireland, the demise of any hopes and dreams I may have cherished. Perhaps, if I had been single-minded, less preoccupied with getting a ring on my finger, if I had been born with a tough ruthless streak in me, not so easily squashed flat, I might have succeeded in smashing through the barriers. I've learnt since, the hard way, that to make it half-way big in this singing lark – never mind how great the voice – these are the qualities you need. Furthermore, as a woman, it helps considerably to have a husband or lover, or even a brother, in the business, a big strong man out there gunning for you, ready and able to chop the bastards down.

There was no work in Dublin at the time, no jobs of any kind, even as a dishwasher. Eventually, feeling pity for me, the management of the ballroom created a job for me working alongside Nancy in the cloakroom. Back to two pounds a week. It was hard: I could hear the band, but I couldn't see them. Instinctively – I couldn't help myself – I would start to sing along with them. And then stop, in tears, unable to get past the first line.

The sensible answer, of course, would have been to hike it across the water to London there and then. But I didn't. Instead, I went to the dogs with Nancy.

The rendezvous was Shelbourne Park. She was a funny one,

Nancy. She'd hunch herself forward in the seat, tight as a ball, eyes focused on the track, oblivious to everything around her, gesticulating and yelling, nails clenched into the fists, exhorting her favourite to make it first to the winning-post.

'Come on, girl, come on! God, would you look at those back legs – the little darlins. Fantastic! Come on, girl, *you* can do it . . .'

I, who knew nothing of dogs and who couldn't have cared less, was fascinated by her, by the whole histrionic performance, in this, my very first encounter with the gambling fraternity. Nancy knew everyone of them. Which was very handy for us, as they could always be relied upon to say, 'What are ye havin', girls?' the minute they set eyes upon us in the bar, the two of us sitting there, waiting, one bitter lemon on the table between us. There was always a meal too, fine generous country men that they were, friends of the father – must look after the little one, give her a good feed, fatten her up a bit. Not forgetting her friend, of course, peculiar though she looked, hair for all the world like a stook of straw on top of her head, and all that fancy get-up of hers. I knew they couldn't figure me out, were a bit anxious about Nancy being seen with me – they'd told her so – but they were always polite. As for the conversation of an evening, I found it agonizingly dull. I really could not, with the best will in the world, drum up the slightest interest in a greyhound. I felt only pity for them, skinny shivering delicate creatures that they were, with their laid-back ears and their round trusting eyes, for having to undergo that haring around in the hope of catching a mere bit of piss in the wind. Besides, with a drink or two in me, I was ready to party. And party we did. There was a plethora of places to choose from. We danced in the Metropole, we danced at the Trinity hops, and early mornings in the low-down night clubs of Leeson Street we grooved till the dawn. Always there was a drink at our elbow. Or two. Or several. As the night wore on we lost count. There were private parties, too, in the colleges, in students' flats, in the Rotunda Hospital. It was there I met a gynaecologist from Cairo. Tenor sax went out the door; in any event he had developed a kind of prudish attitude towards my lifestyle of late, having heard a rumour that I was becoming rather too free and easy with my favours. He was, of course, correct. My new regular boyfriend now was quite old, about thirty-five or so, but charming, and he took me out to proper dinners in the best restaurants and travelled me around by taxi. I was immensely impressed by his job. Once I persuaded him to get me into the operating theatre, on the pretext of being a medical student, in order to watch a Caesarean being performed. It was wonderful. I stood there, fascinated, until I realized that my legs were giving way under me, and I was on the verge of fainting. They had to carry me out, which was terribly inconvenient for all concerned.

It wasn't just the sight of the knife and the abundance of blood that had caused me to feel faint. I'd been having fits of passing-out for some time, but had ignored them, putting it down to the fact that I wasn't eating enough. I'd also had no period for months, but a pregnancy test had come back negative. A second one was negative, too – they said it was stress. That I could well believe! I could easily have been pregnant, though. Way back in May, not long after I had arrived in Dublin, I'd taken a chance. I'd taken chances since then, too, but it was after that first occasion that I'd stopped having my periods. It had been a casual and very drunken coffee-bar pick-up, a boy from one of the Mediterranean countries, a handsome Casanova studying at Trinity. He'd taken me back to his place and plied me with gin. I remembered nothing, except that we'd had sex and I hadn't wanted it but was too drunk to get him off me. I'd seen him several times since. 'I'm pregnant,' I'd whispered the first time. 'Congratulations,' he'd replied and, laughing, turned back to his friends.

The test my gynaecological friend persuaded me to have also came up negative. God, if he couldn't tell, who could? I believed him, but immediately became weighed down by misgivings again when he too announced that he had a wife, this one back in Egypt. He also had a fiancée, he added, living in London, and she was coming over to see him this weekend. Thus was I unceremoniously dropped. I was full of suspicion. Was he afraid that he was the one responsible and had therefore lied to me about the results? There was no way I could be sure. In any event another bastard had hit the dust.

Nancy and I were beginning to have a shambolic time with

landladies. When we'd arrive upon the doorstep of a likely new lodging house, before we'd even stepped across the threshold, they'd take one gawp at me – I didn't have the wit to dress down and anyway, I thought, why should I? – and immediately enquire as to the nature of our occupations. I would say, 'Vocaliste,' and proud of it. Nancy would murmur, 'Dog-trainer.' They were hardly the most salutary of pursuits. Better to have been a nurse or a teacher or a shop girl or – dear Lord, forbid – a post office assistant, like normal people. We couldn't even pretend to be any of those, out and about as we were half the night, and by day snoring away in our beds, sleeping it off. We'd come in about four in the morning, shoes in hand, the worse for wear, giggling, falling over things, hushing each other up in massively loud stage whispers, pissed as newts. The following day we'd be politely requested to vacate the premises . . . 'I run a respectable house here . . .' You'd think the very least we could have done was to turn up sober and keep the roof over our heads. But we hadn't the sense.

Nobody ever mentioned returning any of the rent owed to us. What with that, and the exorbitant monies we were dissipating on our improvident lifestyle, the cash-flow position was beginning to suffer a rather debilitating decline. The standard of the rooms, the only rooms we could afford, began to hit rock-bottom. There were fleas everywhere. Millions of them, eating us alive. I knew about fleas. I was an expert on the subject. I knew that squashing a flea under the soft pad of a finger or even a hard book, thinking to rub him out, achieved nothing. He'd spring up again as soon as look at you, completely resuscitated, and be gone. It was altogether a matter of precision. In order to achieve his unequivocal demise, it behove one to trap him between the sharp edges of the two thumb nails – that is assuming one *had* edges to one's thumb nails – and at the self-same instant, grind into him. The resulting crack was the moment of truth. In the good old days, the days when I had lots of food in my stomach, flea extermination was part and parcel of the daily routine. We'd be back from school, full of bread and jam, and she'd sit herself down at the kitchen table and, patting her skirts, call out, 'Right then Mary. Let's have a look.'

Oh, God, how I hated it, gritting my teeth, so it's a wonder they didn't get totally worn down over the years. I'd be obliged to kneel on the hard linoleum floor, my face stuck in her lap, while my mother went into a trance of flea-picking over the length and breadth of my poor head. She revelled in the exercise, going aah, in a great gasp of satisfaction when she got one in the long scarlet talons, dragging the quicksilvery thing up out of its sleepy burrow, up up, through the length of a single hair, not a hope in hell for it, and me whingeing and squirming and going mad with the pin-point of pain in my skull.

'Keep still,' she'd admonish. 'Still. Stop fidgeting.'

With a kind of soppy fondness, I sometimes wished she was here now. She'd be having a field day.

But the rooms got worse. In one house the deal included 'all meals'. The landlady would ask at breakfast what we would like for tea. If we said fish, she'd present us later with one sardine, *one*, the forlorn centrepiece of a lethargic slice of fried bread. In another place we came back one day to find our stuff moved up to the attic. She had given our room to someone more worthy, a commercial traveller. But we were chucked out of there too, with a lecture to Nancy on how to run her financial affairs.

'I'll set you up on the right road,' the woman advised – she quite liked Nancy.

'Take your capital.' Twenty pounds it was at this point. 'Put it by, and build on that. You mark my words.' As Nancy says now, she had the right idea.

We ended up in a room with a sloping floor over a fishmonger's. The stink of the fish was almost too much to bear, and everything was at an angle, slightly falling down. It didn't make that much difference. When we came home in the mornings, our whole world was at an angle; somehow the two managed to balance each other out. We had both left the Four Provinces and were now seriously looking for jobs. Nancy managed to get one as a cleaner, but walked out after a couple of days. We were so desperate that I dressed up as straight as I could and went back to the woman, the old cow, to ask for Nancy's wages, saying she'd broken her leg and was in crutches and in a terrible way. She gave me a pound. It was a kind of gift horse, so we took it to the dogs.

There was a good little sprinter running that particular night that Nancy knew and fancied. He came in at twenty to one. Obviously, we had to buy champagne to celebrate. The rent would have to wait.

Every day was a new adventure, albeit a trying and tiring adventure, devising a way to raise some money or food, preferably both. Nancy was full of schemes. For a country lass, she was mighty canny. We found a great pawn shop where the man accepted anything, anything at all, from us. You could get half a crown those days for an old skirt. My Gor-ray went. Then some of the jewels, my favourite feather boa, and slowly I began to pawn my beautiful stage clothes. I had no need of them now anyway. The day the black velvet dress went I could have cried, but it bought us a slap-up meal and another week's rent, and the strength for me to get up and go for an interview in a post office out in the suburbs. I didn't get the job.

To cheer ourselves up, we went off to have a meal in Bewley's of Grafton Street, a nice up-market establishment, the best. We chose curried eggs, it being the very latest culinary delicacy. I didn't like them, so we had something else. And more. And more. Then trifle. When the girl came and asked, 'Madam, what would you like next?', we couldn't resist having a second helping. And lashings of fresh cream – the puffed-up sort. Strawberry and vanilla ice cream. And endless cappuccinos.

Nancy went to the ladies' and managed to get out of a side door. But me, they caught. I had chosen to make my escape through some tricky revolving doors, and I can still remember the sick feeling in my stomach as I tried to swing them round and out. But they were swung back on me and I heard the 'Perhaps madam forgot to pay her bill.' There were tears, of course, but no police, which was really charitable of them, considering the exorbitant cost of the food we'd put down us. I made the excuse, 'I forgot my purse and it was my turn to pay. I was going to come back later,' which they pretended to accept, but suggested they look after my handbag until my return. The bag was worth nothing, but it had my make-up in it – my whole life. I went out into the street. Nancy was nowhere, so I wandered up Grafton Street in a total daze, the tears pouring down my face, not giving a damn about anything. This was the end. But within minutes, I heard a familiar voice. 'Mareena! God, what's the matter with you?' It was the piano player from the Four Provinces, a tiny, crinkled, spidery creature, ancient, whom I'd hardly even noticed. I told him the sorry tale and without a word he dug into his wallet and handed me a twenty-pound note. 'Keep it,' he said. 'You need it more than me.'

That old man can't be around today, but when he reads this, up there on his lovely cloudy piano stool, he will understand, clear as crystal, how wonderful he will always be to me.

I got a job then as a day waitress and about the same time Nancy got a live-in one. We were sad to split, but we'd stay friends, we said. For ever and ever and ever. Promise. Times were hard, though. The dancing days were over. Nevertheless, Nancy, come hell or high water – and there was plenty of that in her life – never once forgot to say a prayer for me, every single night of those forty years it took for us to get together again. When she told me this, I realized exactly why she has always been special to me. She has a great line going in guardian angels!

I had started to thicken around the waist. It wasn't noticeable to anyone else, but during the long lonely nights when the world was silent save for the slow heavy tick of the clock in the corner and the blue spluttering hiss from the gas fire lumbering inexorably through the hard-earned sixpences with which I fed the meter, I knew. I was in trouble, the worst kind of trouble. One of the other waitresses, Elpie, a lovely daft Scots girl with whom I had become friendly, gave me the name of an abortionist. I went to see him, in the sleazy dump of a hell-hole in which he lived. He chatted to me. How long had it been since . . . you know . . . the curse? Questions about my sexual habits followed, questions which I considered to be totally irrelevant. I began to wonder what he was about.

'You've got the money?' he said then. I took it out of my bag. Precious notes, precious, precious notes borrowed from Elpie. Blood money. The price of murder. 'Good,' he said as I handed it over. 'Now, let's see. You're nervous, aren't you?' He smiled. I hated his smarmy face, but he reached over and patted my cheek.

'Come now, no need to worry. It's nothing. It'll all be over in a minute.' He hesitated. 'Tell you what. Let's get you relaxed. Makes it much easier for everybody. How about we have a wee cuddle before we start?'

He proceeded to undo his flies. I was out of that place like a shot. Minus the money.

I had no idea what I was going to do, except that I knew I had to save, so I got them to give me extra hours at work. Elpie said I should go to England, but I was terrified. I was frightened of everything now. I couldn't find the courage to make the huge move, get myself across the water for an abortion over there. I knew nobody, knew nothing about anything. Neither did anyone else. There was not one solitary soul who could help – either with advice or with money. I was demented. But I kept up the job, working long hours, hoarding my tips like a squirrel, eating everything I could get my hands on in the restaurant, thieving the stale buns out of the kitchen. Elpie let me sleep on the settee in her place, which, apart from the bed, was about the only piece of furniture around. She was married to Bill, a Scot too, a long drink of bearded water, gentle, silent. He was an artist. She was an actress. The three of us lived on baked beans and bars of Cadbury's milk chocolate and took turns to go out knocking on doors, begging for food and sixpences. The boozing had stopped.

The writing home had stopped too. I had nothing to say to them. They'd be worried sick, I knew. I had to do something. Quick. Then Elpie came up with what we thought was a brilliant idea. She knew someone in Belfast, a circus dwarf who'd made it big. But *really* big. He now owned a chain of picture houses right across the city. He was a good friend of hers, a kindly, caring soul. The perfect solution to my problem – the only solution that we could see – was for me to go up there. He'd give me a job, she was sure of that, and maybe he'd even be able to arrange an abortion for me; it might be easier in Belfast. One thing was for sure, he was an absolute angel of a man. He would see I came to no harm.

And indeed he was. I had sold the last of my possessions, the watch that Kevin had given me, a pack of playing cards stolen from some dump along the way – I hated card games – and a pair of knitting needles. It had been enough to buy me a corset, one of the old-fashioned pink concoctions, laced-up and steel-ribbed, that used to dangle down over the curtains around Minnie Mohan's settle bed. And with my new trim figure, I headed back up North.

He gave me a job in the ice cream and sweetie kiosk, and a mattress and eiderdown on which to bed down of a night, in one of his picture houses. In a few days he would have arranged suitable accommodation. But one thing he would not arrange was an abortion. He was a powerful Catholic. I spent a whole week sleeping on the floor of that cinema, staring up at the blank screen, the shadowy curtains in the dim weird light, listening to the mice – or was it rats? – squeaking and scurrying across the carpet. I was filled with terror, frightened they'd get me, run over my face . . . frightened, frightened of everything. I began to feel tiny rumblings in my belly way late into the night, small flickering movements. Oh, Jesus, sweet sweet Jesus, help me!

It took only that week for my new midget friend to fall in love with me. I sang a song for him one day, 'Danny Boy' – his name was Danny – and he cried his little heart out. From then on, nothing was good enough for me. Together we'd get me through this. Somehow. He asked not one single favour of me, not a touch, not a hand-hold, not even a kiss on the cheek. But he found me a terrific room near the cinema, all flowery and chintz and pink, saying it would do until he was able to organize a proper flat, with two bedrooms. Two. Oh, God!

I immediately wrote home with the new address, an elaborate long-winded bulletin with complicated explanations about jobs and rooms and the whys and wherefores, and how I hadn't wanted to worry them so hadn't written . . . and lies and lies and more lies.

Two days later, as I was resting on my frilly new bed, there came a knock on my door. I opened it. And there was my father, smaller now, cowed-down, eyes on the floor, the picture of absolute dejection. Beside him my mother, standing tall and indomitable, great hoops of scarlet appendages swinging from her earlobes.

And a look on her face fit to kill.

'Where's your good coat?' says she, watching me throw my bits of tat into the bag.

'Oh!' says I. I hadn't thought of that one. The Donegal tweed had gone the way of everything else, pawned, a long time ago. And a fair penny it had fetched, too.

'Actually I lost it. Somebody stole it when I was in Dublin.' Good one, I thought.

'Fine company ye keep.' A muzzled aside from my father, his lips in a thin hard line.

'I have a nice jacket,' I continued. 'But I was about to buy another coat, any day now, here ... in Belfast. What with the weather getting colder, I mean.'

'Your good coat.' She was starting to shout. 'Your good Donegal tweed coat. It cost me a fortune, that did. Some slags they must have down in Dublin. Just as well you're back up here again – in a civilized part of the world. Safe.'

I didn't leave any message for Danny. I would write to him, make sure he understood how grateful I was, how much I thought of him – would always think of him, what a dear, dear human being he was. He would understand. He would know I had no choice, that the matter had been taken out of my hands. I had to go with them now – journey onwards, to my doom.

We had tea before we left the city in a kind of pub-café. As well as the tea, my father had his usual glass of sarsaparilla, laced with a covert dash of something stronger, I suspected, when he suddenly became happy again and started to chat.

'You're lookin' well,' he said pleasantly, leaning back, relaxed. 'Whatever you've been up to it certainly suited you. Must be that sea air, I suppose. Put on a bit of weight, too.'

My mother said nothing. She was always the sharp one. I wondered if she had noticed the shape of me. I wondered if I showed. I was wearing a massive baggy jumper, a wonderful cover-up that I'd got in a second-hand shop for two-and-six. Looking at me, from any angle, you'd be hard put to tell. She was abnormally quiet, and her face didn't exactly have the most benign of expressions. They'd remarked upon my hair almost immediately. My father had enquired as to whether I possessed such a thing as a beret, so I could cover it up, hide it from the neighbours. Why a beret and not a hat or a headscarf? I wondered. I hadn't worn a beret since the convent days. Perhaps the sight of the blond streaks had turned his mind a little. The conversation centred around the café, the decor, the other customers, the price of what we were eating. There was a deliberate veering away from what was really bothering them. Precisely what had I been up to?

She bought me a new coat then. The style of the moment was the A-line, ideal for pregnant girls, especially those who were a trifle reticent about broadcasting their condition. The shops were full of the wide tent-like coats, so it was a natural choice. I still wondered, though. However, the colour she selected, with an involuntary 'Isn't that gorgeous?', was spectacularly bizarre. It too was the very latest fashion fad, shocking pink so startling you could see it a mile away. Had she suspected that my overall appearance would need to adopt a more discreet demeanour in the near future, she would never have chosen this tornado of a colour. One could reasonably conclude, therefore, that she had no misgivings in that direction. She was probably angry with me for leading them a merry dance. Nothing more.

It was a smashing coat and under normal circumstances I'd have preened myself around the long mirrors and twirled the skirt out into a wavy umbrella and tried on a hat or two to match. But I did none of these things. I buttoned it up to the throat and meekly followed my parents out of the shop and on over to the bus station. It was a grey day. I was glad of the coat.

I sat in the seat in front of them. Sixty miles of staring out of the window, desperately trying to hold the tears back, taking in the hedges and the fields and the trees, all – in these desolate October days – surrendering themselves helplessly to the pulverizing atrophy of autumn. There was no going back. I too had surrendered, the fight ebbing out of me, the smart-aleck lip crushed, a half-dead thing with the only life in me the one that was right now fluttering relentlessly deep down within my belly.

The heinous horrible cussed creature that clung on doggedly for dear life, that refused to budge in spite of the interminable punching into it with my fists, the scalding mustard baths. And the pint of neat gin, almost immediately spewed up over everything in sight.

I didn't speak much. My mother was jittery, an edge to her voice. My father seemed calm enough. They were discussing the new house, into which they'd be moving around Christmas. It was one of a row of nearly completed council houses on the edge of the village, on the main road, a garden back and front. My father figured he could do with a bag of that new grass-seed stuff McGuigan's had recently got in – a shop with an eye to the main chance. They'd get the rose bushes in Derry and maybe they could get some violets . . .? They were my mother's favourite flower. Did shops sell violet seeds, or did they only grow wild? Those blue things that were a bit like violets, maybe they would do, the next best thing. Lobella or lobelia or something – they'd make a nice border. That's what they were meant for, he thought, – a border plant. She was wondering if it wouldn't be a good idea to put up net curtains, in the front of the house anyway. Everybody would be able to see in, the walkers-past, the people in the buses and cars, every Tom, Dick and Harry. At the arse end of Mullaghash, there had been no need to bother your head with hazards of that ilk, the hens being the only bodies ever likely to be taking a constitutional around and about. Now and again I'd pass an intelligent remark or ask a pertinent question, like did they know yet who'd got the houses either side? It was altogether very frazzled. Everybody was smoking. A lot. I couldn't wait to get home and hide away in my room, where I could sit down in peace and quiet and confer with my mountain. This time I think my wise friend would have some difficulty in providing a suitable answer.

I didn't even get that far. When we got into the house the brothers were immediately sent off to the village for some messages, which would keep them occupied for a good while, and my father came out with what was bothering them straightaway. My father!

'Tell us, girl, have you ever done anything . . . wrong?'

It was like the time she'd told me the facts of life. 'Has anything happened to you yet?' You were supposed to be a mind-reader, supposed to understand exactly what it was they were referring to.

'No,' I said. 'Good heavens, no! How could you think such a thing of me?' I made myself appear irate, shocked.

'Oh, good. Good. Thank God. That's okay, then.' And he settled into the corner.

Not so her. She was setting out the cups and saucers, making a helluva clatter.

'I don't believe you!' she announced. 'Don't believe you one bit. You look fat to me. *Fat*. God knows what you've been getting up to, the company you were keeping . . . thieving lot. Well, young madam, I am going to get the doctor in to examine you tomorrow, then we'll soon see what's going on.'

My heart went cold. As cold as death. It was over now, finished. There was no need to think of a plan, no need to work anything out, what lies to tell, what excuses to make. It was all too late. Too, too late.

The doctor who came to check me out was not our local one. He was the great loud buddy friend of that bastard Jim Fallon, the gambling, boozing, back-slapping crony of his. I knew him well. He used to come into the pharmacy every day, for one thing or another, and they'd be conferring out the back for ages, exploding sporadically into vociferous cackles of buffoonery. I hated his guts.

'Well, well,' he said, coming into my room and closing the door. I knew my mother was standing in their bedroom the other side, listening.

'So what have we been getting up to in the big wicked city, eh?' He was smiling. Smirking.

'Nothing,' I muttered.

'Well, we'll soon see, won't we, girl? Right. Up on the bed with you then.'

Oh, I was mortally ashamed. I squeezed my eyes tight, squeezed the tears out of them and wished I could die there and then. Oh, God, I so desperately wanted to be dead. Anything rather than this.

'Right,' he pronounced. 'Done. That didn't take long, did it? Your mother was right, of course. Five months, I'd say. Pretty mess you've got yourself into, eh? Pretty bloody mess. You should be ashamed of yourself, bloody hope you are. You know' – he held himself up straight, speaking slowly and low – 'I can't believe you could do this to your parents, your family, a decent respectable family like yours – and your father with the job he has, too. God, if you were mine I'd thrash the livin' daylights out of you.'

I had started to sob. I had a sudden desire to hit him. How dare he? How feckin' dare he speak to me like that? Especially when I knew of some of the things he got up to, or would have liked to have got up to, if snippets of those backroom conversations I'd overheard were anything to go by.

I waited for her to come in. I remember the word 'whore'. I remember the words 'filthy bitch'. I remember her screaming at me like I had never heard her screaming before in all my twenty years – at any of us, for any reason. I kept screaming back at her that I had been raped, but she wouldn't listen. The disgrace of it, the curse I had brought down on this family, my poor poor brothers, how could they hold their heads up in public again? The shame, Jesus Mary and holy Saint Joseph, the terrible terrible shame of it . . . *bitch bitch bitch* . . . I knew he was there, Father, crying himself to bits, saying, oh, my God, my God, what are we going to do? Placating her. Saying, 'Enough. Enough. Calm down. Come on, come on downstairs and see the doctor. He wants to talk to us, make plans . . .'

And then silence.

They wouldn't let me leave my room for a week, except in the dark of night when the two younger boys were asleep. Patrick and Joseph were both teaching in Belfast. She brought me up my food on a tray. She emptied my potty for me. And she spoke not a word. I could hear the murmur of their voices in the night, and I could hear the crying. But I covered my head with the pillow and tried not to hear. I couldn't bear their pain.

I spent the time in bed reading through my old books, or sitting at the window in my pyjamas and big jumper. And, of course, weeping. My face in the mirror was unrecognizable, so swollen and blotched had it become, the hair crowning it with the once-winsome golden streaks now utterly ridiculous-looking, incongruous. Where was the girl who, not so very long ago, had taken centre-stage, whose heart and head had thrilled to the sweet ecstasy of rapturous applause, who had the boys at the snap of her fingertips and the whole wide world at her dancing feet?

She gave me details of the plan of action, standing with her back to me, staring out of their bedroom window, toying with the curtains. She couldn't bear to be in the same room as me a second longer than was necessary. She couldn't even bear to look at me. The hysterics were finished with. Silence had taken over, a terrible cold smouldering snarl of loathing that rendered her speechless, impotent, strangling the very breath in her being, crushing her, bit by bit, hour by wretched passing hour. My heart bled for her. I wanted to reach out and hold her, comfort her, tell her it wasn't the end of the world. Except that it was the end of the world. And there was no escaping it.

It had been arranged that we would be taken to Belfast that evening, after dark. The doctor was organizing everything and the place we were going to was a special home, a house where girls could stay, girls like me. And then, when the time came – she could hardly get the words out – I would go to a private nursing home next door to that place. In due course further instructions, plus any money that might be needed for . . . well . . . certain clothing items, would be sent to me there in the post. I was to write home as usual, but pretend I was in a hospital in Dublin. The brothers had been told that I had tuberculosis, and that none of the neighbours must know. TB was considered a disgrace in those days, especially in our community, a disease most shameful which befell only the poverty-stricken, the malnourished. The boys would appreciate the need for secrecy. As I had already been away for quite long periods over the past couple of years, nobody would suspect anything. The most crucial thing of all, though, the most vital precaution to be taken was that during my stay in Belfast I was on no account to allow myself to be seen by anyone who might recognize me. There were all kinds of people we knew who were living and working in Belfast. Patrick

and Joseph for a start. Friends of theirs, friends of everybody.
Girls who'd been at school with me. Cousins. The streets of
Belfast were riddled with them. For this reason I would remain
inside the home for the four months and would never, never once,
set foot beyond its threshold, not even for Sunday Mass. This last
was a cross I would have to bear. God would understand.
Humph! She tossed her head at this. They couldn't take any
chances by having me go to a public hospital either. I had cousins
nursing in Belfast, which was why, when the time came, I was
going to the nursing home. Jesus Christ, how much was it costing
them?

Smoke curled around the inside of the car in turgid acrimonious
shrouds. We were all of us chain-smoking, but it was cold so
nobody suggested opening a window. There wasn't much conversation of any sort. I had been told to sit in the front. I suppose
they couldn't stand the thought of perhaps touching me by
accident if I had sat beside one of them in the back. I didn't know
the driver and they didn't either; he was some stranger brought in
to deliver the victim to her incarceration. I kept thinking of the
expenditure. Where was it coming from? I knew they couldn't
have any savings. Mind you, my mother had a thrifty streak in
her. She had never been mean, not even what you would consider
careful, like my father. But she was shrewd. I suppose it was
possible she'd managed to put away a small nest-egg through the
years. She'd have been canny enough to have set aside some
money for their funerals, hers and Da's. Even if she had to starve
in this life she'd make damned sure they'd be buried in style.
There'd be no pauper's send-off for them. They had already
bought the grave, a double plot, where my baby brother had been
buried a lifetime ago. Oh, Christ, what was I thinking of? All this
death stuff and graves ... my mind had sunk into a deep black
pit.

They didn't make any effort to kiss or hug me goodbye,
nothing like that. They were crying. I was crying, tears everywhere. I was glad to see them go. Now I could get on with it. Get
on with what?

The dormitory to which I was led had several girls in it,
sleeping. I supposed it must be quite late. I didn't have a watch.

Oh, Kevin, Kevin, why didn't I run off to America with you? You lovely, gentle, soft, innocent boy, what would you say if you could see me now? What would you say if I told you I had pawned your present, bestowed with such love, the precursor to the ring – the ring which would have taken my feet off in a totally different direction, a path of respectability, legitimate children, sanity?

It was like being back at the convent, the self-same white bed, the locker. And the girl in the bed next to mine sitting up and introducing herself, Angela. Even with the coverlet over her, I could see she was huge. My God, was that what I was going to be like in a few months' time? But she was only six months gone. She was just big. I was tiny by comparison. No wonder I'd got away with it for so long. Hah! Had I, then? People are very polite when it comes to a single girl looking a bit fat. Is she, isn't she? Maybe the whole world knew, and my mother hadn't been so clever after all.

I took an instant liking to Angela, and that first night we talked until the dawn, making frequent sorties to the kitchen for coffee and biscuits, which we were allowed to do. It was terrific to have made a friend and already I felt a million times better, even laughing now and again at something one of us would say. She told me who the father of her child was. She'd been going out with him for four years and they were getting married as soon as this business here was over and done with. Naturally, she was keeping the baby. I was horrified when I heard his name, and only barely stopped myself from saying I knew him. He had tried to date me once, tried really hard, at a sports day around about the time I was working in the post office. He was heavily involved with Church affairs, organizing the sound equipment and lighting for religious functions, retreats, stuff like that, and was considered by the priests to be a veritable pillar of the Church. But I knew, from what the local girls said, that he was a real bastard with women. Poor Angela. I held my tongue, though. She'd find out soon enough. In the event, she had a lucky escape. By the time her baby was born, he was already married to someone else.

There were about fourteen girls in the home at any one time, in various stages of pregnancy or, having had their babies, spending a six-week post-natal time in which they were supposed to decide whether to keep their child or have it adopted. It was a stupid system, Angela told me, cruel, this six-week period. The mothers quickly formed an attachment to their babies; it would have been more humane to have them taken from them at birth, preferably unseen. During the night we heard babies crying off and on in the nursery, and the mothers would get up to attend to them. Poor girls. What was I talking about, 'poor girls'? Soon I'd be one of them myself. Poor me!

The establishment was run by the woman who'd received me, a bad-tempered spinster, 'Matron' as she was known. She was universally hated. In her virtuous work, she was ably assisted by 'the committee', a group of young women, 'Legion of Mary' girls. God, didn't I used to be one of them myself, in the good old convent days, with a broad blue ribbon round my neck, a silver medal of the Virgin sewn on to the end of it and a holier-than-thou look across my gob? These were the women who came in every evening to sit with us, talk to us, listen to our problems, give advice. These days they'd be called counsellors, but those days, in that place, they were known as busybodies, patronizing prissy little virgins, every one of them. They, too, were detested. The work – cooking, cleaning, laundry – was done by the inmates. There were no books allowed, no access to a library. But magazines were permitted, and they were strewn about over the common-room, mightily thumbed, chewed up from cover to cover. We gathered in that room every evening where, after seven, smoking was allowed. During the day, moving around the house, you got whiffs of tobacco everywhere. Matron was constantly moaning, flailing her arms through the rooms and corridors, throwing open windows to let in thumping great blasts of the freezing Belfast air. It was here too of an evening that the interminable knitting went on, the matinée coats, the bootees, minute sprigs of clothing for the newly-born, but not beyond. Those who couldn't knit ripped. The mistakes of the knitters. Or wound the wool into balls from hanks hung between chairs. Here we swapped stories, empathizing with each other's sadnesses, commiserating with each other on the demonic destruction of our lives. And here too we laughed, and sang along with the radio – in tune and out of tune – the latest hits. Often we danced, with big-bellied awkwardness, in our blue uniform smocks, gyrating, thrusting our huge mortal sin out before us, proud of it, wobbling the milk-heavy ponderous breasts as if we were strippers, vulgar, obscene. Laughing, laughing, always laughing. In a second, though, one split second, the whole merry scene could disintegrate. It took only one of us to break down, to collapse into a chair in tears, and the laughing would stop, dead. And the entire room just as suddenly be filled with the moaning and rocking and wailing of unutterable despair.

Once a week the girls could go to the pictures. One or two of them would meet up with a boyfriend, the father of her child, and they'd come back, three sheets to the wind, staggering drunkenly in the door. We'd have to shut them up and hide them from Matron. I, of course, couldn't go out. And as for the drink – well, that was a thing of the past. My inexorable downfall. I'd never touch a drop again, as long as I lived.

My job in the house was scrubbing. The floors were both tiled and wooden, hard on the kneecaps, and Matron insisted they be kept immaculate. I didn't mind. This was mortification of the flesh time; atonement had to be made. It was only right and proper to be on my knees, scrubbing my sins away. I couldn't pray.

One of the girls had passed on her wedding ring to me when she'd left, which I now wore, although I wouldn't be needing it. Everyone wore one, even the ones who were superstitious about it. They were a necessary prop for the confinement in the public hospital, and cost two bob in Woolworth's. Stuck in with all the married mothers, our girls were the ones who didn't have visitors, who never received flowers, whose husbands were in the Navy, in America, up a mountain, just died – anywhere – who invented another life for themselves and talked lovingly, and usually at great length, about the absent father of their child, the man who was coming home next week. Always next week. These were the mothers who, in the dead of night, wept silent tears into the pillow. And who, in the end, fooled nobody.

When my time came, I was utterly alone, the only patient in

the nursing home. Another matron, another virago, who kept addressing me as 'miss', hissing it out like a viper, was in charge. In the nine days I stayed there, apart from the cleaning woman, I never once saw or heard another soul. It was the loneliest, most isolated period of my life, without human contact, no radio, no sounds in the terrible empty house save those of the traffic in the streets below. And the crying of my child, my darling boy. My own crying, the absolute heaven and the excruciating hell of holding him in my arms.

There was no earthly reason why I should have stayed in that dump for nine whole days. I was perfectly well. Five would have been enough, and then I could have had the comfort of the girls around me, the massed shoulders upon which to weep. I knew the old harridan would have informed my parents, via the doctor or however it was they communicated, that a nine-day confinement was necessary, so she could get more money out of them. And my parents, so vulnerable at this moment, would naturally agree with everything. They were as putty in her sadistic grasping hands. She made me breast-feed, too. 'You don't think I'm going to go through all that bottle nonsense,' she snorted, 'when you've got a perfectly good supply of milk in you.' I started to argue about how much more difficult it would make the parting, how I'd heard from the other girls that breast-feeding only intensified the bonding, making matters more complicated than was necessary. But she wouldn't listen.

I knew she'd never been married, never experienced the process of bearing a child herself or of giving birth. Or of having to give that child up. She was a cruel bitch, shrivelled, dried up, cold as stone.

I had written home the day the child was born, a short note, a secret one. It was safe. The two younger boys were at college and only my mother would be there to meet the postman. I had told them I'd had a son, a perfect and beautiful boy, and I was going to call him Peter. I'd asked them, begged them, to come and see us. But the letter they sent in reply made no mention of the birth. It stated only that thanks be to God it was over, thank God I was well, but no, they wouldn't be coming to Belfast just yet. Arrangements were being made, however, everything was being taken care of, I would hear from them again shortly. I cried. Bitter tears. There was to be no forgiveness.

The letter when it came was a blessed relief. They were coming to Belfast the following week, and together we would travel by train south, towards Dublin. We'd get out at a town along the way where a car would be waiting for us and would take us to an orphanage in the countryside. And that would be that. Thank God it would all be over.

But of course it wouldn't be over. They knew it and I knew it. The doctor had seen to it that the case would not go through the medical records. They had taken the precaution of changing my name; it was as if the whole unfortunate episode had never taken place. Whatever records there were, whatever the legal eventualities that had to be observed, would apply to someone else. The truth, the whole truth, not even the slightest inkling of the truth, would ever be uncovered. In years to come, in generations to come, no one, no matter how hard he or she tried, could ever succeed in ascertaining the facts. The obliteration had been absolute. Nevertheless, the scars would remain, the shame. Those they could never obliterate – my poor, poor parents.

We nodded to each other only, as I entered the visitors' parlour. Both of them looked haggard, worn, older. Oh, Christ, what had I done to them? The child had already been taken away by one of the Legion of Mary girls. She was travelling with us in the train, but apart from us, in another carriage. No chances of being recognized were to be taken. We saw her immediately, standing in a corner on the station platform, way up the other end, a tiny bundle of white in her arms. They both started to cry and I tried to comfort them.

'It's all right,' I said. 'It's all right. I'm sorry, so terribly sorry. It'll soon be over . . . absolutely over. Don't cry . . .'

My own eyes were dry. I was utterly cried out. Last night I had said my goodbyes to him, rocking him in my arms the night long, finally falling asleep on the floor in the cold dawn light, my head against the railings of the cot. I had sworn my love to him, had vowed that I would find him one day, somehow, some way, somewhere. He had a birthmark on the instep of his foot, another miracle in my life, a light in this terrible tunnel of pain. I would find him. By Jesus and all the saints in heaven, I would find my son one day.

In the train we heard him crying, and without a word, my mother got up and went to him. I was so shocked, I couldn't speak. But she brought him back to our carriage and sat down again beside my father. She handed me some money.

'Go', she said. 'Go and get something to eat. Go with the girl, the Legion girl.'

I went. I couldn't believe it. My heart was singing. She was holding him, nursing him. Oh, God, perhaps she wanted to keep him. He was their first grandchild, after all. She'd always had a soppy heart. Underneath that wicked temper and berating tongue, there slumbered a kind soul. But of course it couldn't be. When we returned to the carriage she handed him back to the girl, and she and my father went to eat.

The orphanage was in the middle of nowhere, a formidable, gaunt grey house set in acres of pasture and woodland, the avenue a mile long. And trees everywhere. Oak trees, stark, barren of their leaves, weeping with me in the falling snow as we drove away. I looked out of the back window at the house, my eyes devouring the sight of it so I could never forget it, and my fingers started to claw at the window. Suddenly I heard screaming, inside the car. It went on and on. I couldn't stop it. It filled my ears and my head and tried to burst into my brain and destroy me. Swallow me alive. Then the car turned a corner and the house was gone and my mother was holding me, rocking me. And it was finally . . . mercifully . . . over.

This time I applied for a job in the post office myself. I couldn't stand being around the house, the new house. Any house. My parents were being kind to me, solicitous of my every need, caring in a way they had never cared before. It was most odd. But the tension was palpable. My guilt was overwhelming. I was bowed down to the ground with it, forever on my knees in the chapel, even though I believed in nothing. Absolutely nothing. I was constantly conscious of money too, how much my mistake had cost them. Their funeral savings had gone down the drain – better the foetus had perished likewise.

The house was nice, especially the bathroom, her first, with its stripy fish and its silver shells and its blue wavesy wallpaper. However I was used to bathrooms now; I had been in and out of so many. She was polishing away as diligently as ever, loving every moment of it, only this time I wasn't being asked to help. The front lawn was all proper, all dug up and raked and ready for the spring planting – the grass-seed, the rose bushes, the lobelia. The back too was being got ready for the vegetables, a couple of washing lines in a precise rigid V across its length. But no chucks. The chucks were gone, where to or how I didn't ask. I had always loved those silly hens and the place wasn't the same without them. You could still see the mountain but at a distance now, so it wasn't the same either. Nothing was. The new school down by the chapel was a monument to modernisim with its brazen red brick and unctuous G-plan. And real flush lavatories and proper toilet paper. Sean the JAM had come up a bit in the world, but he was as dumb as ever. We had absolutely nothing to say to each other, not that we ever had. The old school was being converted into a dance hall. Soon the peaceful dignity of Mullaghash would reverberate with the Friday-night galumphing of rock 'n' roll. The swing was gone from the old oak, but the rope marks were still on the branch. Oh, the songs I sang, the poems I wrote and the dreams I dreamt on that swing.

All gone. It was time for me, too, to be gone.

This post office was even smaller, in such a tiny village you'd be through it before you knew you were there. Falcarragh, an absolute honey of a spot, again on the wild Atlantic coast of Donegal. It too was a fishing village, same old switchboard, same old salmon lunatics, same old boss-type, only in this job it was the grown-up daughter who was the cranky one, ordering me around like I was a simpleton. I didn't care. I could cope with anything. And now, *now*, by God, I would stay with it. I would become a post mistress, even if it killed me. Some way, somehow, I'd make it up to my parents, try to ease their pain and make them proud of me, however impossible that might seem at the moment. The wages were four pounds a week. Two pounds of this I was to send home to my parents to pay or, to *help* pay – I didn't know anything about the costs – for my son's keep in the orphanage. That was the deal.

As it happens, there was a wonderful new dance hall in the village, and I got stuck in there every Saturday night without fail, dancing my heart and soul and guts out in an attempt to get my wits and my life together again. It was there I met a band, a kind of family band, from a town nearby. About six of them, the children, the father all in together, music coming out of their ears and jumping with dynamism and merriment and glorious laughter and mad as hatters. They offered me a gig, singing with them every Saturday night, travelling throughout the county, well-paid, so supplementing my meagre income, but in no way interfering with the day job. It was exactly what I needed.

I clung on to the hope that I could keep my son, that somebody would come into my life and rescue me, create one of my miracles for me. I fell in and out of love constantly, but either they didn't want me or, in the end, I didn't want them. I thought longingly of Paul. After all I had been through, and indeed after the rotten way he had treated me, he was still the one. But he was married now, though not to the judge's daughter. I heard that she'd dumped him not long after they'd become engaged. Someone had told her that he'd been seeing another girl, an actress type. Hah! So he'd married someone else on the rebound and together they were reproducing, nineteen to the dozen. Had I had a lucky escape? I wasn't sure. Kevin was still in America, still single they said. But the memory of him did nothing for me and anyway he wouldn't want me now. *Nobody* would want me. I was soiled goods.

My son was nine months old when the adoption papers came through. I took them with me on a cold November evening to sit on a rock by the Atlantic and think it over. The couple who wanted him were wonderful, the nuns in the orphanage said. They were rich, too. They had been making his acquaintance for some time now, and they adored him. They could offer him everything. Everything I didn't have. I had nothing to give him, nothing whatsoever. Not even hope. The choice was simple, in fact there was really no choice. Carefully I signed my name, this time my *real* name, in my very best handwriting. It was important that it looked good, neat and tidy. I signed him away, out of my life for ever. And dropped the envelope in the box when I got home. Like I would a casual letter to a friend.

I stayed for two years in the lovely Falcarragh, finally realizing my ambition of becoming a post mistress. It meant I had a slightly more superior position in life, quite snazzy really. Head Office sent me around the county to work as a relief sub-post mistress, taking over from the bosses when they needed a holiday, maternity leave, or a sojourn in the asylum to cure their mental breakdown brought on by pressure of work. To begin with I loved it, especially the travelling, new places, new faces and the excitement of living out of a suitcase again. And I was able to continue with the singing. After about a year of this, however, I'd seen the lot, done everything. I began to weary of the practical-ities, the poky dark dreary rooms with bars on the windows, the long hours, the same plain boring country folks with their pullulat-ing bunions and their prolapsed wombs. Even the dance band had lost its novelty. The sameness of my situation had started to pall. It was time for a change of scene.

The job I found myself next was again on the coast of Donegal, but in a jewel of an hotel, the Rosapenna, famous world-wide for its superlative eighteen-hole golf course and its excellent salmon-fishing. It was as up-market as you could get, and I felt perfectly at home there working in reception, learning the business and aiming – very determinedly – for the position of head receptionist, or higher even. The hotel was truly beautiful, like a Swiss chalet dolls' house in white-painted wood, probably seventeenth- or eighteenth-century. It had been transported piece by piece from Norway or somewhere like that, and rebuilt on a wild and lonely promontory of smooth lush flats leading to a honeycomb of humped sand dunes and on to a pale yellow strand, speckled with shells, stretching for miles to the distant mountains. The sea was everywhere, with massive cliffs and treacherous labyrinthine caves and a wayward ruggedness that was fearsome and unpredictable and merciless as it was beautiful.

In my first month there, a Dutch vessel with six sailors on board crashed on those rocks. We took them in and we tended to their wounds, and we bedded them down and we fed them fresh

salmon until it was coming out of their ears. And then we bedded
them properly. At least I did. Only one of them, though. They
were big and blond and bronzed and speechless, not a syllable of
English between them, and overnight they became a tourist attrac-
tion, the talk of the land. The press were everywhere and radio
reporters with dinky tape recorders, and visitors in buses came by
the tonload to gawk. They went swarming up and down and
across the dunes to go and look at the wreck and pick at it and
bombard the local pubs with an abundance of trade and a great
deal of jollity and partying. Everyone had a smashing time, not
least the sailors who had, of course, never experienced Donegal
hospitality and didn't know what had hit them – never mind the
rocks. It lasted a whole month until another Dutch ship docked at
Belfast and called them to heel. For me, it was a most auspicious
beginning. Things could only get better. Gone were the dark old
days. We were getting back to being our old self again.

The Rosapenna was owned by an elderly couple and their
daughter, landed gentry, who lived in private quarters and made
an appearance occasionally in order to pass the time of day with
the guests or the workers. They were pleasant, inoffensive, really
quite nice, but a world removed from the staff, Irish all of them.
It wasn't important. What *was* important, at least to me, was the
presence of their niece, one Miss Wilson, of true blue English
blood, who was the hotel manager and ruled with an iron fist in
an iron glove and a tongue on her that could slice ice. Although
she'd hired me, she disapproved of me, of my appearance mainly,
so I set about straightening myself up, ironing my clothes, polishing my shoes, going easy on the make-up. It worked. The hours
were savage, seven in the morning until ten at night, with an
afternoon break and one day off in the seven. There were two of
us and we were run off our feet. There was the reception work
itself, which included organizing golf tournaments, establishing
fishing rights and sundry other bits and pieces – complaints,
phone messages, reallocation of rooms. Behind the scenes was a
switchboard and a big tabular ledger, in itself enough paperwork
to constitute a full-time job for one person. Nevertheless, throughout everything, one could find an intermittent moment in which
to make a little eye contact, one could indulge in a flirtatious

conversation, however slight, one could establish that one was a woman, and an available one at that. Available for the right person, of course – one was learning. But there were plenty of those.

During the busy summer season, after dinner – for which the full-length gown and dinner jacket were obligatory – there was dancing every evening in the ballroom. It was excruciatingly grand. We used to watch through the windows, us lesser mortals, from the smooth damp lawns. It was like a fairyland, these creatures from another world, this thoroughbred assemblage drifting about under the candelabra, the women graceful, poised, glittering, their menfolk, husbands and sons, regal, attentive to their every whim, so handsomely elegant. Oh, Lord, if I could just get one of those sons to fall for me I could have all this and more – the big houses, the stately cars that some of them brought over with them from England strewn across the front drive, holidays in the Bahamas, the frocks, the jewels, the sheer shininess of their hair and complexions, procurable only from the top salons in Europe. It was indeed another life.

I did get to know someone from that other life. It was a shy beginning. He was a shy boy, Rupert, one of the incredibly good-looking sons of the Carrington family. They were regular visitors to the Rosapenna and Rupert and I became acquainted through evening excursions to the public houses in the village.

When the dancing was over and the reception closed, I would go off most nights with a bunch of the guests to one of the local pubs, where the merry-making for them would continue and for me commence, although sometimes I'd have had a glass or two sneaked in to me from the barman during the course of the evening – a body needed it to cope with that tabular ledger. We'd drink and sing and dance until the small hours, the pubs delighted to have the custom, the Gardai turning a blind eye – the winter was long and hard – and night after night I wouldn't get to bed until nearly dawn. It was a bit like the Big-Band days, although now I had to get up in the morning and work the whole day long. It didn't matter. I coped, somehow. And I was happy.

So Rupert and I became friends, though never lovers. I doubt that we had anything in common, save that we rather enjoyed being together. And strangely, that was enough. There were nights when we wouldn't go out, and he'd come to my room and sit on the end of the bed and we'd talk and talk late into the night. Sometimes he would polish my shoes for me, *spit* and polish – he was at military college – and I use to sit and watch him, the care he exercised, the meticulous way he rubbed in the polish with a drop of spit in a hard tight circular movement, bit by bit, until the whole surface of the shoe gleamed like a ripe chestnut. He'd hold it out to catch the light, proud of his workmanship, and look at me with this gorgeous bashful smile when I told him how wonderful he was. How special. It was a kind of loving, the kind that made you want to cry, a trembling silver thread shimmering tentatively between us, a thread that could strengthen, given time and the right circumstances. Or a rope to bloody hang myself with. Which is precisely what I did. I took him home to meet the parents.

Why I did it, I'll never know. I suppose I wanted to impress them, show them the kind of company I was keeping these days. Whatever the reason, he was delighted to accompany me – it was my day off – driving me there in his father's luxurious automobile, taking me to a nice restaurant along the way, treating me indeed as I had so often watched the gentlemen treat their consorts in the ballroom. The family were returning to England shortly, but we had planned to write to each other, and anyway he would be back.

When we reached the village and I saw the row of council houses and the neat square patch of lawn and the blooming roses, I suddenly saw it through his eyes. Oh, dear God, what an idiot I was! Why couldn't I simply have left things as they were, let him imagine my background, my family? Indeed, I doubt if he'd ever thought of them until now; he'd seemed happy enough to accept me the way I was. Why hadn't I trodden more carefully instead of charging in with hob-nailed boots, given him the chance to get to know me better, allowed the love to grow? Slowly, slowly.

My mother was in her element. Out came the best china, the cakes, the works. I prayed, prayed so hard, that my father would have the gumption not to ask him what school he'd been to. But he did ask. It was after tea, when the pipe was lit and the situation had become more relaxed. Rupert, calm as you like, answered politely, 'Actually, sir, I'm at Sandhurst.'

'Well, well. Is that right, then?' said my father, puffing away. Nervous again. If I'd had a gun, I'd have shot myself.

And that, I'm afraid, was the end of the lovely Rupert.

But there were others, men who were notorious or infamous or both, a couple of MPs, who shall of course remain nameless. That first winter in the Rosapenna could have been boring, but it wasn't. There was always someone interesting around, something to keep me amused. I was promoted to the position of head receptionist, which now that I had achieved that status meant very little except a small salary rise. The job was as hard as ever. A new manager was taken on, a smart young Frenchman, ex-Gleneagles. He would inject some fresh energy into the place. At first Miss Wilson resented him, although she wasn't in any way demoted. It was simply that she didn't see the necessity for changing anything. After a while, though, she herself started to change. In the beginning it was her skirts. She shortened them, showing, for the first time, a fine pair of sticks. Then there were the shirt blouses, white or cream always, sober in the extreme, quite butch really. These were replaced by whimsical fripperies of colourful chiffon, displaying a modicum of cleavage. She went on a trip to Belfast and came back with a new hairstyle, a silly feathery affair which took ten years off her. Even her face began to take on a different look, the eyes losing the cold steely stare, the thin line of mouth opening up with a soft rosy lipstick. The day she requested me to call her Susan instead of Miss Wilson I knew for sure that something had got into her. It was of course the Frenchman.

He had taken to bringing her up breakfast in bed, *her*, and not appearing back down again for an hour, longer sometimes. We timed him. I, who could have done with him myself, thought it was disgraceful behaviour. She was old enough to be his bloody mother, for God's sake, I said. That's what I said then. I wasn't to know in those days of course how sweet it is to find yourself with a nice young lover in middle age. In fact, she married her Frenchman. And I suppose they lived happily for many a long day.

Early May and we were getting ready for another season, taking on a young trainee in reception for Susan had decided that the hours were far too long and we must have extra staff. I was in fine fettle. And then it happened. I became pregnant again. At this point, I would ask you not to throw the book at me! It must be understood that in Donegal in the late fifties, and indeed for years to come, there was not the slightest hope of finding anything pertaining to birth control, and that my lifestyle included getting paralytic every weekend and sometimes, too, during the week. I was looking for love and if someone wanted to *make* love to me, then I was sure it meant he loved me. I was under pressure, too, from the parents to get married. At twenty-six, I was considered to be very much on the shelf, an old maid. They were desperate for me to marry and terrified, naturally enough, that I might 'get into trouble' again.

There was no doubt in my mind this time about my condition. I didn't even bother to have a test. I knew what I had to do. Over the past year I'd been to see a local doctor a couple of times about my extremely heavy and painful periods. He'd suggested having a D and C, a scraping-around job, I suppose to loosen things up a bit. More often than not, he said, it did the trick. Now I planned an interesting trick of my own.

I dressed carefully, made myself look really good, and went to see him again. He was a kind old dear, a bit dithery, and I knew he liked me. He played golf regularly on our course.

'I have a week's holiday coming up,' I said. 'Next week, in fact. It's the last break I'll get before the season starts, and we're going to be so busy this summer I *cannot* afford to take a day off if I'm feeling bad. Do you think you could possibly slip me in somewhere for that little operation . . . please?' I looked him straight in the eye, the picture of innocence. He didn't even bother to examine me and rang a friend of his in the town, a surgeon who had his own private hospital and who also happened to play golf with us, and knew and liked me as well.

'Sure,' he said. 'Get her to pop in Monday morning. Won't take a minute. We'll have her right in no time. Can't afford to do without her in the Rosapenna, the place would collapse without her.' I could hear him, quite clearly, down the line. There was to be no cost.

Which is why I found myself waking up from the anaesthetic in a small beautiful room, rather like a nun's cell, a crucifix shining on the wall opposite in the faint afternoon sun. The hospital was indeed run by nuns; they had prepared me for the operation, cheerfully placid starched individuals steeped in purity and God's good grace. I hadn't allowed myself to think – not for one single second had I allowed myself to think. Now I was wearing a thick wad of sanitary towel. I could feel it. The deed was done. Thanks be to God.

I was sitting up having a cup of tea when he walked in, the surgeon. One look at his face and I knew I was in trouble. He didn't mince his words.

'*Out*,' he said. 'I want you out of here. How dare you do that to me, to all of us, fool us like that? Lie to us. You *knew*, didn't you? You *must* have known. My God, I can't believe what I've done. One hour, right? I want you out of here within the hour.' And he was gone.

I had a terrible sickness in the pit of my stomach. Fear. He wouldn't tell anybody, would he? His anger was awful. But of course he wouldn't. He *couldn't*. By rights – probably by law – he should have examined me first, done a pregnancy test. But he'd trusted me, taken me at my word. It wouldn't have dawned on him that I'd been having him on. To be honest, I'd never for a moment considered the possibility that he would detect the presence of a six- to eight-week-old foetus. What size was it, for God's sake? Nebulous. A tiny squiggle, minuscule, completely obscured by the rest of the murky stuff that was in there. But obviously he had noticed and by the time he'd seen it, it was too late. He was a Catholic, a staunch upright Catholic surgeon, who had this day, however inadvertently, performed an abortion. That, for him, constituted murder.

I could have gone back to the Rosapenna, but they had very kindly given me a whole week's holiday, getting somebody to stand in for me. I could hardly come traipsing back again after only one day. Besides, and this was the real dilemma, I was *afraid* to go back in case either my doctor or the surgeon would walk in, as they were bound to do before long. The thought of a confrontation with them filled me with terror. In fact, I wasn't sure that it would be a clever move on my part to return to the hotel at *any* time. I'd have to think about it, reassess my situation. And where better to untangle the muddle I was in than in the peace and quiet of the mountains? It was spring. I would go home. The break would do me a power of good.

Nevertheless, the bus journey was fraught with difficulties. I kept feeling sick – the aftermath, no doubt of the anaesthetic – and the bus was obliged to stop frequently for me. I blamed it on food poisoning and everyone was kind. But it was a terrible journey and I was glad to be home and tucked up in a good comfortable bed with a hot-water bottle.

'It's the flu,' pronounced my mother, taking over. 'You look ghastly.'

'Like Belsen,' added my father. 'Absolute skin and bones, she is. What are they feeding you on there?'

I managed a laugh. 'Fresh salmon.' They laughed too. Oh, it was good to be home. Safe. Wonderful, too, to be so thin for them – they who must always now live with the fear that I might appear back on the doorstep as a big fat lump.

'We eat salmon all the time,' I went on, by way of conversation. 'Even for breakfast. The guests catch it and hand it over to the kitchen. There's nothing else they can do with it. So it's coming out of our ears. I don't think I want to see salmon again as long as I live.'

I tried to stay in bed, but I wasn't really ill, had stopped feeling sick, didn't have a temperature, so it was difficult to pretend. The only thing that was wrong with me was that I was having a period, and there was certainly nothing wrong with that! It was perfectly normal. I could see that my mother was delighted when she realized I was using sanitary towels. She was singing away, polishing away, and the atmosphere in the house was great. I went for long walks over to the old school, walked for miles indeed, even halfway up the mountain. I needed to think. The second pregnancy had shocked me. It shouldn't have happened. It had been the safe time of the month for me and I'd presumed that there wasn't the slightest possibility of me being caught. But I had been caught. And next time I might not be so lucky – except that there wouldn't be a next time. I was positive about that. But what to do now?

Perhaps it was the walking, perhaps the surgeon had stopped halfway through the operation in a panic, perhaps for God knows what reason, but suddenly one day as I came in the door I started to bleed badly. There was nobody in at the time, which was just as well. I charged up to the bathroom in a panic, feeling the hot rush of blood down my legs, and there in the bowl my whole insides fell out. Or so it seemed to me. I nearly went out of my mind. Jesus Christ, I was dying. The man had killed me, knifed me to bits in his rage. But common sense took over. Perhaps he *had* stopped short of a full abortion, but the stirring up had caused it to come away anyway, and this was it – here in the lavatory pan before my very eyes. Or maybe even I had only myself to blame. I knew I should have taken to my bed properly, stayed there, rested for a few days at least, especially as I'd spent that first day – and that almost immediately after the operation – travelling in a bumpy bus and wandering around smiling at everybody, as though I was perfectly fit.

Whatever was happening to me, the bleeding showed no signs of stopping. I was passing big clots every time I went to the lavatory, haemorrhaging in fact, and it was becoming increasingly difficult to hide it. I was also growing weaker, my face taking on a grey cadaverous appearance which no amount of Panstick could hide. Then came the morning when I found myself unable to get out of bed. What was worse, horrific indeed – the kind of nightmare I couldn't have thought of in a million years – I was lying in a pool of blood. My mother's first words, 'It looks like a miscarriage to me', ominous though they were, didn't even frighten me. I was dying. My life was over now. I was paying for my sins. May God in His mercy forgive me.

What they told the neighbours I can't imagine, but an ambulance isn't exactly the least conspicuous of vehicles, especially when it's screaming its brains out. The whole village would have seen and heard, and very quickly the entire countryside would know. I presume the explanation they gave would have something to do with the food-poisoning story: complications had arisen, I'd burst a gut – my mother was an expert, an old hand, in the art of fabrication.

In the hospital in Derry to which I was whisked away, they

performed another D and C, this time a thorough clearing-out. It was the only thing that could save my life. But they were smart in Derry. They asked questions, and although it was all very rushed, even with the pre-med, until the very last minute when I was put under, they probed, 'Who did this to you? Tell us his name, his name, name . . .'

But I didn't tell. Even in my dopey state, I didn't tell.

Back home, the situation was quiet. My mother would never know whether I had been pregnant or not, but there could only be blessed relief I suppose, that, whatever it was, was no more. She was distant though. There was a marked change in the way she looked at me, cold, hard. Any feelings of love she may have harboured for me, any maternal tenderness that still lingered, were gone. Dead ... as the foetus that had resided for such a short space of time within the comfort of my womb. She was never to look on me with love again.

When I told them I was returning to the Rosapenna they seemed pleased, although I got the impression they'd have been happier had I informed them that I was departing for America. Or perhaps Australia. Anywhere far, far away, out of their sight. We had nothing to say to each other these days. I had changed. They knew that, but couldn't put a finger on precisely how. They understood only that I was trouble. But then I had *always* been trouble, right from the word go. In some peculiar way, which they would never understand, I was a misfit. And at this moment, in this summer when I was twenty-six and a half, my time had run out. They had come to the decision that I'd be better gone. Out of it. Gone for good.

I rang the Rosapenna and left a message with the new girl in reception that I wouldn't be back. She could have the pretty clothes I had left behind in my room, or they could be thrown out. Whatever. I didn't care. Then I took the bus to Belfast. My precious sweetheart was waiting for me, the dwarf, Danny. I'd been writing to him over the past few years, intermittently, and sometimes he'd rung me. Always his words were the same: whatever happened, however much trouble I was in, he would be there for me. Had his feelings for me been purely those of friendship I could have taken him up on it, but he loved me with a passion that had lessened not a jot and I – however much I adored him – could never return that love. Neither could I hurt him. He had recently acquired a share in a small hotel. I wondered in passing if it had anything to do with me. I wouldn't put it past him to have bought it so he could set me up in style in a business I now knew quite well. That was the strength of his love for me. But that wouldn't be the answer for me. It might be fine for a time, a challenge certainly, exciting. But, too soon, I knew I'd feel trapped. I wouldn't be able to move; it would be like being back in the mountains. I'd never get away from the big sorrowful brown eyes of him staring up at me, begging almost, for a glint of recognition.

'You want to go to England, don't you?' he asked that first evening.

'I don't know,' I replied, quite truthfully. 'I don't know what I want.'

'I think you'd be better off there. In London. It would do you good to get away, see the world a bit. There's lots of opportunities across the water. You should try it at least. In any event, you can always come back here if things don't work out, but I think you should give it a go. I've decided anyway I'll give you a return plane ticket . . . no, no,' as I started to object, 'take it as an early birthday present, and I'll arrange a nice girls' hostel for you to stay in until you get on your feet. Okay?'

'I'll think about it,' I replied, too overcome to say more.

Other people might have considered it odd that all I had to show for my twenty-six years was a three-foot midget man waving me goodbye and godspeed at the airport. But I knew differently. In that small body was a heart as big as my mountain, a heart as solid too. I had kissed him for the first and last time. Farewell. We were never to meet again.

The captain's voice came over the tannoy, announcing our progress. We were passing the Isle of Man. I looked out, but couldn't see anything. Ah, well. It didn't matter. Nothing, but nothing, could cloud the excitement that was in me. I was wearing my new costume, a fine trim bottle-green Donegal tweed with little flecks of all the colours of the rainbow. Danny had bought it for me. It was *class*. I'd have need of that, he'd said. It was vital to be properly turned out, going to the big city. No necessity to look like a culchie. A hat was important as well. The straw boater was on my lap, set off with a wide green satin ribbon and an old damask rose. The tweed was possibly a trifle heavy for a June day – we were actually in the middle of the blistering heatwave of the summer of 1960 – but Danny always knew what was best.

It was the captain's voice again. Not long now. All was smooth, no turbulence. And we might be delighted to know that the temperature in Heathrow at this moment was ninety degrees. Whew! Ninety degrees.

And that, me darlins, was only in the shade.